Aaron M

732 - 494 7636

Flash of Insight

Related Titles
of Interest

Group Design and Leadership: Strategies for
Creating Successful Common Theme Groups
Henry B. Andrews
ISBN: 0-205-16197-9

The Active Self in Psychotherapy: An Integration of
Therapeutic Styles
John D. W. Andrews
ISBN: 0-205-12580-8

Planned Short-Term Psychotherapy: A Clinical Handbook
Bernard L. Bloom
ISBN: 0-205-16155-3

Helping People Change: A Textbook of Methods, Fourth Edition
Frederick H. Kanfer and Arnold P. Goldstein (Editors)
ISBN: 0-205-14382-2 Paper   0-205-14383-0 Cloth

Child and Adolescent Psychotherapy: Process and Integration
Robert M. Leve
ISBN: 0-205-14907-3

Integrative Paradigms of Psychotherapy
Ted L. Orcutt and Jan R. Prell
ISBN: 0-205-14823-9

Small Groups: Process and Leadership, Second Edition
Barbara W. Posthuma
ISBN: 0-205-16169-3

Flash of Insight

Metaphor and Narrative in Therapy

Stephen S. Pearce
University of San Francisco

Allyn and Bacon

Boston • London • Toronto • Sydney • Tokyo • Singapore

Copyright © 1996 by Allyn & Bacon
A Simon & Schuster Company
Needham Heights, Massachusetts 02194

Library of Congress Cataloging-in-Publication Data
Pearce, Stephen S.
    Flash of insight : metaphor and narrative in therapy / Stephen S. Pearce.
    p. cm.
    Includes bibliographical references and index.
    ISBN 0-205-14572-8
    1. Metaphor—Therapeutic use. 2. Storytelling—Therapeutic use.
I. Title.
RC489. M47P43   1996   95-5923
616.89'16—dc20   CIP

Printed in the United States of America
10 9 8 7 6 5 4 3 2   99 98 97

This book is dedicated with deep gratitude to my wife Laurie, who is my most uncompromising and intelligent critic. In every aspect of the development of this book, she helped me struggle with ideas and challenged me to reach farther than I ever could have expected. Without her editing skills and her intuitive feel for language and metaphor, this book never would have appeared.

Contents

Foreword

Storytelling in its various forms allows us to listen, take in information, understand, comprehend deeply, interpret, and integrate new information at numerous levels with both the conscious and unconscious minds. The conscious mind tends to process the content through the usual and habitual patterns and defenses. However, the unconscious mind, with its more open and creative orientation, provides a receptive place for new and old ideas to form and reform in a variety of ways. Sometimes this happens by pushing the limits or stretching the previous learnings to perceive in different paradigms.

Now, narratives, storytelling, anecdotes, teaching tales, and metaphors all have taken their recognized, legitimate place in the world. They help to transmit cultural heritage, values, language, philosophy, and spiritual traditions—and yet they do so much more.

As individuals with limited conscious minds, filled with all the rules of society and our own consciously or unconsciously chosen protective walls and defenses, we tend to get in our own way or impede our personal growth and development by holding onto old habits and adaptations to life. Yet metaphor can be a gently effective and easy way to promote change with fresh perspectives.

As a young child, I listened to many teaching stories, some with puzzles to solve within the story. Over time, I realized that these stimulating stories had taught me to think in many different ways and patterns and had enriched and broadened my perspectives. Now, in my private practice, metaphor is constantly present in stories, in "homework" assignments (such as exploring new behaviors), in the language I use with clients, and even the accoutrements of the consulting room. For example, one of the clocks is fast and slow at the same time. In time, with the use of this book, you will come to understand this even better.

In this book, the author approaches the area of metaphor in a number of simple, practical ways. Often parents, teachers, and therapists find that when a metaphorical story is needed, it is easy to go blank. However, with the easy, logical, informative approach to using metaphor provided here, the construction and use of metaphor becomes demystified and is made readily available.

The book provides a history of narrative use in various cultures and tells us what can be learned from this historical review. The book provides a rich understanding of how teaching tales and narrative and metaphoric material skirt the defenses and make it possible to speed up the therapeutic process. In addition, the book highlights the potential shock value of narrative and metaphoric material to help a client gain a different, better, or broader understanding of his or her problems.

The book relates metaphoric material to altered states of consciousness, including hypnotherapy, and provides a simplified understanding of the hypnotic power of such material. It also provides an opportunity for the practitioner to understand the relationship of the bicameral mind, communication modalities, and the power of specific language in these stories.

The book provides a detailed outline of some of the creatively useful contributions of my father, Milton H. Erickson, M.D., to therapy. These include puns, indirection, humor, "shaggy dog" stories, and paradox along with altered states of consciousness.

The author addresses the separate components of metaphor as well as the styles of delivery to further enhance the efficacy of the stories and metaphors for the benefit of the client or student. The logical step-by-step process provided enables anyone to develop and utilize narrative, storytelling, and metaphor in teaching or in therapy.

Included here is an encyclopedic catalog of specific narrative and metaphoric material arranged in more than sixty categories for use in therapy. Each narrative category provides detailed stories, fables, anecdotes, fairy tales, brief quotes, aphorisms, and other metaphors. Although some of these are brief stories, they give the narrator the opportunity to weave in background and details to build and enrich the metaphor for specific individual applications.

This book also contains a glossary of words and terms, as well as an extensive bibliography for those who wish to pursue further research. Dr. Pearce's book provides broad applications in fields other than therapy. It is a useful tool, as well, for clergy, educators, anthropologists, sociologists, and storytellers.

And that reminds me of a story about losing and finding one's self in a story about a book about a story.

Carol A. Erikson, L.C.S.W.
Director, Erikson Institute
Berkeley, California

Preface

What is a metaphor? Metaphor is a way of knowing—one of the oldest, most deeply embedded, even indispensable ways of knowing in the history of human consciousness. It is, at its simplest, a way of proceeding from the known to the unknown. It is a way of cognition in which the identifying qualities of one thing are transferred in an instantaneous, almost unconscious, flash of insight *to some other thing that is, by remoteness or complexity, unknown to us. (Nisbet, 1969; emphasis added)*

With the words, "It's only a story," people attempt to defend themselves against narrative's power, real or perceived. The refrain softens the chilling reality of tales and prevents the metaphoric content of narrative from encroaching into the conscious realm, where it affects thought and behavior. Narrative and metaphor provide a buffer against the tensions created by the experiences, personal concerns, problems, and storms of life. These words of comfort lessen the impact of the impulsive, instinctual world of imagination and shadowy unconscious, but cannot eliminate them entirely. Metaphor deeply permeates those realms of an individual's psyche that harbor ideas that would otherwise be repugnant or unacceptable. In the subconscious, stories find a venue where they can reside until the individual is ready to admit the story and its messages to his or her conscious being.

Narrative and metaphor afford individuals the opportunity to distance themselves from events in their own experiences and become the protagonist in their own lives' narratives. Metaphor and narrative enable them to rehearse potential solutions until they achieve insight and new direction. Once material previously deemed intolerable is thought and rethought, it can gently, softly knock on the door of consciousness and say, "Here I am." A metaphor is a story that allows people to bridge the gap between what is and what should be.

Narrative and metaphor accomplish these tasks by virtue of the processes by which they are transmitted, received, and processed. The human mind, bicameral in structure and operation, admits numerous possibilities for the incorporation of stimuli into the conscious and unconscious realms. Each hemisphere of the brain has its own style of receiving and processing information. Whereas order, logic, and clearly defined rules reside in the left hemisphere, the right hemisphere is home to subjective and liberating activity. The right hemisphere tolerates ambiguity and flourishes in the world of emotion, symbol, imagery, and narrative. It is in the right hemisphere that vision takes shape, giving form to both the concealed and the revealed. Here metaphor is welcome, providing shadow and color to thought and emotion. The right hemisphere admits material that is automatically excluded by the left hemisphere, until it traverses the isthmus to the left side and is incorporated into conscious-level thought.

The nature of communication within each of the two hemispheres mirrors their characters. On the left side, messages relayed in digital communication invariably have only one referent, one stimulus, and one response. Multiple referents, stimuli, and responses are the work of analogic communication, centered on the right side of the brain. It is through the latter that metaphoric material finds expression.

Metaphor's multiple meanings result in a myriad of responses. Some of these responses are expected; many are not. All are potentially therapeutic. Metaphor stimulates the tension between what is and what can be, a conflict that can find resolution with the passage of time. Metaphor is a particularly useful tool because of its universal nature and its intimate connection to narrative. All human beings have experience with stories and have stories of their own. Traditionally, stories have been used to heal and cure. Stories do not require any sophistication, psychological mind set, or professional terminology to allow the client access to their healing properties.

To substantiate the power of narrative for therapeutic intervention, note should be made of its informal use by the medical community and allied professions in hospital settings since the turn of the twentieth century. Physicians and psychiatrists praised its value (Shiryon, 1978). An 1853 article entitled "On Reading, Recreation and Amusements for the Insane" may be the first published work on what has come to be called *bibliotherapy*. "The Therapeutic Use of a Hospital Library," published in 1919, was the first article to use the term bibliotherapy. After Karl Menninger published *The Human Mind*, he received many letters claiming that the work had therapeutic value. Some of these letters contained requests for a bibliography of narrative materials for use in therapy. He published the results in *A Guide to Psychiatric Books*. In the early 1970s, Shiryon (1977, 1978, 1992) coined the comparable term *literatherapy*. Although the vast number of articles published, by clinicians and nonclinicians alike, under the rubric of bibliotherapy and literatherapy claim positive results, they are anecdotal and not systematic in application, methodology, or data collection. In general, the procedure applied involves the prescription of a variety of selections from literature, followed by a discussion of the applicability of the selections to the reader to help this client achieve insight, catharsis, and identification with the narrative characters (Shrodes, 1978). Shiryon (1977) summarized the application of literature to therapy in these words: "A story has direction and impact, and elicits reactions from the reader." The chief distinction between the bibliotherapeutic approach and more recent therapies is that bibliotherapy relies heavily on insight and interpretation and offers little in the way of indirect suggestion, which serves as a cornerstone of the methodology offered in this book.

Despite their accessibility, stories are not passive. They can aggressively disrupt and even shatter accepted understanding and modes of behavior. Yet, they offer the opportunity to circumvent client resistance. They allow for what Watzlawick, Weakland, and Fisch (1974) call the "gentle art of reframing," which involves the shifting of an experience from one context to another. This book is designed not only to help the practitioner understand the many strands that combine to foster the use of narrative, but it provides a seven-step protocol for using narrative in therapy, (1) identifying a problem; (2) selecting a sensory preference or personal frame of reference for delivery of the metaphor; (3) planning the delivery of the metaphor, taking into account pace, narrative style, rhythm, tone, pause, and transition from a specific topic into the metaphoric model; (4) employing focused words; (5) using embedded commands; (6) including multiple-level metaphors; and (7) delivering the narrative without explanation.

This seven-step approach is the centerpiece of this book. The detailed presentation of the methodology in Chapter 3 is designed for ease of use. Several illustrations provide examples of its application to therapy. The anthology at the end of the book presents and catalogs a brief sample of metaphoric material for therapeutic use. The selections, though few in number, represent topics practitioners frequently confront and give the practitioner access to a topical array of metaphors for therapeutic use.

Chapter 1 surveys the various attempts, from the age of Aristotle to modern times, to define the metaphoric content of narrative and to demonstrate its ability to convey information. To clarify the nature of metaphor, both cognitive and affective characteristics are presented. The connection between metaphor and narrative is seen as integral. Metaphor is a quality of narrative, whose complex and multiple interpretations are the result of subjective responses of the recipient to a variety of cues. The chapter illustrates how metaphor clarifies an individual's concerns and problems and how it enables unrelated thoughts, feelings, and information to be experienced, processed, confronted, and understood.

Because narrative is such a basic component of society, it is no wonder that it has an unusual ability to transcend cultural differences, move among cultural groups, and find expression in hundreds of variants, each bearing the unique stamp of its host culture.

The universality of narrative enables individuals to establish a sense of cultural identity through recovering a mythologically instructed past. In cultures that maintain strong narrative traditions, narrative is frequently believed to be physically and emotionally curative and redemptive. Both the religiously instructed and the psychoanalytic communities have long recognized the curative value of narrative. Religious traditions, even those that exist without or prior to written traditions, as well as Freud and his successors, regularly employ narrative in the curative process. Freud's disciple, Jung, developed the notion that there are universal patterns of human experience that come from the metaphors in the collective unconsciousness of humankind. Bettelheim (1976) is credited with reawakening interest in narrative for therapeutic purposes with his landmark work, *The Uses of Enchantment.*

Chapter 2 considers the impact of the legendary psychiatrist Milton Erickson, who provided the greatest practical and inventive applications of metaphor to therapy. This chapter discusses five of Erickson's approaches to the therapeutic use of metaphor: (1) indirection, (2) humor, (3) paradox, (4) utilization, and (5) altered states of consciousness. Digital-analogic communication and its relationship to left-brain and right-brain communication are also highlighted.

The chapter also discusses several factors that must be taken into account in developing a metaphor for therapeutic use: the client's style of communication, packaging, reframing, isomorphism, the creation of new metaphors, and metaphoric content.

Chapter 3 introduces a systematic approach to the methodological implementation of metaphor in therapy. An explicit seven-step technique provides both the novice and the experienced practitioner with ways of using this material most effectively. Specific, hypothetical case studies demonstrate ease of use. The approach is designed to overcome client resistance quietly and quickly in order to accomplish a great deal therapeutically in a short period of time. The implementation of any or all of the seven steps creates opportunities to magnify the power of narrative's metaphoric content. The seven steps can be summarized as follows:

Step 1 identifies the nature of the client's problem, a standard practice in beginning any therapeutic relationship.

Step 2 identifies the determination and implementation of visual, auditory, and/or kinesthetic modes of delivery of metaphoric or factual information.

Step 3, the method of delivering the metaphor, gives therapists an opportunity to pay careful attention to rhythms, tones, pauses, and other techniques used in communication in order to amplify the impact of a message. By selectively preparing the delivery of the metaphor, varying the pace and style of delivery, and paying careful attention to the listener's responses, the effectiveness of the metaphor is greatly increased.

Step 4 explores how to select and implement focused words, phrases, and sentences chosen because of the symbolism they contain and the feelings they evoke. Words and phrases selected for special attention and focus are interspersed through the therapeutic session. The objective is to direct clients' attention to the symbolism attached to the words and to stimulate new associations.

Step 5, the use of an embedded command created by inserting the client's name into a communication, focuses the patient's attention. Adding such emphasis to a statement changes the way in which it is received. This emphasis may also be accompanied by a shift in voice from third to second person.

Step 6 involves the concurrent use of two or more metaphors. These metaphors vary in length or narrative type and may involve an aphorism or quote embedded within a longer metaphor. These metaphors combine to provide multiple-level communication.

Step 7 involves delivering the metaphor without any explanation or commentary, to enable the client to ruminate and use the metaphor for both conscious and unconscious deliberation.

Chapter 4 is a compendium of narratives, including anecdotes, myths, fables, quotations, and stories, which provide practitioners with a thematic inventory of material to use in therapeutic situations. This anthology is by no means comprehensive, but it does provide an initial collection to which therapists can add their own favorite material. The bibliographic references suggest areas and sources to which therapists may look for additional narrative material from a wide variety of sources.

Acknowledgments

This book never would have been created without the initiation and encouragement of my teacher and friend, Dr. Vincent D. Foley. His warmth, good humor, and realistic evaluations of so many situations provided a wonderful model for me as therapist, teacher, and author. Special thanks go to Janine M. Bernard of Fairfield University, Fairfield, Connecticut; Vincent D. Foley of Jamaica, New York; and Ted L. Orcutt of San Diego, California, who provided worthwhile suggestions for the final preparation of the manuscript. Personal thanks must also be given to Carol Erickson of Berkeley, California, for her willingness to write the foreword for this book and for her insightful suggestions.

Many people at Allyn and Bacon deserve praise for their help in the editing and production of this book. Of particular note are the contributions of Mylan Jaixen, associate publisher, and Susan Hutchinson, editorial assistant. The meticulous copy editing of Judy Ashkenaz of Total Concept Associates greatly refined this book.

My work has been greatly enriched by the writers of prose and poetry who have provided me with imaginative understanding of the language and metaphors that speak clear truths through and between the lines of their stories.

I owe a debt of thanks to many people who generously shared their stories and the application of them to therapeutic opportunities. I am especially grateful to friends, colleagues, and family who offered ideas and encouragement. Special thanks go to my friends, Gladys and David Catterton, for their support in this endeavor, and to Muriel Cohn for her skilled assistance.

About the Author

Stephen S. Pearce was born and raised in the New York metropolitan area, and worked there until 1993, when he assumed the post of senior rabbi of The Congregation Emanu-El of San Francisco. For twenty years he was a faculty member in the Human Relations Department of the Hebrew Union College–Jewish Institute of Religion in New York City. He also taught at St. John's University, where he received his doctorate in counselor psychology in 1977. In addition to his rabbinic position, he is currently on the faculty of the University of San Francisco. Dr. Pearce is the author of numerous articles and two children's books, and has addressed conventions of major professional organizations.

▶ 1

Introduction: The Meaning and Message of Metaphor

Metaphor "is central to our understanding of our selves, our culture, and the world at large" (Lakoff & Turner, 1989). Yet its use as a therapeutic technique is so complex and expansive that one needs to define the terms and the parameters of the frameworks in which it operates in order to apply the technique effectively. Metaphor is fundamentally a literary technique found in all types of narrative, be it fairy tale, drama, story, saga, or legend. All of these literary forms preserve metaphoric content suitable for use in therapy; many examples are presented in the thematically arranged anthology of this book.

Metaphor is a significant technique of narrative. Economy of language is its hallmark; it says much in few words. However, clinicians should not be fooled by its apparent simplicity, for metaphor is multifaceted. The multiplicity and depth of its interpretations stem from the subjective response of the listener to a variety of cues—tone, plot, character, and moral, among other features.

Because it is easier to talk about metaphor than to offer a single, comprehensive definition thereof, here we consider only some of its characteristics in order to establish a general working definition. The characteristics fall naturally into two broad categories: one that encompasses qualities of metaphor functioning on the cognitive level and one that includes those operating primarily in the affective realm. These groupings enable us to appreciate the features shared in several theoretical statements of the nature of metaphor, while at the same time providing a useful vehicle by which we may apprehend the differences among therapeutic techniques.

Metaphor's economy of expression compresses communication, thus organizing and conveying large quantities of information. Bruner (1979) pointed out that metaphor is one of a number of shorthand symbols that compress and simplify language, thus facilitating the processing of vast quantities of information. Failure to employ metaphor to compress information traps the individual "in a confined world of experience … or an overload of information" that would render all stored information inaccessible and therefore useless.

By expressing one idea in terms of another, metaphor can expand literal meanings that are not otherwise easily defined or articulated. This characteristic is most apparent when language is inadequate to bridge a gap between the abstract and the concrete. The etymology of the term itself reflects this quality. A derivative of the Greek words *meta*, meaning "over," and *pherin*, meaning "to carry," the word *metaphor* denotes the transfer of knowledge from one context to another. This can, by extension, imply movement from the concrete world to the abstract. In his *Poetics*, Aristotle (1972) offered the first recorded discussion of metaphor as an explicit subject matter. He believed that "A good metaphor implies an intuitive perception of the similarity of dissimilars."

Metaphor enriches and enhances communication and amplifies linguistic expression precisely because it expands on what is explicitly said. When the response to the question, "What is it?" includes the reply, "It is like …," this is the simplest form of metaphoric usage in operation (Jaynes, 1976). In this context, metaphor is a decorative, expansive way to transfer information and to define the abstract in ways that are concrete and easily understood. Metaphor provides a simplified way of ordering language and information used in communication.

An illustration may prove instructive. A woman who says that she is looking for a man with silver in his hair and gold in his pocket is utilizing metaphor in this way. The phrase immediately conjures a host of attributes in addition to the explicitly stated maturity and wealth. The woman who utters this metaphor covertly expresses her interest in someone who is mature, dignified, seasoned, experienced, worldly, capable, wise, and successful. The phrase speaks volumes about what she is looking for; it conveys even more information than would an extended conversation.

Metaphor links two unrelated events, ideas, or characteristics and produces an unexpected result. By this process, metaphor communicates that which can be said in no other way by compensating for what Hoffman (1986) termed "insufficient idiom." Metaphor is such an integral part of human communication that this use is unavoidable (Bal, 1991). Metaphor attempts to define what no dictionary provides. Poetry relies heavily on metaphor to supplement language's insufficient vocabulary. Referred to as a *speech act* or *language event* by linguists, the utterance of a metaphoric narrative creates new reality.

Metaphoric narrative contains polarities: struggles between good and evil, love and hatred, cowardice and heroism, fear and safety, black and white. It establishes a dramatic tension between current behavior and potential change. When the metaphoric narrative is successful, that tension finds resolution with the passage of time.

Metaphor functions in the affective realm despite the fact that it is delivered and apprehended by the cognitive, intellectual realm. Metaphor is a vehicle for the understanding of communication, events, or ideas from the cognitive world to the affective world of feeling. It is what Bateson called "the pattern which connects" (Capra, 1988). It enables an individual to access the unconscious realm, where problems and concerns are pondered and are explored in a hypothetical environment that neither makes demands of nor denigrates the individual who is not ready to transform thought into action.

Precisely because metaphor straddles the worlds of cognition and affect, it expedites thought process in the world of feeling. Metaphor can, from its position in the unconscious realm, initiate behavior change. Through the mediation of the unconscious realm, accessed by implementation of metaphor, behavior can change the patient's conscious awareness of either the process or the fact.

Metaphor, according to Coles (1989), demonstrates the mimetic power of literature, with its ability to inspire reflection and movement. Metaphor enhances individuals' introspective search for greater understanding of themselves. Thus, metaphors not only point us in new directions; they admonish us, "offer us other eyes through which we might see, other ears with which we might make soundings" (Coles, 1989). Lewis (1966a) sums up this metaphoric attribute: "…it can give us experiences we have never had and thus, instead of 'commenting on life,' can add to it."

Cameron-Bandler (1978) summarized research on the use of metaphor in therapy by stating that "it contains a solution or set of solutions which instruct the client's unconscious mind in specific techniques to generate new choices regarding the situation or problem they came for help with, without the client's conscious mind being aware that the metaphor is intended to provide a solution."

Therapeutic metaphor enables clients to transform a painful or unresolved experience by enabling them to transfer the meaning of such events beyond critical junctures, resulting in an improved destiny or frame of reference.

Siebers (1992) went one step further and suggested that metaphor challenges the listener to struggle with its message:

> The better the story, the more work it does, but stories demand that we do work as well. They present us with a task, and to accomplish it, we must pass time together. All stories have moral lessons to give us, just as morals tell a story, but to uncover the practical relation between stories and morals demands patience, and it is never without its contradictions, questions, and paradoxes.

He added:

Literature is a form of work because it makes us think about what is work to think about. It stirs astonishment, thoughtfulness, and memory.

The use of metaphor is similar to the administration of a projective test, where various meanings evolve from the inner states of the client. Just as each person finds distinctive images in an ink blot, so, too, the listener draws unique and unpredictable meaning from metaphor. Projective tests and metaphors do not produce exact results. Rather, they produce results that are spontaneous and capricious. This view was posited by Bettelheim (1976):

> The fairy tale is therapeutic because the patient finds his *own* solutions, through contemplating what the story seems to imply about him and his inner conflicts at this moment in his life. The content of the chosen tale usually has nothing to do with the patient's external life, but much to do with his inner problems, which seem incomprehensible and hence unsolvable. The fairy tale clearly does not refer to the outer world, although it may begin realistically enough and have everyday features woven into it. The unrealistic nature of these tales (which narrow-minded rationalists object to) is an important device, because it makes obvious that the fairy tales' concern is not useful information about the external world, but the inner processes taking place in an individual.

Each of these qualities of metaphor carries suggestions for the implementation of metaphor as a therapeutic technique. Awareness of the implications of metaphor's characteristics will strengthen and deepen the therapist's ability to employ this technique effectively.

Metaphor is readily accepted because clients have prior experience with stories, particularly in their formative years—a time of freedom and wonderment. Stories, a relevant feature of clients' experiences, facilitate immediate intervention in the therapeutic process. Stories allow clients to retain their known world view. They do not force the client to consciously confront a different mind set. Valuable time is not devoted to establishing a psychological framework or defining psychological terminology. Metaphor's quality of broad, nondirected interpretation allows individual clients to select what they require for their therapeutic expedition instead of having to contend with a gestalt imposed upon them by the therapist. Thus, both client and therapist, freed from the constraints of preconceived therapeutic assumptions and traditions, can concentrate on addressing particular concerns instead of struggling with the overriding rubric of the therapeutic model.

In describing their particular set of circumstances, clients tell their stories. Roberts (1990) pointed out that it is not possible for a client to speak about a problem without telling a story. Thus, clients employ a format with which they are familiar, that they understand, and to which they can relate. A story implies movement and possibility. Just as the characters in a story can and do change, a story "begs an experiential participation from the client" (Lankton & Lankton, 1983).

Watzlawick, Weakland, and Fisch (1974) utilized a metaphor from the martial arts to explain how metaphor facilitates therapist–client dialogue:

> ...where the opponent's thrust is not opposed by a counter-thrust of at least the same force, but rather accepted and amplified by yielding to and going with it. This the opponent does not expect; he is playing the game of force against force, of more of the same, and by the rules of his game he anticipates a counter-thrust and not a different game altogether.

In part, because metaphor liberates both client and therapist from preconceived notions of what form or direction the therapy should assume, it enables clients to reaccess a stage in their lives when learning and experience were unconstrained, natural, and without predetermined course.

Thompson (1990) asserted that narrative accesses childhood modes of learning and memory skills, which may not be consciously present in adults. In particular, she believed the "traits of curiosity, WONDER, openness, and trust" enrich and broaden experience.

Narratives continue to stimulate thought and understanding as a child journeys from immaturity to maturity. Bettelheim (1976) himself employed a metaphor to explain this notion:

> [It] may be compared to a scattering of seeds, only some of which will be implanted in the mind of the child. Some of these will be working in his conscious mind right away; others will stimulate processes in his unconscious. Still others will need to rest for a long time until the child's mind has reached a state suitable for their germination, and many will never take root at all. But those seeds which have fallen on the right soil will grow into beautiful flowers and sturdy trees—that is, give validity to important feelings, promote insights, nourish hopes, reduce anxieties—and in doing so enrich the child's life at the moment and forever after.

Change is facilitated by returning to the developmental stage in which the client is receptive to learning. In addition to providing clients with the means to regain access to the open, accepting state of childhood, metaphor also provides them with an agent of change. Metaphor propels clients to consider the future by revealing new goals, insights, and probabilities. When myth is employed as therapeutic metaphor, it serves as "the way of working out the problem on a higher level of integration. This is the *progressive* function of myths" (May, 1991).

Although metaphor does not compel clients to linger in the past, some therapists consider a contemplation of the past necessary to a consideration of the future. For Heilbrun (1990), the new emerges from hearing the old.

Metaphor encourages clients to reflect upon their situations. Through its extraordinary power, metaphor reveals the messages concealed from each individual. In a chapter entitled "The Education of the Intuitive Mode," Ornstein (1972) wrote of metaphor's mysterious and veiled content that can serve as reflection points. "Often an action caught in a story forms a pattern which is also present on another level of consciousness, as when an electron-microscopic photograph contains the pattern which can be seen in a photograph of a river taken from an airplane, or in a picture of the earth seen from a satellite."

Although the reflection metaphor initiates may superficially resemble that for which traditional psychotherapy strives, the accessibility of metaphoric language to the client signifies an important departure of the Ericksonian conceptual framework from the traditional model (Watzlawick, Weakland, & Fisch, 1974). The methodology, as developed by Milton Erickson, demands that clients be afforded the opportunity to express themselves and their problems in their own terms:

> *"Take what the patient is bringing you"* is one of Erickson's most basic rules for the resolution of human problems. This rule stands in sharp contrast to the teachings of most schools of psychotherapy, which either tend to apply mechanically one and the same procedure to the most disparate patients, or find it necessary first to teach the patient a new language, to have him begin to think in terms of this new language, and then to attempt change by communicating in this language. By contrast, reframing presupposes that the therapist learn the *patient's* language, and this can be done much more quickly and economically than the other way around. In this approach it is the very resistances to change which can best be utilized to bring it about.

Metaphor permeates, facilitates, and, in some ways, redefines the client–therapist relationship. Metaphor lays "a non-threatening ground for the relationship" between clients and counselors (Combs & Freedman, 1990). Metaphor shifts the responsibility of progress and change from the therapist to the client. Clients search their catalogs of experiences and associations to create personal meaning from the received metaphors. Clients work harder to resolve the ambiguity that the narrative creates. An immediate result is that clients may be inclined to listen more than they speak. Franzke (1985) discovered this response in his own practice: "I never fail to be surprised by the experience of how confrontation with fairy-tale material leads to such strong inner involvement, and how inner forces are set free at such moments."

It should be emphasized that the outcome of the delivered metaphor signals clients that the potential exists to solve their supposedly insoluble problems. The recognition of a potential solution is liberating or, at least, encouraging. Lewis (1966a) highlighted this feature of metaphor in these words:

> I thought I saw how stories...could steal past a certain inhibition which had paralysed much of my own religion in childhood. Why did one find it so hard to feel as one was told one ought to feel about God or about the sufferings of Christ? I thought the chief reason was that one was told one ought to. An obligation to feel can freeze feelings.... But supposing that by casting all these things into an imaginary world, stripping them of their stained-glass and Sunday school associations, one could make them for the first time appear in their real potency? Could one not thus steal past those watchful dragons? I thought one could.

In freeing individuals from the exclusive realm of logic and rationality, metaphor places the individual in an unaccustomed province. It is as if the client joined Alice in her adventures in Wonderland, where the incongruities and departures from a known reality assume, with the passage of time, a degree of familiarity and normality. The addition of metaphor to the repertoire of therapeutic techniques frees the therapist from literal and logical intervention. Because the therapist has no need to assign meaning or offer interpretation to the metaphor, clients freely select (and reselect at later dates) the most useful interpretation. This releases the therapist from a model requiring substantial left-brain thought process. Erickson commented: "Too many therapists think that they must direct the change and help the patient change" (Rosen, 1982a).

From the client's perspective, the use and effect of metaphor is not what is usually expected in therapy. Metaphors appear to stray from the purpose of therapy and appear, at times, so far afield of the discussion that clients sit up and take notice.

This position was summarized by Wilk (1985):

> Stories require the listener to shift his orientation to reality. To follow a story, we focus awareness away from the external world and direct it toward the narrative. More than that, following a narrative requires transporting ourselves to the particular reality being described. This orientation to another place and time...is characterized by a decreased awareness of external events and an increased absorption in the inner experience. This altered direction of attention facilitates clients' search through their largely unconscious repertory of personal resources, resources that they can use to solve their problem.
>
>   ...What may be hard to take when slapped down in front of us as a raw assertion, may be more palatable, even relished, when tastefully

served up in the form of a piquant story or a spicy joke. And, any point that can be flatly stated can also be turned into an intriguing story.

Protinsky (1986) emphasized the capabilities of metaphor for

interrupting habitual patterns and creating an unconscious search for a new frame of reference. Thus, for example, indirect suggestions given in the context of a metaphorical story fixate attention, suspend habitual frameworks, and produce an unconscious search for a new perspective.

Thus, metaphor has the capacity to "re-define and re-describe reality" (Ricoeur, 1975). From an Ericksonian perspective, a primary goal of metaphor is to challenge, shock, and surprise to produce rapid change.

TeSelle (1975) described what she called the *parabolic experience* as

a way of believing and living that initially seems ordinary, yet is so dis-located and rent from its usual context that, if the parable "works," the spectators have become participants, not because they want to necessar-ily or simply have "gotten the point" but because they have, for the moment "lost control" or as the new hermeneuts say "been interpreted."

Expanding upon the notion of the powerful influence of metaphor on the in-dividual, Frye (1993) wrote of the "counterenvironment" formed by metaphor, which is "antipathetic to the civilization in which it exists." He suggested that lit-erature "conveys a sense of controlled hallucination... where things are seen with a kind of intensity with which they are not seen in ordinary experience."

Crossan offered a similar perspective on the use of narrative in the field of theology. In *The Dark Interval,* Crossan (1975) insisted that the role of narrative is to startle the listener. New Testament parables serve not to maintain or order reality but rather to disrupt all accepted meaning. Crossan's point is that "stories... shatter the deep structure of our accepted world and thereby render clear and evident to us the relativity of story itself." Crossan assigned the term *transcendence* to this purpose of parable. It is designed to allow the reader to bridge two distinct worlds:

The surface function of parable is to create contradiction within a given situation of complacent security but, even more unnervingly, to chal-lenge the fundamental principle of reconciliation by making us aware of the fact that we made up the reconciliation. Reconciliation is no more fundamental a principle than irreconciliation. You have built a lovely home, myth assures us; but, whispers parable, you are right above an earthquake fault. (Crossan, 1975)

Hoffman (1986) summarized the essence of Crossan's position: "It entails a reversal of normal expectations, an overturning of a world-taken-for-granted, a disrupting challenge to cherished assumptions." In the search for absolute truth, the reader of narrative discovers that even this thought leads to a shift in expectations. Funk (1988) summarized this position:

> The world in which we live is a narrative world, created by and in our stories. We like to think that there is a world out there, quite concrete and objective and reliable, only to discover that that thought, too, is just another story. And so we go on proliferating stories in the vain hope that we will eventually arrive in some story that is quite literally and permanently and unalterably "true."

From a different perspective, the goal in using metaphor, according to Combs and Freedman (1990), is to establish rapport with a client, to gain access to the client's emotional states or attitude, to suggest ideas or solutions, and to embed suggestions for further internal development. Combs and Freedman also advocated the use and provided extensive instruction in their development of the therapist-created metaphor. In addition, they emphasized the use of metaphoric ceremonies as an opportunity to promote change, as more fully developed and popularized by the Milan therapeutic approach (Palazzoli, Boscolo, Cecchin, & Prata, 1978).

Both the client and the therapist are beneficiaries of metaphor. Ozick (1986) pointed out the reciprocal, universalizing power of metaphor that allows each participant in the experience to understand the other better:

> Through metaphor, the past has the capacity to imagine us, and we it. Through metaphorical concentration, doctors can imagine what it is to be their patients. Those who have no pain can imagine those who suffer. Those at the center can imagine what it is to be outside. The strong can imagine what it is to be weak. Illuminated lives can imagine the dark. Poets in their twilight can imagine the borders of stellar fire. We strangers can imagine the familiar hearts of strangers.

Metaphor is particularly useful because the therapist often views his or her role as an attempt to understand the larger meaning of the client's stories/histories. Thus, the mind set of both participants is oriented toward metaphor's many forms of expression.

Despite the benefits of metaphor, the counselor should be aware its fluidity often makes practitioners uncomfortable with the use of metaphor in therapy. Because the telling of a narrative does not guarantee a particular response on the part of the client, the therapist must anticipate a large number of interpretations and reactions. When metaphor is delivered effectively, the therapist establishes an inner tension, both in himself or herself and in the listener. The tension in both parties results from the uncertainty of not knowing exactly where the metaphor may lead. Multiplicity of meaning is apparent when a therapist, hoping to convey a particular meaning to the listener, finds that the client has accepted the face value of the story or has applied an entirely different meaning from the one intended. It is often difficult for the therapist to articulate the results of metaphoric use and to assess its benefits because so much of it occurs in the unconscious mind. Clients, responding to allegorical meaning, may attribute their changed behaviors to something entirely outside the therapeutic process. The skilled user of metaphor must be prepared to acknowledge that the client may not credit the intervention of the therapist or the therapy for the changes that have taken place because they have occurred in the subconscious. The client may not be able to articulate, in the logical language of the left brain, the changes. Thus, the therapist must be alert to changes indicating that the unconscious mind has influenced changes in the client's behavior.

> No matter how well designed according to a metaphor protocol a specific story may be, clients can respond idiosyncratically in a way that isn't expected but provides valuable information to the observing therapist. (Lankton & Lankton, 1989)

Haley (1976) expressed one note of caution in applying metaphor to therapy. Typically, assessment focuses on digital communication, so that "Evaluating a change in a metaphor is a problem with an undeveloped methodology." The use of the analogic mode for evaluation needs to be refined in order to comply with quantifiable expectations of the therapeutic community.

Metaphor is worth hours of conversation in uncovering the client's past. Through metaphor, client and therapist meet and feel understood. In one way or another, many forms of therapy make use of metaphor. It is a multifaceted resource that can provide rich rewards for the client and the therapist alike.

CULTURAL IDENTITY: VALIDATION OF THE INDIVIDUAL WITHIN SOCIETY

Narrative has long enabled members of a particular society to feel connected to long-held rites, rituals, social practices, and traditions, as well as to each other. Narrative defines both the group and its individual members. Narratives, termed *transformative texts* by Bruner (1968b), legitimate societal arrangements and provide a sense of security, particularly in times of bewildering change.

Foremost among the anthropological studies that demonstrate the power of narrative to link members of a society and to define its social institutions are those of Bronislaw Malinowski. Working primarily with the natives of the southwestern Pacific Ocean islands, particularly of the Trobriand Islands, Malinowski coined the term *functionalism* to describe society as an interdependent, organic whole. Everything pertaining to that society, including all myths and cultural material, has the practical function of assuring the survival of the institution (Malinowski, 1936/1962).

Among those cultural appurtenances are myths that, for Malinowski, constitute "a warrant, a charter, and often even a practical guide to the activities with which [they are] connected." Charter myths are active components of culture, certifying the legitimacy of social arrangements. They are lived realities, fulfilling the sociological function of acting as a warrant for those institutions. They are indispensable and vital, the "backbone of primitive culture," without which it cannot survive (Malinowski, 1926/1954).

Malinowski developed the notion that the intrinsic meaning of a narrative comes not from the narrative itself but from the meaning given to it in cultural context. Thus, as much as individuals are defined by their myths, so the myths are defined by the society. Simply stated, narratives are texts in context. Because Malinowski believed that the meaning of myth lay not in its literal messages but, rather, in what myths did for individuals and societies, he turned to the behavioral consequences of certain stories: "If we really want to understand myths, look at what myths *do*, not what they *say*" (Strenski, 1992).

Kluckhohn (1942) applied the work of Malinowski to the Navaho. He affirmed the belief that narrative in the form of myth establishes and sustains cultural identity, promotes social solidarity, formalizes values, and provides for the transmission of culture. Thus, for the Navaho, returning home to hear cherished narratives provides the opportunity to revivify spiritual life, exercise community connection, and experience a feeling of security. Navaho myths provide firm values and definite answers to puzzling questions of life and death (Kluckhohn & Leighton, 1951). One Navaho told Kluckhohn and Leighton (1951), "Knowing a good story will protect your home and children and property. A myth is just like a big stone foundation—it lasts a long time."

The usefulness of narrative among members of the same cultural group stems from the fact that "people who share a complex knowledge about their worlds can assume a common background and speak through allusion" (Rosaldo, 1986). The use of such "telegraphic shorthand" cannot be employed where the recipient of the narrative is culturally unrelated to the teller. Not having the luxury of common cultural, ethnic, and religious background, moderns must make explicit all details so that their listeners, who do not share a common background, can make all the connections, be they cultural practices, physical landscape, or linguistic innuendo, that a member of the speaker's cultural group automatically assumes. The advantage of both listener and narrator belonging to the same culture is that the narrator need not make significant digressions to make his point. The member of the community brings his or her prior experience to the story; in turn, the story validates and strengthens that individual's place in society.

In addition to transmitting a cherished cultural heritage, providing security and connectedness to a culture, narratives also provide a sense of self-worth. Bruner (1986a) believed that "stories are interpretive devices which give meaning to the present in terms of location in an ordered systematic sequence." When he applied this theoretical construct to Native American stories, he stated that these stories enable the Native American to "construct an Indian self." He found the differences between Native American stories dating from the 1930s and those from the 1970s particularly indicative of change in Native American self-apperceptions: "In the 1930s and 1940s, the dominant story constructed about Native American culture change saw the present as disorganization, the past as glorious, and the future as assimilation." The more recent story views the present as "a resistance movement, the past as exploitation, and the future as ethnic resurgence." Although these themes appear to diverge, Bruner focused his analysis on the ordering of the common components of each narrative. Contained within the story of "past glory, present disorganization and future assimilation" of the 1930s are suppressed elements relating to "present resistance [and] future resurgence," which dominate the story of the 1970s. It is the relative importance of each element in its respective narrative that defines the tone of the narrative as a whole. Each narrative is a reflection, a statement, of the Native American experience and identification at a particular point in history. The power of Native American narrative derives from its ability to transform itself and to define cultural self-perceptions. The story assumes a life of its own as past conditions yield to the present.

The notion that a narrative can be transformative, enabling an individual to reexperience his cultural heritage, thereby defining personal identity and providing a sense of personal security, is one that is quite suggestive for the therapeutic setting. To clients, it emphasizes the importance of understanding personal and cultural backgrounds, not only in order to understand who they are and how they got to be that way, but also to be able to build on those features of their past that serve as sources of strength, encouragement, and dynamic direction. Narratives that enable patients to revalue their worth because of insights gained from their cultural heritage provide a transformative tools that can shape how they feel about themselves and where they are headed.

Narrative's power to define a cultural milieu, to identify an individual's place therein, and to create a sense of personal security is not limited to modern cultural settings. Ancient texts and religious practice also must be included in order to understand how narrative historically has been utilized by religious communities. The therapeutic community can benefit from the powerful changes that religious narrative has effected for the faithful throughout the centuries. Early recorded narratives demonstrate the force of the written word to empower a listener through past experiences of his cultural tradition.

The Gilgamesh epic is the longest and greatest literary composition of ancient Mesopotamia. Although it is difficult to ascertain the purpose for which the work was written, Dalley (1989) suggested that it was probably written for entertainment.

In an analysis of a portion of the Old Babylonian version, Abusch (1993) suggested that Gilgamesh's speech at the death of his companion, Enkidu, carries "the speaker and the audience back to the experience itself. It presents the event as if it were ongoing and causes the audience to share in it."

To a Western reader, a more immediate example of narrative as a means of societal and personal validation is found in the role of narrative in the Judeo-Christian tradition. Joseph Campbell, one of the great popularizers of mythological studies, spoke of the corpus of images, identities, and models that provide the "mythologically instructed community" with patterns for growth (Bruner, 1979). Bruner (1979) stated that narrative, in the form of myth, provides the members of the mythologically instructed community "with a library of scripts upon which the individual may judge the play of his multiple identities."

Numerous examples illustrate the ability of narrative to make listeners feel that they have personally relived and reexperienced the particular historical event in question. An example of this phenomenon can be drawn from the Christian sacrament of baptism.

The baptismal liturgy is replete with references to the identification of the candidate for the sacrament with the community that holds that sacrament valid. Prior to the baptism itself, during the Thanksgiving over the Water, the celebrant (or the child's parents, in the case of an infant) confirms the central role that water played in the history of the community, from the moment of Creation through the release from Egyptian slavery to the time of the baptism of Jesus by John. Candidates themselves experience part of the history of the Christian faith with the recitation of these (or similar) words:

> We thank you, Father, for the water of Baptism. In it we are buried with Christ in his death. By it we share in his resurrection. Through it we are reborn by the Holy Spirit. (Church Hymnal Corporation, 1979)

Words that confirm the candidate's acceptance as a member of the community, even as "Christ's own for ever," accompany the performance of the baptism. Thus, the administration of this sacrament, accompanied by a retelling of part of the Christian experience, formally unites candidates with the Church and initiates their participation in the entire Christian experience.

In the biblical book of Exodus the prescription for the Passover celebration is designed to associate for the Jewish listener that festival with the experience of freedom.

The consumption of unleavened bread serves as an additional reminder of the liberation from slavery:

> Seven days you shall eat unleavened bread, and on the seventh day there shall be a festival of the Lord. Throughout the seven days unleavened bread shall be eaten; no leavened bread shall be found with you, and no leaven shall be found, in all your territory. And you shall explain to your son on that day, "It is because of what the Lord did for me when I went free from Egypt." (Exodus 13:6–8)

As if anticipating the needs of future listeners, the author of the book of Deuteronomy commands the listener to repeat the events of the Exodus to his progeny, thereby uniting two generations in the historical experience of the Israelites:

> When, in time to come, your son asks you, "What mean the exhortations, laws, and norms which the Lord our God has enjoined upon you?" you shall say to your son, "We were slaves to Pharaoh in Egypt and the Lord freed us from Egypt with a mighty hand.... It will be therefore to our merit before the Lord our God to observe faithfully this whole Instruction, as He has commanded us." (Deuteronomy 6:20–25)

Rabbis of the Talmudic period (third to fifth centuries A.D.) cited Deuteronomy 6:23 in support of the notion that each generation participates in the Exodus from Egypt:

> Not only our ancestors alone did the Holy One redeem but *us* as well, along with them, as it is written: "And He freed *us* from Egypt so as to take us and give us the land which He had sworn to our fathers." (Bronstein, 1974)

When they created the Haggadah for the Passover celebration, rabbis of the Talmudic period increased the force of their exhortation to recite the Exodus narrative to one's children by suggesting that it be told on four different levels to suit a child's level of understanding:

> Four times the Torah bids us tell our children of the Exodus from Egypt. Four times the Torah repeats: "And you shall tell your child on that day..." From this, our tradition infers that there are different kinds of people. To each we respond in a different manner, according to his question, his situation, and his need. (Bronstein, 1974)

In a contemporary context, Myerhoff's study (1986) underscored the importance to members of a particular societal or ethnic group of having vehicles through which to experience and express their communities of origin. Her study focused on a community of aged immigrant Jews of Eastern European extraction who were living at a Venice, California, senior community center. The participants of this center lived far from their children, felt a lack of self-worth in the eyes of their community, and faced the prospect of impending death and disappearance without being remembered or having made a permanent contribution by which they might be remembered. Myerhoff was intent on helping them achieve feelings of self-worth, and an opportunity to be noticed and remembered after they were dead through their presentation and interpretation of their own history and culture. Myerhoff developed what she called *definitional ceremonies* designed to help these elderly people deal with their invisibility within the larger, alien culture by bringing public notice to their individual and collective worth, vitality, and existence. Under her direction, members of this group displayed and dramatized themselves in many forms, informal and formal, planned and spontaneous: by storytelling, making scenes; by positioning themselves to be noticed, recorded, listened to, and photographed.

In addition to using verbal means to recall and retain their connection to their communities of origin, group members created a mural that was a visual storytelling of their pasts and places of origin. This mural and these definitional ceremonies allowed the center members to watch and be watched, bear witness to their stories and those of their fellow compatriots, and give new and lasting meaning to their frail lives.

As in society at large, the religious community has long provided a powerful means of enabling individuals to define themselves and feel linked to a larger community that offers support, understanding, and continuity. Building on these sources of strength, a therapist can utilize religious and other narratives to help clients deal with their difficulties and secure greater meaning and self-worth.

NARRATIVE'S POWER TO HEAL

Physical and Emotional Healing

Just as narrative validates the position of individuals within the society and provides identity and security to those individuals, it also has the power to physically, spiritually, or psychologically heal members of that society. Traditionally, healers have believed in the curative power of words and ideas.

A rabbi, whose grandfather had been a disciple of the Baal Shem, was asked to tell a story. "A story," he said, "must be told in such a way that it constitutes help in itself." And he told: "My grandfather was lame. Once they asked him to tell a story about his teacher. And he related how

the holy Baal Shem used to hop and dance while he prayed. My grandfather rose as he spoke, and he was so swept away by his story that he
himself began to hop and dance to show how the master had done. From
that hour he was cured of his lameness. That's the way to tell a story!"
(Buber, 1947)

Ideas can provoke ideodynamic physiological responses. The term *ideody-*
namic designates relationships between ideas and the physiological responses of
the body (Erickson & Rossi, 1981; Rossi & Cheek, 1988). Gold (1990) noted the
relationship between physiological responses and narrative. He suggested that
reading a story can produce the same physiological response as an actual life situation because the same signals are sent to our nervous system in both real and
imagined experiences. This is the basis for the success of erotic writing as well
as that of suspense fiction. Fantasy, fear, lust, laughter, and anger are all pro-
grammed into our genes to create a deeply felt inner experience.

The Navaho, probably the most widely studied and best known of all Native
American groups, express the potential for curing physical and emotional illness
through their myths and rituals. Kluckhohn and Leighton (1951) summarized the
qualities that characterize this form of curing and healing: "The fundamental
principles which underlie most Navaho magical practices are those of 'like produces like' and 'the part stands for the whole.' "

Kluckhohn (1942) believed that the word *restore* was the best English translation of the Navaho word used to define what a ceremony does for a recipient.
These ceremonies act not only as a cure for physical illness but also as a remedy
for antisocial tendencies. "The associated myths reinforce the patient's belief that
the ceremonial will both truly cure him of his illness and also 'change' him so
that he will be a better man in his relations with his family and his neighbors."

Traditional tales about healing and successful cures provide assurance that
help is available. In addition to myth and ritual, Navaho ceremonies also employ
sand painting, song, herbal medication, and prayer. Navaho healing ceremonies,
called *chants* or *sings,* are complex amalgams of all facets of myth-related activity. Kluckhohn and Wyman (1938) cataloged twenty-six of the major ceremonies
used in connection with curing by a *practitioner,* the term that subsumes singer,
curer, and diagnostician. These elaborate, mythologically based chants detail
how the chant itself was obtained from the gods and refer to typical applications
for healing a wide variety of ailments, including muscle soreness, tiredness,
lameness, paralysis, drowning, deafness, colds, fevers, rheumatism, abdominal
pain, constipation, gall bladder trouble, internal pain, mental disease, sore throat,
kidney and bladder trouble, heart and lung infection, body itching, eye trouble,
boils, sores, and venereal disease. Kluckhohn and Leighton (1951) compared the
officiant's task in the presentation of a nine-night chant to the memorization of a

Wagnerian opera, including "orchestral score, every vocal part, all the details of the settings, stage business, and each requirement of costume."

Brief descriptions of several chants illustrate the interrelationship between illness, myth, and curing. The chant entitled "Hail Way" is indicated for musculoskeletal disabilities and infirmities. It is based on the mythic hero Rain Boy, who suffers such ailments at the hands of his enemies. The protagonist, Night Way, threatened by physical and emotional problems centered in the head, is central to the "Night Way" chant used to cure related medical concerns. The heroine of "Beauty Way," troubled by a variety of afflictions, becomes the paradigm for dealing with snake bites and problems of the internal organs.

Sander (1979) suggested that the efficacy of the medicine man's power, which is the heart of the Navaho system of healing, derives from the shared belief of the practitioner and his patient in the healing processes of their culture based on ritual and myth rather than on physiology. Both "cause and cure are seen against the supernatural background of a man's life." In an alien culture, the practice would not only be misunderstood, it would be meaningless. This unique relationship between client and healer is responsible for the efficacy of healing simply because both participants affirm specific cultural beliefs and rituals.

In addition to the importance of the relationship between patient and healer, Kluckhohn and Leighton (1951) emphasized the interrelatedness of the mind–body connection: "The whole Navaho system of curing clearly takes it for granted that you cannot treat a man's body without treating his mind and vice versa."

The use of healing narrative by a small group of Eskimos who occupy St. Lawrence Island, the largest island in the Bering Sea, is also well documented. Until 1955, when acculturation to Western ways and conversion to Christianity was complete, these Arctic aborigines relied on a shaman, a practitioner of healing rites, for treatment of certain illnesses which they believed were caused by the loss of the patient's soul as a result of sneezing or sudden fright. Séances, histrionic possession by spirits, and a wide variety of magic and tricks were hallmarks of the shaman's efforts to recover the lost soul. Included in the séance was adventure storytelling, where "the narratives usually involve great feats of strength, endurance, perspicacity, and sometimes even a struggle between the evil spirit who wants to keep the patient's soul in thrall and the shaman's spirit who wants to release the soul and thus return the patient to health" (Murphy, 1964).

The medicine men of the Yoruba tribe of western Nigeria regularly employ both simile and illustrative stories to deal with physical and emotional problems and problems related to the life cycle. These stories are employed in addition to rituals of incantation and magic, performance of blood sacrifice, the use of magical potions and herbal medicines, and the introduction of certain substances into the blood by incision at the site thought to be most closely related to the illness. The application of simile might involve the use of an illustration related to the hoped-for cure—for example, "As the river always flows forwards and never back, so your illness will never return." A story is employed that is the expansion of a verse and is accompanied by one or two short chants. They generally refer to ancient equivalents of individuals who were beset by similar problems, which were ultimately resolved (Prince, 1964).

Buckley (1985) studied the Yoruba and found that the cultic priests know a large number of verses by heart. These verses contain incantations that describe medicinal ingredients. One of the cultic priests described the purposes of these verses: "They take care of human beings by curing their sickness, giving them children, giving money to them, and protecting them from their enemies" (Buckley, 1985).

Islamic tradition employs what is known as "spiritual medicine," in which physical illness may be cured by recitation of prayers or readings from the Qur'an. Although the primary outcome of this activity may be the creation of sustained faith, curative powers are thus ascribed to the verses of Islam's holy book. As early as the ninth century A.D., a text entitled *Miraculous Properties of the Qur'an* discussed the curative properties of virtually each Qur'anic passage. Furthermore, each chapter, read in a different fashion, results in different benefits (Rahman, 1987).

Sufism, an outgrowth of the Islamic ascetic, mystical tradition, has increasingly found popularity among therapists for the perceived therapeutic quality of its tales. Ornstein (1972) and Fellner (1976), among others, referred to the writings and anthologies of Shah as rich resources for therapeutic tales. Fellner (1976), commenting on the similarities among stories of the Sufi, Zen, and Hasidic traditions, noted that the multidimensionality of the stories enables them to "carry a message or comment on several levels, not only of understanding but also of impact."

"The Worm and the Toothache," a short, cosmogonic text from ancient Mesopotamia, combines a creation story with directions to a dentist for curing a toothache. The mythological section of the story offers an explanation of how toothaches came into being. The instructions to the dentist include ritual incantations along with this admonition:

Fix the pin and seize its foot.
Because thou hast said this, O worm,
May Ea smite thee with the might
Of his hand. (Pritchard, 1958)

The strong association of mythological and ritual material is indicative of the healing power of narrative.

In the Hindu tradition, hymns and tales explain the origins and character of disease, offer instruction for curing, train healing initiates, and validate the power of the medical practitioner.

Beck, Claus, Goswami, and Handoo (1987) reproduced a tale from the Saurastra area of Gujarat, India, in which villagers afflicted with mumps seek contact with the descendants of the protagonist of this tale in order to alleviate the pain associated with the illness.

Chaplin (1930) reported that Hindus attempt to cure emotional problems by reading and by having the client meditate on a fairy tale that depicts their problem. One popular tale tells how the god Dhanvantari overwhelms the destructive power of venomous snakes. This narrative features a spiritual teacher whose protective healing occurs through the use of charms and magic. Thus, the tale discloses the power of the practitioner and gives the suppliant confidence in his healing. Through tales of this type, an individual is "apprised of what he needs to know to preserve health and long life…" (Zimmer, 1948).

Chaplin (1930) suggested that in Hindu tradition, mental and physical disorders are perceived as related and intertwined. She described the methodology of Hindu mind-healing when applied to psychotherapy as including the use of specially arranged tales tailored to meet the specific requirements and difficulties of the particular patient.

Bettelheim (1976) made passing reference to the Hindu use of fairy tales to "medicate" a disoriented person in the hope that the tale would help the individual visualize both the nature of his problem and the potential for its solution. The tale is applied in these cases with the expectation that the client will find himself, just as the protagonist in the tale did.

A remarkable application of the psychological curative power of storytelling emerges from the oriental saga, *The Thousand and One Nights*. The stories in this collection are set within a frame narrative relating how the noble Scheherazade cured the king Shahryar's madness which resulted from witnessing his wife's infidelity. The outraged king murdered his adulterous wife and, over the course of the next three years, nightly massacred his subsequent brides.

When Scheherazade proposed marrying the king, her father could not dissuade her. He did, however, give a vital message to his daughter by telling her what appear to the reader to be two irrelevant, though beguiling stories, which, in fact, modeled the paradigm for controlling the king's murderous rage, namely: Tell an unending story.

Shahryar agreed to delay his new wife's execution in order to hear the end of the tale she had begun on their wedding night. He was so intrigued by her story that he kept delaying her execution in order to allow her to continue on each of the successive one-thousand nights. At the completion of this cycle of stories, Scheherazade and the other women of the kingdom are spared, and Shahryar is cured of his madness and is restored to his former reputation as a just ruler.

Clinton (1986) attributed Scheherazade's success to a "talking cure" that "conforms to the expectations of Bagdad, not Vienna. That is, the doctor does the talking, not the patient, and tells tales that address the patient's concerns." Thus, Shahrazad included tales centered on the relationship between men and women, unjust retribution, the virtuous character of some women contrasted with the vile nature of a woman who would betray her spouse, treatment of women, and assurance that punishment should be appropriate to the crime. One of the stories mirrored the king's unfortunate experience with his first wife, but concluded with a different destiny than the murders of his spouse and of the other women.

The view that narrative has healing power is summarized by Kluckhohn (1942), who suggested that both myths and rituals constitute "a cultural storehouse of adjustive responses for individuals." Most notably, he spoke of their role as socially sanctioned palliatives for mental ills that may alleviate anxiety and direct antisocial feelings into socially appropriate, safe channels.

Several New Testament references indicate the power of narrative in healing. Scripture has numerous examples of Jesus' use of parable in his activities. Jesus' reputation as a healer and preacher is indicated by Matthew (4:23–24; similarly, 9:35):

> And he went about all Galilee teaching in their synagogues and *preaching the gospel* of the kingdom and healing every disease and every infirmity among the people. So his fame spread throughout all Syria, and they brought him all the sick, those afflicted with various diseases and pains, demoniacs, epileptics, and paralytics, and he healed them. (emphasis added)

Specific healing incidents are related in the Gospel of Matthew. In the first case, a centurion sought help: "Lord, my servant is lying paralyzed at home, in terrible distress." Jesus responds with this metaphor, which heals the servant:

> I tell you, many will come from the east and west and sit at table with Abraham, Isaac, and Jacob in the kingdom of heaven, while the sons of the kingdom will be thrown into the outer darkness; there men will weep and gnash their teeth. (Matthew 8:11–12)

Word spread of these miraculous healings, and Jesus employed the use of "a word" to heal.

> That evening they brought to him many who were possessed with demons; and he *cast out the spirits with a word, and healed all who were sick.* This was to fulfill what was spoken by the prophet Isaiah, "He took our infirmities and bore our diseases." (Matthew 8:16–18; emphasis added)

The Gospel of Luke contains several references to the notion of healing and preaching. As word of Jesus' healing powers spread, the following interchange (Luke 7:20–22) took place between the disciples of John and Jesus:

And when the men had come to him, they said, "John the Baptist has sent us to you, saying, 'Are you he who is to come, or shall we look for another?' " In that hour he cured many of diseases and plagues and evil spirits, and on many that were blind he bestowed sight. And he answered them, "Go and tell John what you have seen and heard: the blind receive their sight, the lame walk, lepers are cleansed, and the deaf hear, the dead are raised up, the poor have good news preached to them..."

Luke (9:1–2) chronicles Jesus' commission of the twelve disciples to preach and heal:

And he called the twelve together and gave them power and authority over all demons and to cure diseases, and he sent them out to preach the kingdom of God and to heal.

The sophisticated Johannine metaphor replaced the Hebrew scripture's depiction of a vengeful deity with "God is love" (1 John 4:8). By equating God with Love, John enabled people to experience the power of the deity as children experience the benevolent love of a parent. Thus, the notion is immediate, experienced by most members of the Christian community. Even those who fail to experience the unequivocal love of a human parent for its child are, in accepting Christian doctrine, guaranteed the love of the Father of mankind.

Mark (4:34) simply states that Jesus never spoke without a parable. It must be remembered that in the New Testament, preaching is most often associated with the telling of parables. Thus, these two activities are closely linked.

Though not central to the biblical or rabbinic traditions, healing through narrative was employed by using a technique known as *bibliomancy*, the practice of using biblical words and verses for divination or magical cures. Deuteronomy (6:8–9; 11:18) admonishes the Israelites to bind certain verses on their hands and foreheads because of their protective qualities and for talismanic purposes. A selection of scriptural verses, including a large number of psalms, were prescribed for curing a wide variety of psychological and physical illnesses, including bleeding, fever, pain, heart disease, eye diseases, obsessive behavior, and alcoholism. Beyond medical concerns, such literature could be utilized for an expansive collection of nonmedical problems (Grunwald, 1901–1906/1963).

Rich examples of healing through narrative are found in later Jewish mystical and Hasidic sources. A Hasidic story speaks of the redemptive quality of stories and their abilities to heal the psychological wounds of an individual:

Whenever there was a crisis, the Baal Shem Tov would go to a specific place in the woods, light a fire, say a prayer and catastrophe would be averted. A generation later, the Maggid of Meseritz, the Baal Shem Tov's disciple, faced with similar concern, would go to the same location and say: "I do not know how to light the fire, but I can say the prayers." Again the threat lifted. A generation later, Rabbi Moshe Leib of Sasov, next in the line of Hasidic leaders, faced crisis by returning to that place in the woods and saying: "I do not know how to light the fire, nor do I know the prayer, but I know the place where this all happened, and this must suffice." And it was sufficient. Finally, when catastrophe faced Rabbi Israel of Rishin of yet a later generation, he sat in his study and said: "I do not know how to light the fire and I cannot say the prayers and I do not even know the place in the woods, but I can tell the story." And once again the emergency was lifted. (Adapted from *Kenesset Yisrael*, an early twentieth century anthology of tales collected by Reuven Zak and available in English in Buber, 1948, and Frankel, 1989)

Religious Healing and Redemption from Sin

In the context of organized religion, healing may occur when the narrative serves as a vehicle for individual or societal redemption from sin. The following examples demonstrate the redemptive power of stories in various traditions.

In Jewish tradition, the ritual retelling of the story of the binding of Isaac (Genesis 22) in the context of the Jewish New Year's observance is equivalent to acceptance of sin offerings for atonement:

> ...for the sake of Abraham's compliance with the divine command of offering up Isaac, God would accept hereafter sacrifices of animals as an atonement for the people's sin. When Abraham asked, "What will happen if they will no longer be able to bring such sacrifices?" God replied, "Let them recite it before me, and it will be for me like unto the sacrifice." (Gaster, 1928)

The rabbinic commentaries regarded the hearing of the ram's horn at Jewish New Year commemorations as sufficient grounds for absolution:

> ...I will sit in judgement upon them on the New Year's Day. If they desire that I should grant them pardon, they shall blow the ram's horn on that day, and I, mindful of the ram that was substituted for Isaac as a sacrifice, will forgive them for their sins. (*Midrash Tanhuma*, cited in Ginzberg, 1909–1961)

A Hasidic tale emphasizes that hearing stories can offer spiritual healing or redemption:

> Before the death of the Baal Shem Tov, his faithful assistant inquired about how he would earn a living after the death of the great master.

The Baal Shem Tov replied, "You will travel about telling stories about me and you will become rich."

Following the death of the Baal Shem Tov, the assistant reluctantly pursued this new calling, earning only a subsistence living. Never having given up faith in the Baal Shem Tov's word, he heard one day that there was a rich Jew who would pay generously to hear any story. He told him this story:

"There was once a notorious anti-Semite who inflamed crowds and instigated pogroms against the Jews. One day, the Baal Shem Tov came to this town and found that all the Jewish homes and businesses were shuttered up and bolted tight because this man was going to provoke the local people into going on the rampage. Unafraid, the Baal Shem Tov sent for the man. When they met face to face, the man told his story to the Baal Shem Tov. The Baal Shem Tov rebuked him for his cruelty when he learned that he was an apostate. Shocked to his senses, the man wept and asked: 'O rabbi, how can I be redeemed, having yearly shed innocent blood?' The Baal Shem Tov told him that repentance would make God's redemption and forgiveness possible. The man insistently asked how he would know that he had finally been forgiven for his sins.

"He replied, 'You will know that your soul has been redeemed when one day you hear your own story.'"

The Baal Shem's assistant was richly rewarded for telling this redemptive tale. (Adapted from *Adat Tzaddiquim*, a nineteenth-century anthology of tales collected by Michael Levi and available in English in Buber, 1955, and Patai, 1980)

In many instances, Christian parable enables the listener, through active participation, to become a party to the creation of the metaphor's meaning (Funk, 1966; Wilder, 1964). Thus, the participant may, at the same time that he identifies with the historical experience of the church and community, experience spiritual renewal and redemption from sin.

The Eucharist is perhaps the best known example of a metaphor that offers participatory healing and renewal. As the ritual officiant offers the bread and wine, he evokes for the participants the Last Supper, the Passover meal at which Jesus instructed his disciples to eat the matzah and drink the wine, which, through transubstantiation, had become his body and blood. Acceptance of the Eucharist affords the modern participant an opportunity to experience God personally. In each celebration of the Eucharist, these transformations are viewed as wondrously continuing. In some churches, the words "Do this in memory of me" accompany the offering of the Host. Tracy (1987) described the healing nature of this act:

Neither by the blood of goats and calves, but by his own blood, he entered at once into the holy place, having obtained eternal redemption for us. For if the blood of bulls and of goats, and the ashes of an heifer sprinkling the unclean, sanctifieth to the purifying of the flesh; how much more shall the blood of Christ, who through the eternal Spirit offered himself without spot to God, purge your conscience from dead works to serve the living God?

Similarly, the retracing of the stations of the cross, both in churches and along the Via Dolorosa in Jerusalem, in reenactment of the Easter Passion, affords the faithful a physical opportunity to be reassured of resurrection and eternal life.

The Psychoanalytic Use of Myth

The adherents of the psychoanalytic school of thought acknowledged the power of metaphor to provide a pathway to healing and gave this vehicle widespread expression.

Freud recognized that traditional myths and legends contained important psychological insights. He categorized many of the tensions his patients experienced in terms of pressures experienced by mythic figures, notably Oedipus, Electra, and Narcissus. This approach was designed to make people aware of "the inescapable cauldron of emotions which every child, in his own way, has to manage at a certain age"(Bettelheim, 1976).

Freud and other early psychoanalysts turned to folklore, fairy tales, and other forms of imaginative literature to label and categorize symptoms they documented in their numerous case studies (Grolnick, 1986). Indeed, Freud's masterful narrative ability enabled him to record his early case histories in terms of the mythic and folkloristic metaphors he observed in each patient's story. Case histories with such allusive titles as "Little Hans," "The Wolf Man," and "The Rat Man" provide fascinating reading. Grolnick (1986) summarized Freud's development of a treatment method using the folklore model in which "the patient and the analyst tell and retell, interpret and reinterpret the story of the patient."

Freud believed myths and fairy tales contained symbolic language derived from the unconscious. However, they were "only the expression of irrational, antisocial impulses rather than the wisdom of past ages expressed in a specific language, that of symbols" (Fromm, 1951).

In addition to imaginative literature, Freud frequently extracted dynamic metaphors "of energy and force, flow and resistance, repression and conversion, defense and aggression..." from social and political life, as well as from "the fields of physical dynamics and hydraulics, physiology and natural history, anthropology and mythology, archeology and ancient history, military life and technology, the classics and popular literature, and from other realms as well" (Leary, 1990). Richards (1974) provides a compilation of these metaphors and analogies. It is also important to note that Freud catalogs what he considered to be universal symbols and metaphors that patients reported were present in their dreams. So pervasive is Freud's use of metaphor in the development of psycho-analysis that Nisbet (1969) stated that classical psychoanalytic theory, stripped of its metaphors, has little remaining significance: "Divest classical psychoana-lytic theory of its metaphors—Oedipus complex, etc.—and there would not be a great deal of substance left."

Fromm (1951), like Freud, believed that dreams and myths share a universal symbolic language of inner experiences, feelings, and thoughts different from conventional daytime logic: "It is a language with its own grammar and syntax, as it were, a language one must understand if one is to understand the meaning of myths, fairy tales and dreams."

When dreams, daydreams, and unconscious thought are viewed in this light, it is possible to discover connections between the client's metaphors and his or her pathology. Freudian psychoanalysis adopted this as its major focus: to uncov-er the relationship between myth, the id, ego, and superego, and the unconscious mind. Discovery of this connection is viewed as a key to understanding and in-terpreting motivation and behavior in each patient.

Jung, one of Freud's first disciples, synthesized a unique understanding of the mythological level of the unconscious. He expressed it in the notion of arche-types, original patterns that manifest themselves throughout individual and soci-etal behaviors through all time. Archetypes account for universal patterns of human experience and reflect the collective unconscious of humanity.

Jung described the collective unconscious in this way:

> We can distinguish a *personal unconscious*, comprising all the acquisi-tions of personal life, everything forgotten, repressed, subliminally per-ceived, thought, felt. But, in addition to these personal unconscious contents, there are other contents which do not originate in personal ac-quisitions but in the inherited possibility of psychic functioning in gen-eral, i.e., in the inherited structure of the brain. These are the mythological associations, the motifs and images that can spring up anew anytime anywhere, independently of historical tradition or migra-tion. I call these contents the *collective unconscious*. Just as conscious contents are engaged in a definite activity, so too are the unconscious contents, as experience confirms. (Jung, 1921/1971)

Dieckmann (1986) wrote that the collective unconscious is "the world of mythological, primordial images, and it can, if rightly understood, direct the in-dividual to modes of experiencing and to possibilities of emotional functioning which lie outside the range of his personal experience."

Jung delineated many archetypes, among them birth, death, power, the hero, the child, mother and father, natural and man-made objects. These largely uncon-scious motifs manifest themselves in fantasy, dream, myth, fairy tale—what Jung termed *parable*—that powerfully influence all behavior.

There are as many archetypes as there are situations in life. Endless repetition has engraved these experiences into our psychic constitution… representing merely the possibility of a certain type of perception and action. (Jung, 1934/1959)

For Jung, the primary expression of the archetype was the parable or metaphor. He suggested, for example, that the sun can be identified with

the lion, the king, the hoard of gold guarded by the dragon, or the force that makes for the life and health of man, it is neither the one thing or the other, but the unknown third thing that finds more or less adequate expression in all these similes, yet—to the perpetual vexation of the intellect—remains unknown and not to be fitted in a formula. (Jung, 1958)

The power of an archetype is derived from the affective response to it. Through responses to the emotionally charged symbol, sense can be made out of life's tensions and challenges. Archetypes help channel primitive, instinctual drives into cultural and spiritual values. "They only emerge into consciousness when personal experiences have rendered them visible" (Jung, 1978). In short, it is personal experience that creates the content of the archetype.

Rites for fertility, protection from outside forces, health, strength, and success in war are but a few of the situations in which the metaphoric meaning of archetype is employed in primitive and modern societies. Archetypes help ensure fulfillment of desired goals. For Jung, such parables or metaphors serve a clear purpose, which he termed *canalization* (Jung, 1928/1960).

Jung's accomplishments brought the collective unconscious and its archetypes to a prominent position, and his theories generated extraordinary interest in myth. The central focus of his work, however, was on interpreting and understanding this material rather than applying it to help initiate change in the individual.

The publication of Bettelheim's *The Uses of Enchantment* (1976) was a watershed for the theoretical developments of the Freudian school. This work created a heightened awareness of the means by which narrative could be utilized for therapeutic work with children and adults. Bettelheim suggested that narrative provides individuals with means to mature and to understand themselves and the world. For Bettelheim, stories provide growth opportunities to work through life's great mysteries in a socially acceptable way because "the most difficult task in raising a child is helping him to find meaning in life."

Bettelheim (1976) suggested that the focus of a story must do more than arouse curiosity or entertain:

…it must stimulate his imagination; help him to develop his intellect and to clarify his emotions; be attuned to his anxieties and aspirations;

give full recognition to his difficulties, while at the same time suggesting solutions to the problems which perturb him.

For Bettelheim, stories conveyed problem-solving messages to the unconscious and conscious mind by dealing with concerns that preoccupy the individual:

> They speak about his severe inner pressures in a way that the child unconsciously understands, and—without belittling the most serious inner struggles which growing up entails—offer examples of both temporary and permanent solutions to pressing difficulties.

This sentiment was echoed by MacIntyre (1984), who suggested that a social interaction deficit exists in those children whose formative education excludes experience grounded in narrative:

> It is through hearing stories about wicked stepmothers, lost children, good but misguided kings, wolves that suckle twin boys, youngest sons who receive no inheritance but must make their own way in the world and eldest sons who waste their inheritance on riotous living and go into exile to live with the swine, that children learn or mislearn both what a child and what a parent is, what the cast of characters may be in the drama into which they have been born and what the ways of the world are. Deprive children of stories and you leave them unscripted, anxious stutterers in their actions as in their words. Hence, there is no way to give us an understanding of any society, including our own, except through the stock of stories which constitute its initial dramatic resources. Mythology, in its original sense, is at the heart of things.

For Bettelheim, the telling of the myth or fairy tale is the therapeutic activity. The goal is the growth and development of the child and his emotions, the clarification of his anxieties, and the development of problem-solving techniques. Children can return to these narratives over and over, each time enlarging their previous understanding of the metaphor.

Haley (1976) commented that metaphor is the means by which variant schools of psychology are provided with common ground, despite their differences in the applications of the metaphor or analogy. In the psychoanalytic school, for example, the analyst applies therapist-generated analogies to explore the connections between the client's metaphors. Similarly, the metaphors that emerge from dreams are exposed to free association in order to uncover metaphors that relate to the patient's life.

In general, the practitioner of the psychoanalytic school is most interested in discovering and having the patient unearth personal metaphors that are analyzed and searched for insight into the patient's past and problems. This usage relies on the client as the source of metaphor which might be arrived at not only by means of free association but also by emphasis on dream analysis. Although a great debt is owed to the discovery of the unconscious and the metaphors that emanate from it, that is by no means the central focus of this work. The premise that is the basis for the approach offered in this book involves the more active use of metaphor by the therapist, who initiates its use by the client; it is the client who is expected to reflect on its content, as opposed to the converse in psychoanalysis. The central focus is not client-initiated metaphor at all. This different use will become clearer in the next chapter, which begins by focusing on the work of Milton Erickson, whose innovative use of metaphor has brought landmark changes to the understanding of narrative and metaphor in therapy.

▶ 2

Narrative as a Therapeutic Resource: The Creative Influence of Milton Erickson

The spread of the use of metaphor in clinical practice can be largely attributed to the work and life of Milton Erickson and his many students. Erickson has been called "one of the most creative, perceptive and ingenious psychotherapeutic personalities of all time" (Zeig, 1980). Nevertheless, his inventive approach is difficult to systematize and comprehend. His use of multifaceted, complex, and highly theoretical constructs has created a loyal cadre of disciples who have attempted to quantify his techniques, although most admit this to be a difficult task (Haley, 1981).

Haley (1981) summarized the complexities inherent to comprehending Erickson: "…if I understood more fully what Erickson was trying to explain about changing people, new innovations in therapy would open up before me."

Because Erickson's innovations and therapeutic techniques were not formulated in a systematic way, the interested student must discover a great deal on his own (de Shazer, 1985). Paradoxically, the seemingly elusive and vague qualities of Erickson's interventions are paradigmatic and prescriptive for the successful use of metaphor in therapeutic settings.

Wylie (1990) offered an eloquent appraisal of Erickson's unconventional therapy:

If Freud was a philosopher-priest from Vienna, Erickson was a samurai warrior from Wisconsin, whose stories accumulate like legends around a fabled knight-errant. Optimistic, active, aggressive, Erickson did not wait for the slow dawning of insight in the fullness of time. "If you do not, I will do," he said to his patients; if they were unable to move or change themselves, he pursued, cajoled, manipulated, or bullied them out of their dilemmas. On occasion, he told them what to eat, how to dress, what to do and say, where to go. But much of his therapeutic activity was in the form of indirect suggestion—stories, metaphors, riddles—delivered while the patient was in trance. Erickson was not particularly interested in helping patients consciously understand their predicaments; he thought insight and interpretation were largely useless. The goal of therapy was change, which occurred when patients learned what they already unconsciously knew, though they might never know *why* they had changed.

The reverence in which Erickson is held rivals that accorded great philosophers, psychologists, and religious leaders. Trainees visiting Erickson would be convinced that a story, metaphor, or remark was directed specifically at each one of them, even though Erickson had been speaking to an entire group—this despite their diverse backgrounds, perspectives, and experiences and even despite the fact that Erickson might have also used the same metaphor on numerous other occasions (Haley, 1981). The mystique that surrounds Erickson only seems to magnify with the passage of time.

ERICKSON'S THERAPEUTIC PHILOSOPHY

Seven major and distinct differences between the Ericksonian model and the traditional psychoanalytic model highlight the contrasts between these approaches. These include:

1. The view of the individual
2. The role of the client's past
3. The understanding of the unconscious
4. The role of insight
5. Client goals
6. The role of the therapist
7. The evaluation of outcomes

Central to Erickson's work, and standing in sharp contrast to the psychoanalytic model, is the prominent view of the individual's uniqueness. Until Erickson began employing his novel approach, most psychologists who studied the human condition emphasized similarities, and accordingly grouped personality characteristics. Freud, for example, grouped development and personality types into oral, anal, phallic, and genital. Conversely, Erickson chose to focus not on the similarities people manifest but, rather, on their unique differences. Rosen (1982b) cites the response of the allergist told by Erickson to sit in an open field:

> After about three hours, the allergist returned to Erickson and said, "Did you know that every blade of grass is a different shade of green?" In telling this story, Erickson was pointing up the value of noting distinctions. Every person has different shades of any characteristic we can define. Erickson encouraged us to treasure those unique shades.

The second major difference between the psychoanalytic and Ericksonian approaches is the role that the client's past plays in therapy. Erickson abandoned the psychoanalytic model, which required a lengthy and painstaking global search of the client's past, in favor of a model that centered therapy on a specific problem. This became the basis for what has come to be called *strategic therapy*. In contrast to traditional psychoanalysis' focus on the past, the focus here is on the present and the future.

The understanding of the role of the unconscious in therapy constitutes the third way in which Erickson differed from the psychoanalytic model. Classical psychoanalysis considers the objective of therapy to be the monitoring and uncovering of the unconscious in order to free individuals from their pasts. It views repression as the singular means by which the mind deals with unacceptable negative forces that the individual encounters.

In contrast, Erickson believed the unconscious to hold a positive source of wisdom, knowledge, and common sense, beyond that contained by the conscious mind. Because Erickson was more interested in helping clients find their own strengths and solutions and in putting the unconscious to work as a positive force for change than he was in diagnosis, his target was the sharpening of the therapist's skills to effect change. This approach was tailor-made for the use of metaphor, which was frequently delivered while patients were in trance states of varying degrees. Metaphor is seen as an agent of change to propel the patient into the future, one that does not compel him to linger in the past. A citation from Erickson's 1979 teaching seminar makes his view of the unconscious explicit:

> Now, the unconscious mind is a vast storehouse of your memories, your learnings. It has to be a storehouse because you cannot keep consciously in mind all the things you know. Your unconscious mind acts as a storehouse. Considering all the learnings you have acquired in a lifetime, you use the vast majority of them automatically in order to function. (Zeig, 1980)

Related to the understanding of the unconscious is the role insight plays in therapy. Whereas psychoanalysis viewed insight, the logical understanding of a situation, as a chief goal, Erickson found insight and its application to be of little use in therapy. Furthermore, he found insight often presented an impediment to the therapeutic process by keeping the therapeutic relationship restricted to the cognitive level. This "safe" therapy created a wider chasm between intellect's world of ideas and affect's emotional world (Yapko, 1990). In the use of metaphor, Erickson found a significant tool for bridging the gap between those two worlds.

The goals of therapy differ widely between the psychoanalytic and Ericksonian approaches. From the psychoanalytic perspective, the goal is to uncover unconscious thoughts, memories, and feelings. Once the patient brings these to a conscious level, he is then able to utilize the insights to foster change. For Erickson, the primary goal of therapy was the rediscovery and harnessing of the hidden capacity for problem solving and curiosity for learning that people have as children. Change would occur when patients learned what they unconsciously knew about problem solving, although these resources might never be understood or acknowledged on a conscious level. Therefore, unlike the patient in psychoanalysis, Erickson's client might never know or even understand why change had taken place. Erickson would frequently comment to his clients that "you know more than you think you know" (Lankton & Lankton, 1983). He expected clients to take responsibility for their own lives by employing problemsolving techniques. Failure to employ these underutilized inner resources was, in Erickson's perspective, the source of pathology.

The role of the therapist in psychotherapy and in Ericksonian therapy are diametrically opposed. Because Erickson believed in working outside the patient's awareness—in contrast to the psychoanalytic model, which believed in bringing the unconscious into the patient's conscious mind—he would frequently issue directives and would emphasize communicating in metaphor (Haley, 1973). Erickson frequently presented clients with opportunities and options for change that they might not understand or to which they might even object. He would, however, permit clients to elect not to implement the suggestions offered. This might reveal the extent to which a client really wanted to change. Despite this highly directive approach, Erickson always respected his clients' ability to find the inner resources for change.

A telling example of Erickson's ability to manage patients' treatment by finding their own inner resources for change is that of the depressed woman whom Erickson encouraged to increase the number of African violets she cultivated. Prior to Erickson's intervention, her only interest was in her church. During a visit to her home, Erickson saw three African violets and a single leaf in a pot being used to cultivate a new plant. Building on her devotion and her green thumb, Erickson urged the woman to send an African violet to any member of her church who celebrated a wedding, funeral, or other life-cycle event. This kept her busy and depression-free for over twenty years. When she died, she was known as the "African violet queen" to her numerous friends. As in this example, Erickson's active interventions were frequently viewed as unconventional.

Finally, the manner in which therapeutic outcomes are evaluated also provides an opportunity to examine very different theoretical and practical considerations. Quite simply, under the psychoanalytic rubric, the client fails if change does not occur. Erickson, however, believed the converse to be true; as a therapist, he assumed responsibility for change and therefore took direct responsibility for the success or failure of therapy.

ERICKSON'S METHODOLOGIES

Do you know about the ways white people and Indians hunt? White hunters gather on one edge of the forest, stationing only one or two hunters on the other border. The troop then charges loudly through the forest, banging the trees, flushing out the prey toward the guns of the waiting hunters. Alternatively, white hunters will make a great production of tracking, using dogs, binoculars, four-wheel vehicles, a vast array of technology.

The Indian hunter goes alone into the heart of the forest, sits on a rock with his face toward the wind, and quietly watches and waits for the animal to come to him. Now, that's how I do therapy. (Frykman, 1985)

Erickson offered this metaphor to describe the methodology he employed for accomplishing therapeutic goals. Much of Erickson's theory and practice evolved from his intuitive, highly developed sensitivity to and understanding of human nature. This quality appeared at an early age. Rossi (1982) related that, even as a child, Erickson seemed to have an almost magical understanding of human nature, an ability to notice and utilize even the most subtle nuances in human behavior. The following illustration depicts how, as a youngster, Erickson made use of the technique that has come to be known as the *double bind:*

His father was trying to pull a stubborn calf into a barn, and young Milton laughed at him. His father, still pulling the calf into the barn, yelled at Milton, "Do you think you could do better?" Milton went up and pulled on the calf's tail and, of course, the calf, to escape the worse of the two evils, immediately trampled over the father into the barn.

In response to this description, Rossi asked: "Now this was a young lad, not yet in puberty—what kind of consciousness was this?" The answer is that Erickson was an intuitive child who would grow up to incorporate the events of his life, as well as a panoply of observations and experiences, into his life's work.

Erickson's clear memory of and respect for his formative childhood experiences also enabled him, in his adult life, to call on the playful and even mischievous characteristics of his childhood. Erickson often used homespun metaphor of farm and small-town values from his own life to teach clients about turning adversity to advantage.

His severe case of polio ultimately enhanced his use and control of his body. The memory of how, prior to his illness, he had used combinations of muscle groups enabled him to recover, learn to walk again, and attain physical mastery over his debilitating illness. Erickson hoped others would see the instructive side of their disabilities, just as he had learned from his own illness. He urged people to see that the past does not doom them to remain the same forever. The unconscious storehouse of learning could be the wellspring for changed and new behavior. Erickson employed metaphor to access these forgotten, inner worlds. The qualities Erickson possessed are not unlike those of metaphor, with its capacity to enable individuals to reconsider their lives, reactivate long-forgotten resources, and harness them for present and future experiences.

Because Erickson could appreciate rather than defend or deny idiosyncratic behavior, faults, and symptoms, and because he could see the commonplace in new ways, virtually every phase of his work brought new approaches to therapy. Erickson was one of the early progenitors and champions of family therapy. He was among the earliest advocates of family therapy who believed that therapy should not be only client-centered but should also examine an individual's home environment and family of origin. Erickson understood that there was more to a person's problem than just the presenting symptoms. In the days of the then-fledgling field of family therapy, he observed that symptoms also manifest themselves through overt and covert familial contracts. He was among the first to bring other family members into the therapy session with the patient. He became a master at bringing reluctant but significant relatives into his office for exposure to and inclusion in the therapeutic process. Because Erickson viewed them as part of the problem, he utilized these other family members as part of the solution. For Erickson, as for other family therapists, no symptom existed in a vacuum; the interplay of familial relationships had to be examined for effective solutions to be created.

In addition to his ground-breaking work in family therapy, brief note must also be make of his equally progressive work in the field of what is now called "sex therapy." Erickson was among the first therapists to discuss sexual matters freely and to recommend specific therapeutic intervention, long before the recent development of interest and research in this therapeutic approach.

Erickson will also be remembered for the unique techniques, both nonthreatening and memorable, he developed to encounter patients. He was a master at putting clients at ease, bypassing resistance, and calming fears. His ability to reframe and redefine problems enabled patients to turn adversity into advantage, debility into tools for change, and seemingly embarrassing situations into something to laugh at and enjoy. Of the many techniques he developed and embraced to accomplish these seemingly impossible feats, five have been selected for discussion and illustration to highlight a number, though by no means all, of his creative problem-solving techniques. These are used to demonstrate how metaphor pervaded all phases of Erickson's work.

Indirection

> *A disciple once complained, "You tell us stories, but you never reveal their meaning to us."*
> *Said the master, "How would you like it if someone offered you fruit and chewed it up before giving it to you?"*
> *No one can find your meaning for you.*
> *Not even the master. (White, 1982)*

Erickson favored a strategy that subtly moves clients toward goals in ways that are neither obvious nor expected and that leads clients to do their own thinking and problem solving by introducing nondirect ways to a solution. This approach lends itself to the application of metaphor into the therapeutic setting because the client is already expecting to make associations between two or more apparently nonrelated inputs.

Erickson believed neurotic and highly disturbed clients to be indirect in their communication and resistant to direct communication from others. He reasoned, therefore, that treatment likewise had to be indirect. The more resistant a client was to attacking a problem head on, the more Erickson applied metaphor. In its simplest and most accessible form, many individuals apply the popular term *negative psychology*. Encouraging a person to do the opposite of the desired behavior, in effect, forces him or her to reconsider his actions.

Through indirection, Tom Sawyer reinterpreted his tedious task of whitewashing thirty yards of board fence into such a desirable task that all his friends clamored and even paid for the opportunity to take a turn. In Tom's own words: "Does a boy get a chance to whitewash a fence every day?" (Twain, 1876/1991). This example also illustrates how indirection can be a component of the reframing process, discussed later in this chapter.

In a story drawn from his own family, Erickson talked about how his sons, Bert and Lance, planted a garden for him.

> ... I paid for the garden produce the same price I paid at the vegetable stand.... That's how they got their spending money—they WORKED for it. I had a potato patch. Thirty rows—LONG rows...and to HOE

them is a *great big job*. How can you get two little boys to *hoe* a great big field? You have them hoe row by row and the field is STILL as big…Have them hoe a diagonal line, from here to *here*, and hoe a diagonal line here and across and down the middle and kept [sic] cutting that field down into little pieces, and making more and more designs, and it's FUN to make *designs*. They transferred hard work into *play*. (Gordon & Meyers-Anderson, 1981)

Later in her life, Erickson's daughter, Roxanne Erickson (1986), described the frustration she had felt at her father's use of indirection to enable her to learn Spanish in a nonclassroom setting. When Roxanne reported that she was not eligible for the Spanish class she wanted to take, Erickson questioned her about the Spanish-speaking children in her school: their extracurricular activities, their lunch habits, where they lived, and so on. He discovered that some native Spanish-speaking children were enrolled in the school's free lunch program. Erickson suggested that the family go on an austerity program and take advantage of the school's free lunch program. Roxanne could save 50 cents each school day; lunch would cost her 25 cents less than it normally would, and Erickson would match the 25-cent cost of lunch on those days. Roxanne couldn't quite figure out what all this had to do with learning Spanish, but she agreed. Daily, she ate lunch with the children in the free lunch program. Immersed in a Spanish-speaking environment, she learned the language better than the children who took the course. She remembers swearing that she would never be indirect, but finds that she uses the same techniques with her children.

Another example of a family story in which indirection was applied is that of "Robert's Blood," which Erickson told to a client suffering from migraine headaches as an indirect way to get the client to accept the notion that pain is controllable (Erickson, 1986). This is Erickson's description of his son's accident (Erickson, 1983):

Several years ago my three-year-old son, Robert, fell down the back steps and drove a tooth up into the maxilla. Now being just three years old he was quite frightened and suffering a great deal of pain. He lay on his back on the pavement, crying to high heaven his expectations for a lifetime of agony in blood.

His mother and I ran out to the backyard to see what all the hullabaloo was about. As I looked down at Robert screaming and crying, I knew one thing that he did not know: I knew that there is a right time to speak to a child and that time is when the child is able to listen to you. While Robert was screaming he would not be listening to me, but I knew his wind would run out and that he would have to take a deep breath to recharge his battery. So when he paused to take that breath, I said, "And it hurts just terribly, doesn't it, Robert?"

Now at that point he knew I was talking sense. Most parents do not talk sense to their children. Robert went on with the screaming and took another breath, and I said, "And it will keep right on hurting." That was exactly what Robert was worried about. He was afraid it would keep right on hurting, so again I had spoken intelligently.

Then when he paused for breath the third time I said, "Maybe the pain will go away in a minute or two." What three-year-old hasn't heard the phrase, *a minute or two*? That was old stuff to Robert, but it did give him a faint ray of hope.

When Robert paused for the next breath I signaled his mother and we both looked at the blood stains on the pavement, and I said, "Mother, is that good, red, strong blood?" She looked as worried as I did. We both looked at the blood, and Robert's eyes bugged out as he looked at it. Mother and I debated the issue of the quality of Robert's blood, and then I reasoned:

"You know, Robert, the color of the pavement makes it difficult to see if your blood is the best kind of good, red, strong blood. You've got to see the blood where it is nice and white."

So Mrs. Erickson and I picked up Robert and took him to the bathroom and let his blood dribble into the nice, white sink. And you know, it was good, red, strong blood, and Robert was just as interested as I was.

Next I wondered, Would Robert's blood mix well with water and make the right color of pink? I washed Robert's face and it did make the right color pink.

Then I broke the really bad news to Robert. "You can count to ten easily," I reasoned. "You can count to twenty easily, but, you know, when the doctor puts the stitches in your lip I don't think he could put in twenty stitches that you could count. I don't think he could even put in ten. But you go ahead and count the stitches and see if he can put in at least ten."

So Robert went off to the doctor's with a wonderful goal in mind: he was going to count those stitches!

When we arrived at the doctor's office the surgeon said, "I don't want to inject a local and I don't want to give him a general."

"Just go ahead and sew it up," Mrs. Erickson directed.

And so he did begin to sew up Robert's injury, and Robert dutifully began to count: "One ... two ... three ..."

In the end, Robert got only seven stitches, and all the while the surgeon kept looking from Robert to Mrs. Erickson and back to Robert. (He just didn't understand a three-year-old child wanting *more* stitches!)

Erickson engaged his client's attention with the story of "Robert's Blood" in order to allow his client to direct his unconscious to resolve and alleviate his pain.

Specifically, Erickson wanted to teach the patient that he could control his pain in much the same way that Robert had. He was directed not only to be brave, but even to ignore his pain. Thus, through the use of metaphor, Erickson subtly and carefully moved his client, in an unexpected way, toward his goal of relief from pain.

Erickson cataloged family incidents and employed these and other metaphoric stories in the therapeutic technique of indirection. The metaphoric quality of stories derived from Erickson family experiences gave him new opportunities to expand his treatment through the use of metaphor.

Humor

Erickson championed the use of humor and challenged his clients with puzzles and riddles. He believed that humor was not only welcomed but also facilitated the progress of therapy and put patients in a more pleasant frame of mind "because your patients bring in enough grief, and they don't need all that grief and sorrow" (Zeig, 1980). Erickson believed that well-placed humor could ease pain, enable an individual to confront disturbing situations, and facilitate change. Humor led his clients in unexpected directions and instructed them that life is often richer and more complex than they had ever believed. Furthermore, Bergman (1992) suggested that a humorous metaphor or joke, which is a structured, compact narrative, plays a specific therapeutic role: "It makes a point with power, generally by surprise. A good story is exceedingly hard for anybody to forget."

Rosen (1982b) described Erickson's use of humor in this way:

Anyone who has ever seen the twinkle in Milton Erickson's eyes, who has noted the secret smile on his face as he talked, or who has heard him chuckle about the many practical jokes that were played within his family knows the large role that humor played in Erickson's life. His own and his listener's laughter frequently punctuated his stories.

Of the use of humor, Erickson (1992) taught:

Instead of treating that resistance seriously, as if it were a desperately serious problem that had to be dealt with, why shouldn't I laugh about it? Why shouldn't the patient laugh about it? No reason at all, because patients really ought to show some resistance to you. They come to you, and they know that you are going to change them in some way, but they don't know how. They have no idea of how thoroughly you understand their problems; but they know very well that *they* don't understand their problems, so how could a perfect stranger understand them? They are justified in having resistance. Therefore, *they ought to show that resistance as a part of their symptomatology, and the therapist ought to re-*

spect it, but he also ought to put it in its rightful place in a therapeutic situation.

Humor pervaded Erickson's experiences, right to the time of his death. Rosen (1982b) says that his favorite of all Erickson's turns of phrase was Erickson's response, shortly before his death, to a former student who had expressed concern over the rumor that his teacher was dying. Erickson responded: "I think that is entirely premature. I have no intention of dying. In fact, that will be the last thing that I do."

Erickson described his use of a humorous metaphoric message in a case in which an alcoholic woman was having difficulty dealing with her college-age daughter. She pinpointed the onset of her daughter's difficulties to a ride she had taken in a convertible. While yawning, the daughter had caught bird droppings in her mouth and had been ashamed and difficult ever since. Erickson asked if the daughter had a sense of humor. The client said that the daughter did, but it had gone unused for a few years. Erickson replied:

"Well you must have a lot of humor dammed up behind that capable person. So do you mind if I do a little therapy long distance?" The mother said, "No I don't mind." So I mailed the girl a postcard from Philadelphia advising her about the *perils of yawning* while riding in a convertible. The girl got that card and said, "Who is that man and how did he EVER find out about it? I know *I never told him*. Did YOU tell him?!!" She said, "What's his name?" The girl said, "It's signed M. H. Erickson." And the mother said, "I've never BEEN to Philadelphia. I don't know of anybody who lives in Philadelphia by THAT name. Isn't it rather a funny thing?" The girl burst into laughter and said, "It certainly *is*." And she laughed, oh, uproariously for quite some time. And resumed normal living. It was just friendly advice. (Gordon & Meyers-Anderson, 1981)

Erickson used humor to help the daughter see beyond her embarrassment and unhappiness over her trauma. Although the daughter did not get to know this "M. H. Erickson of Philadelphia," he put her resistance in its rightful place and conveyed humanity and humor to her. He retold and presented her with her own story in such a way that she could laugh at it and at herself. In doing so, she realized the humor in her own situation.

O'Hanlon (1987) suggested that humor can be used indirectly to "make points that would have been pedantic or resistance-provoking if made directly." He noted that an overbearing parent would probably respond better to humor containing metaphoric meaning than to direct advice and admonition on child rearing. He offered, as an example of ironic humor, the metaphor of the unmarried speaker who titled his lectures on child-rearing practices "Ten Commandments for Parents." After his marriage and the birth of his first child, he changed the title to "Ten Hints for Parents." The birth of a second child brought a further emendation to "A Few Tentative Suggestions for Parents." Following the birth of his third child, he gave up the lecture circuit (Rajneesh, 1978).

Erickson used riddles to challenge patients to look beyond their problems and accustomed reference points to see things from a fresh perspective. Erickson challenged clients to connect three rows of three dots with four straight lines without lifting the pen from the paper. Similarly, he would challenge people to design an orchard with ten trees containing five straight rows and four trees in a row. (Solutions appear on page 47.) In his playful manner, he would give people a sheet of paper with the number 710 or 7734 and challenge them to read it every way possible. Few would think to turn the paper upside down to read OIL or hELL. He would tell people that they could not be sure which their left and right hands were. After telling a person to place his left hand behind his back he would ask: "Which one is left?"

As with humor, Erickson hoped that puzzles, riddles, and other conundrums would challenge individuals to look beyond their current situation. The effectiveness of these techniques stems from their origin in the right hemisphere of the brain, the same domicile as metaphor. By tapping the myriad resources housed therein, Erickson could activate his clients' most creative powers for the healing process.

Paradox

One technique Erickson favored to produce change in a patient was the use of paradox. Like humor, puzzles, and riddles, paradox capitalizes on behaviors that often appear absurd, preposterous, and contradictory. Paradox is often used to play out a situation to absurdity. Erickson and Rossi (1979) explained that paradox is effective because, like any experience that produces shock or surprise, it fixates attention and interrupts previous patterns of association. This experience of the unrealistic, the unusual, the fantastic, or even the bizarre provides an opportunity to alter the way in which information is received. Often this makes individuals more open and receptive to new learning and experiences. Rossi (1972) succinctly stated that the use of paradox results in a break in an individual's "habitual pattern of awareness." He called this instant insight *a creative moment.*

Erickson particularly enjoyed the use of paradox because, although patients thought he was providing them with a choice of how to proceed with their lives, he understood that either choice would achieve the desired effect he expected. His use of what has come to be called the double bind merely provided Erickson's patients with the illusion of choice. Two powerful examples of paradox illustrate Erickson's use of the double bind. In the first, Erickson presents an overweight woman with choices that make it impossible for her to *not* lose weight:

A woman came to see me and she said, "I weigh 180 pounds. I've dieted successfully under doctors' orders hundreds of times. And I want to weigh 130 pounds. Every time I get to 130 pounds I rush into the kitchen to celebrate my success. I put it back on, right away. Now I weigh 180. Can you use hypnosis to help me reduce to 130 pounds? I'm back to 180 for the hundredth time."

I told her, yes, I could help her reduce by hypnosis, but she wouldn't like what I did.

She said she wanted to weigh 130 pounds and she didn't care what I did.

I told her she'd find it rather painful.

She said, "I'll do anything you say."

I said, "All right. I want an absolute promise from you that you will follow my advice exactly."

She gave me the promise very readily and I put her into a trance. I explained to her again that she wouldn't like my method of reducing her weight and would she promise me, absolutely, that she would follow my advice? She gave me that promise.

Then I told her, "Let both your unconscious mind and your conscious mind listen. Here's the way you go about it. Your present weight is now 180 pounds. I want you to gain twenty pounds and when you weigh 200 pounds, on my scale, you may start reducing."

She literally begged me, on her knees, to be released from her promise. And every ounce she gained she became more and more insistent on being allowed to start reducing. She was markedly distressed when she weighed 190 pounds. When she was 190 she begged and implored to be released from her own promise. At 199 she said that was close enough to 200 pounds and I insisted on 200 pounds.

When she reached 200 pounds she was very happy that she could begin to reduce. And when she got to 130 she said, "I'm never going to gain again."

Her pattern had been to reduce and gain. I reversed the pattern and made her gain and reduce. And she was very happy with the final results and maintained that weight. She didn't want to, ever again, go through that horrible agony of gaining twenty pounds. (Rosen, 1982a)

The technique worked because the woman was caught in the paradox of either disregarding her promise and not losing weight or keeping her promise and losing weight. Given her strong desire to change her lifelong pattern, she had no choice. Previously, she resented having to lose weight. Through paradox, her mind set was reframed so that she would, then and subsequently, resent gaining weight.

In the second example, Erickson paradoxically reframed a mother's eating problems by utilizing her desire to be a good parent:

One mother came in and said, "I'm overweight. I've got four children. I'm setting a bad example. I'm *ashamed* of myself. I'm always *too busy* to go anywhere with them. The truth is I'm too busy EATING! I keep having to go to the store to buy candy and cookies to eat—I NEVER have time to take my kids anywhere." I said, "I'm sorry for your poor kids growing up in ignorance…never discovering what the Botanical Gardens look like, and to never ONCE have the chance to climb Squaw Peak, never ONCE going to the Grand Canyon, never once seeing the Petrified Forest or the Painted Desert or the Meteor Crater or Casa Grande or Pueblo Grande or old Tucson. I think it's terrible to do *that* to your kids. Now go home and paste to your mirror a piece of paper that bears the wording 'Let the damn kids grow up ignorant' and leave it there. You have good reason NOT to look in the mirror. But there'll be no way for you to forget what's on that paper pasted on the mirror." Two years later she called me up. "I'm down in weight now, my kids have visited every sight in Arizona. Can I take that piece of paper off the mirror?!!" I told her she COULD take it off, but she ought to look not in the mirror but at the growth and development of her children. It took two years of practice learning to enjoy them, enjoy Arizona sights. I think that sort of treatment is much more helpful than trying to dig into a long forgotten past that CAN'T be changed. (Gordon & Meyers-Anderson, 1981)

The paradox in this case alerted the client's attention to the fact that if she remained overinvolved in eating, she would neglect her children's education. Forced to confront the enormity of that possibility, she directed her energies to where they truly belonged. As the attention was redirected toward her children's education, she no longer focused on her eating patterns and weight problem.

Erickson employed metaphor to exploit the potential of paradox. Haley (1973) described one of Erickson's paradoxical uses of metaphor in dealing with a couple who were unable to discuss openly their conflict over sexual relations:

He might, for example, talk to them about having dinner together and draw them out on their preferences. He will discuss with them how the wife likes appetizers before dinner, while the husband prefers to dive right into the meat and potatoes. Or the wife might prefer a quiet and leisurely dinner, while the husband, who is quick and direct, just wants the meal over with. If the couple begin to connect what they are saying with sexual relations, Erickson will "drift rapidly" away to other topics, and then he will return to the analogy. He might end such a conversation with a directive that the couple arrange a pleasant dinner on a particular evening that is satisfactory to both of them. When successful, this approach shifts the couple from a more pleasant dinner to more pleasant sexual relations without their being aware that he has deliberately set this goal.

Certainly a couple coming for therapy for sexual conflict and ending up talking about dinners and eating styles must, on an unconscious level, sense the tension between their problem and the solutions that are talked about, even if they appear unrelated on a conscious level. Such a metaphor creates an interruption of their problem and results in a *creative moment* that leaves them open to new and creative learning.

Utilization

Via the technique known as *utilization*, Erickson could incorporate any of a client's symptoms into his therapeutic strategy. Erickson selected metaphors based on his client's preconceived notions and responses. In Erickson's own words,

> Any 52-year-old woman who starts calling me "sonny" has a sense of humor. So I made use of that.
> In other words, whatever your patient has, make use of it. (Zeig, 1980)

O'Hanlon posited that the utilization technique is one of Erickson's most lasting contributions to therapy:

> Erickson held the view that the therapist should, like a good organic gardener, use everything that the client presented—even things that looked like weeds—as part of the therapy. The "weeds" of "resistance," symptoms, rigid beliefs, compulsive behavior, etc., were essential components to be taken into consideration and actively used as part of the solution. (O'Hanlon & Weiner-Davis, 1989)

A striking example of utilization involved Erickson's agreement to see, only once, a ten-year-old autistic child who could communicate only by mouthing sounds, making grunting noises, and twisting and acting peculiarly. All other forms of treatment had failed. Erickson describes that meeting:

> And the girl made a number of weird sounds and so I REPLIED with weird sounds, and we grunted and groaned and squeaked and squawked for about half an hour. And then the girl answered a few simple questions and very promptly returned to her autistic behavior. And we really

had a good time squeaking and squawking and grunting and groaning at each other. And then she took the patient back to the hospital. In the night time she took the patient for a walk. She told me later, "that girl almost pulled my *arm* off, yanking me down the street, she wanted to see *you*...the one man who could really talk her language." (Gordon & Meyers-Anderson, 1981)

One of Erickson's best known metaphoric applications of utilization involved his work with Joe, a florist by occupation, who was terminally ill with cancer and suffered extreme pain. Erickson utilized Joe's occupation and deep interest in growing plants to help him manage his pain. Erickson placed Joe, who had a strong dislike of hypnosis, into an hypnotic trance, in which Erickson told him an extended metaphor about growing a tomato plant. This is a brief excerpt from his induction:

Now as I talk, and I can do so *comfortably*, I wish that you *listen to me comfortably* as I talk about a tomato plant. That is an odd thing to talk about. It makes one *curious. Why talk about a tomato plant?* One puts a tomato seed in the ground. One can *feel hope* that it will grow into a tomato plant that *will bring satisfaction* by the fruit it has. The seed soaks up water, *not very much difficulty* in doing that because of the rains that *bring peace and comfort* and the joy of growing to flowers and tomatoes.... (Erickson, 1966/1980)

Erickson reported that Joe was able to return home from the hospital and not have to continue to consume large doses of pain killers. On those rare occasions when Joe experienced a surge of pain, he was able to control it with aspirin or 25 milligrams of Demerol. Joe was now able to enjoy his remaining time with his family in productive activity rather than spend that time hospitalized and heavily sedated. By speaking of something to which Joe could relate, Erickson utilized Joe's profession to help him enter a trance state, in spite of his resistance. To do this, Erickson offered a comparison between the way a tomato plant pushes up through the soil and how the root system "must make the tomato plant *feel very good, very comfortable*," and his ability to make himself more comfortable. Erickson believed that this metaphor extended Joe's life and permitted him brief physical improvement and freedom from chronic pain.

Erickson demonstrated to a client the idea of utilizing inner cues and resources for problem solving by telling the client one of his own favorite metaphors. He reported that as a child, he volunteered to return to its rightful owner an unidentified, runaway horse that had wandered onto his family's property. He mounted the animal, led it to the road, and kept it from veering off the road into the surrounding fields. He successfully returned the horse to its home several miles away. When asked by the owner how he knew where the horse came from, Erickson replied, "I didn't know, but the horse knew. All I did was to keep him on the road" (Gordon & Meyers-Anderson, 1981).

Altered States of Consciousness

At the same time that he was developing the centrality of metaphor to his work, Erickson began to use hypnosis and a wide range of other techniques considered outside of mainstream therapy. Erickson used metaphor in conjunction with a broad range of states of consciousness, including hypnotic trances, full alertness, and meditation. Erickson frequently led his patients to a condition of altered awareness or light trance, akin to daydreaming, that he termed the *common everyday trance* (Erickson, 1927/1980, 1983, 1985, 1986, 1992; Erickson & Rossi, 1979, 1981), in which "we are all open and receptive to the new within us as well as suggestions from the outside" (Erickson, 1927/1980). This receptive state was utilized by Erickson to reinforce a new frame of reference. In this state, there is a heightened awareness of internal mental activity and sensory experience; external stimuli recede into a less prominent role during that time frame (Rosen, 1982a).

This common everyday trance, also termed *conversational trance* (Protinsky, 1986), results from a natural oscillation of different levels of consciousness, part of the ninety-minute ultradian cycle of natural body rhythms, "during which we may find ourselves daydreaming or just taking a break" (Rossi & Cheek, 1988). It is a cycle in which people are inwardly focused approximately every ninety minutes. They "are probably under the sway of parasympathetic and right-hemispheric processes" (Erickson, 1985).

Katz (1985) suggested that a trance state is actually normative and the waking state is the exception. He commented that it takes more work to stay out of what Erickson termed this *inner state of absorption* than it does to stay in. Katz summarized this approach by stating that most trances are momentary:

> You read my words and they remind you of something. Subsequently, you are not reading my words because you are absorbed in reverie. Then you come back to what you are reading.
> Attention wavers. It moves from outer stimuli to the inner world.

Gordon (1988) suggested that the telling of a story is in itself "inherently hypnotic" and will automatically induce a trance depending on the way the story is told. Thus, metaphor may transport an individual deep within himself, to a place where the application of problem-solving techniques may become more inner-directed than might otherwise occur in a normal state of consciousness. Yapko (1990) stated that the very act of telling a story produces the opportunity for "the deeper messages embedded in the story's structure" to communicate more directly with the unconscious and "to activate the client's unconscious ability to response in a significant way."

So pervasive was his use of trance induction that Erickson would tell his clients,

> my voice goes everywhere with you, and changes into the voice of your parents, your teacher, your playmates and even the voice of the wind and the rain.... (Lankton & Lankton, 1983)

Late in Erickson's life, he required those who made the pilgrimage to see him to climb 1,100-foot Squaw Peak. He offered no further guidance or explanation. It was an open-ended, metaphoric ceremony that produced different results for each climber. Haley (1990) suggested that anyone Erickson sent to the summit of Squaw Peak always came back changed—less rational and logical, more spiritual. The power of this call compelled Gene Combs to make the journey one year after Erickson's death. He briefly described that journey in *Symbol, Story and Ceremony: Using Metaphor in Individual and Family Therapy* (Combs & Freedman, 1990).

Combs and Freedman (1990) employ a similar, though not as physically demanding, Ericksonian metaphoric ritual of sending each of their new clients to the public library to select an interesting book, the title of which is new to the client. During the subsequent session, therapist and client discuss the book, how the client selected it, and what in its contents would be relevant to the client's therapeutic goals.

Erickson's influence on contemporary psychotherapy has been so monumental that it is impossible to measure. There is virtually no aspect of treatment and theory that he did not investigate and expound. In the last decade, his work has been the inspiration for numerous publications. Chief among Erickson's contributions was the reawakening of the use and application of metaphor as a tool, not only for a deeper understanding of human motivation and function but also as an instrument for the transformation of lives. His gift of the knowledge that narrative material is transformative and healing is his most enduring memorial. His influence extends throughout the field of therapy and continues to provide seminal guidelines for treatment of a wide variety of emotional and physical symptoms, the administration and utilization of hypnosis, and continuing research in virtually every area of psychological and mind–body study. His voice does, indeed, travel with those who knew him. It extends to those who did not personally have contact with him but who are continually influenced by his students, his teachings and writings, and tapes of his hypnotic voice.

Solutions to Puzzles Posed on Page 40

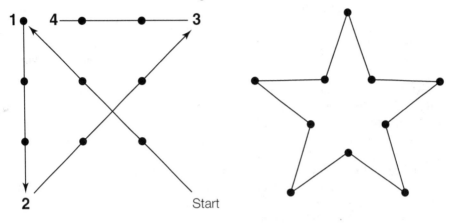

1 4 3

2   Start

METAPHOR VIEWED THROUGH DIGITAL–ANALOGIC
AND LEFT-BRAIN/RIGHT-BRAIN COMMUNICATION

The efficacy of metaphor as a therapeutic intervention depends, in large measure, on the organization and functioning of the brain. Erickson's frequent use of paradox, pun, and humor indicates his understanding and appreciation of the bicameral organization of the human brain. Before turning to a discussion of the power of metaphor as a therapeutic tool, it is imperative to understand the nature of left- and right-brain processing and communication.

For more than a century, researchers have collected evidence of the malfunction of the hemispheres of the brain as a result of trauma, illness, and injury. Meyers and Sperry (1953) and Sperry (1964) observed experimental animals and patients with severed neural connections between the left and right hemispheres of the brain. Earlier observations, combined with their research, led to the conclusion that, in general, damage to the left hemisphere often interferes with or destroys language ability. Damage to the right hemisphere interferes with spatial relationships, emotions, musical and artistic ability, recognition of familiar faces, or even perception of body image (Ornstein, 1972).

Each hemisphere has its own style of processing information. The left hemisphere is an ordered world of logic and carefully defined rules. It is literal and does not allow for contradictions. It insists on clearly formulated conduct, policy, reason, explanation, interpretation, and procedure. The left hemisphere employs logic, syllogism, and formal argument in a step-by-step fashion; it is the home of analysis, reason, and mathematical functioning.

In contrast, the right hemisphere is nonlinear and subjective in nature. Through the right side of the brain, we discover emotions, recognize faces, and have knowledge of imagery, including body image. The right hemisphere is the home of pun, paradox, ambiguity, allegory, allusion, aphorism, and metaphor. It is the seat of nonverbal language and of the appreciation of art, poetry, and drama.

Metaphor's domicile in the right side of the brain gives it unrestricted access to the region of the brain that processes information in the most uninhibited manner. "Metaphor is probably the most powerful of the right-hemisphere techniques because it makes explicit the process by which learning occurs" (Williams, 1983).

Ornstein (1972) viewed the dichotomy between analytic left-brain communication and right-brain holistic communication as the distinction between the "rational" and "intuitive" sides of a person. Bruner (1986) compared the interaction of the two sides of the brain in this way:

> One is the landscape of action, where the constituents are the arguments of action: agent, intention or goal, situation, instrument, something corresponding to a "story grammar." The other landscape is the landscape of consciousness: what those involved in the action know, think, or feel, or do not know, think or feel. The two landscapes are essential and distinct: it is the difference between Oedipus sharing Jocasta's bed before and after he learns from the messenger that she is his mother.

Bruner (1979) expressed his fascination with the bicarmeral organization of the human mind. When the metaphoric reference is made to each hemisphere, the results demonstrate the anatomical fact that activity in the right hemisphere is manifest in the actions of the left side of the body, and vice versa.

> Since childhood, I have been enchanted by the fact and the symbolism of the right hand and the left—the one the doer, and the other the dreamer. The right is order and lawfulness, *le droit*. Its beauties are those of geometry and taut implication. Reaching for knowledge with the right hand is science. Yet to say only that much of science is to overlook one of its excitements, for the great hypotheses of science are gifts carried in the left hand.

Bruner further argued that the two modes of function should not be alien to one another, that "the scientist and the poet do not live at antipodes." Such separation "cripples the contemporary intellectual as an effective mythmaker for his times."

The clear distinction between the nature of the two hemispheres of the brain has been variously described by Watzlawick (1978):

The one, in which for instance this sentence is itself expressed, is objective, definitional, cerebral, logical, analytic; it is the language of reason, of science, explanation, and interpretation, and therefore the language of most schools of psychotherapy. The other... is much more difficult to define—precisely because it is not the language of definition. We might call it the language of imagery, of metaphor, of *pars pro toto*, perhaps of symbols, but certainly of synthesis and totality, and not of analytical dissection.

Since the two hemispheres of the brain function in such independent ways, it is not surprising that communication can be perceived in at least two ways, depending on which part of the brain dominates in receiving the message. One useful means for understanding the differences between communication styles is through the terms *digital* and *analogic*, corresponding to the left and right hemispheres, respectively.

Watzlawick, Beavin, and Jackson (1967) distinguished "digital communication," message content, from "analogic communication," the relationship quality of a message. Haley (1976) contrasted these terms in this way:

Digital communication consists of that class of messages where each statement has a specific referent and only that referent. Something happens or it does not happen; there is *one* stimulus and *one* response.... Each message is about *one* thing and not about something else as well. ...When a message has multiple referents, it... is analogic, in that it deals with the resemblances of one thing to another. It is a language in which each message refers to a context of other messages. There is no single message and single response but multiple stimuli and multiple responses.... The analog can be expressed in a verbal statement, as in a simile or verbal metaphor. It can also be expressed in action—the showing of how something is by acting it out. A message in this style cannot be categorized without taking into account the context of other messages in which the message occurs.

Haley explained this difference by invoking the paradigm of a newspaper halftone illustration. The dots that make up the picture represent digital communication, whereas the entire collection of dots that makes an image recognizable represents analogic communication. At the moment that the picture becomes identifiable, the communication switches from digital to analogic.

Metaphor appears, on the surface, to be a clear message about a specific occurrence or set of events. It delivers its impact to both hemispheres of the brain, through digital and analogic communication. The power of metaphor emerges from its ability to inform clients on many different levels about what is occurring and to enable them to comprehend the gestalt of the communication.

Metaphor functions in the right-brain world, distilling and refining discrete units of information provided by the left hemisphere. In the right hemisphere of the brain, the allegoric message of a metaphor finds its way into the unconscious mind. The metaphor sets the right hemisphere into motion; the message continues to affect feelings and behavior. The left hemisphere, which may not yet be ready for interpretive material, views metaphor strictly as a story. The left hemisphere accepts the narrative at face value and tries to compare and relate it to reality in a logical way. The left hemisphere remains unaware of what is concurrently taking place on the right side, where insight and clearer understanding develop.

Erickson and Rossi (1976/1980) termed the operation of metaphor on different planes or dimensions the *two-level theory of communication*. The left hemisphere arranges all the individual puzzle pieces in the correct places, whereas the right hemisphere perceives the holistic, simultaneous, complete picture (Mills & Crowley, 1986). When the left-hemisphere mode of information processing is confused or bewildered, the brain switches to the right-hemisphere mode of information processing in an attempt to draw together the various associations to uncover the gestalt of the puzzle pieces.

With this basic introduction to left- and right-brain communication, it is now possible to explore the suitability of metaphor to therapeutic settings.

CONFIGURING NARRATIVE FOR THERAPEUTIC USE

Despite the fluidity inherent in metaphor, the metaphor for each therapeutic situation must be carefully crafted and presented in order to be effective. Here the components of metaphor and various stylistic considerations that influence the effective development of metaphor are considered.

Style of Communication

All truly wise thoughts have been thought thousands of times; but to make them really ours we must think them over again honestly till they take root in our personal expression. —Goethe

It is of paramount importance that the therapist determine the communication style a particular client employs. The therapist's skill in making this determination will, to a large extent, determine the success of the therapeutic process. There is widespread agreement that client and therapist must communicate in similar styles in order to facilitate their relationship and the outcome of the intervention.

Watzlawick (1985) detailed a benefit of "learning and using the client's 'language.'" He believed that this technique provides assurance that the client will experience a hypnotic effect although no formal trance induction precedes such language use.

Bergman (1985) spoke of the importance of same-style communication to meet the client on his home territory. He makes a concerted effort to respond metaphorically to those who employ metaphor. "When families and I use metaphor, we have 'right-hemisphere' conversations, which I find emotionally-connecting, informative, emotionally rich, and fun."

Gardner (1971) used what he termed the *mutual-storytelling technique* with children. He asks a child to tell him a story. He listens for psychological themes and unresolved conflict. Gardner then tells the child a story that is constructed around these tensions and provides the characters with a more appropriate manner for handling such contention. His hope is to furnish the child with a newly revised personal myth that will prove more effective than the one he hopes the child will abandon.

Conversely, addressing the client in a frame of reference to which that client cannot relate or that is not facilitative for that client leads to a therapeutic impasse. Difficulties in communication often result when the speaker and the listener utilize different communication styles. A speaker operating in one modality may have difficulty communicating with a listener experienced only in another. Grinder and Bandler (1976) suggest identifying the natural language predicates the client utilizes to describe experiences. When a therapist joins the client's representational system by utilizing the client's predicates, he is, essentially, "speaking the client's language." Doing so allows therapy to proceed in a "strategically more beneficial way."

Mills and Crowley (1986) expressed the concern that failures in communication can hamper therapeutic progress because a therapist fails to employ language preferences that are natural to the client. No matter how compassionate the therapist may be, he or she simply is unable to connect with the patient because each is "on a different wave length."

Once the therapist has determined the communication mode best suited to a particular client, he or she can begin to select, design, and implement therapeutic interventions in the corresponding mode.

Packaging

A certain important man of learning said to a Sufi:

"Why do you Sufis always use analogies? Such forms are good enough for the ignorant, but you can speak clearly to people of sense."

The Sufi said:

"Experience shows, alas, that this is not a matter of the ignorant and the wise. It is a matter of that those who are most in need of a certain understanding, or even a certain part of understanding, are least able to

accept it without an analogy. Tell them directly and they will prevent
themselves perceiving its truth. (Shah, 1972)

Truth walks about naked, dejected, embittered and shunned by all, and
cannot find any place where he is accepted for what he is. Walking aim-
lessly, he meets Parable dressed in wonderfully colored, patterned at-
tire. Parable asks why Truth is disheartened. Truth explained that no
one seems to want to have anything to do with him because of his age.
    Parable reprimanded Truth. "Look, I am just as old as you are and
the older I get the more beloved I become. I will tell you the secret of my
popularity. What people prefer is seeing everything dressed up, dis-
guised. I will lend you my attire and you will see that people will love
you as well."
    Truth followed Parable's instruction and ever since then, they go
hand in hand, equally revered by all. (Adapted from "A Parable on the
Parable," in Newman, 1962)

A corollary to the concept that the client will receive suggestions presented in
a manner accessible and comfortable to him or her is that therapists find appropriate metaphors and deliver them in accessible language. Presentation inappropriate
in content or style may call the client's defensive mechanisms to action. This is
because confrontation of a problem through facts and logic may challenge a client's ability to face difficult situations long before he or she is prepared to do so.

To avoid this potential impasse, the possibility of encountering resistance
must be eliminated. Zeig (1990) referred to this bypassing of resistance as *pack-*
aging, the efficacy of which may be directly responsible for the extent to which
a client accepts the message offered.

The indirect presentation inherent in metaphor makes it difficult for clients
to resist what they do not immediately understand. Even if the allegorical message is unacceptable to the listener, metaphor can be taken at face value, simply
as a story. Regardless of how the metaphor is received, the unconscious level is
simultaneously stimulated with ideas calling for transformation of thought and
emotion. Metaphor supplies the therapist with an opportunity to deliver an "embedded" message to a client via a nonthreatening means.

Gordon (1988) emphasized the importance of packaging as a means of cir-
cumventing client resistance. The metaphor he devised to explain this phenomenon can be paraphrased as follows: Suppose a person wanted to get an elephant
inside a train station, but the station master said he would not allow it inside under
any circumstance. Short of trying to crash through the doors with the elephant,
the individual must focus on packaging the elephant in a form acceptable to the
station master. He puts the elephant in a boxcar and rolls the boxcar into the station with the station master's approval. Once inside the station, the boxcar is
opened. When the station master is confronted by the pachyderm, he can do one

of two things. Either he can admit it to the station, or he can order the elephant out of the station.

Gordon's understanding of metaphor is that it operates through the packaging of experiences. It is an efficient and effective way to have ideas, behaviors, and perspectives that might not otherwise be accepted bypass the client's resistance. Frykman (1985) also believed that narrative is the vehicle for indirect suggestion. Nothing is expected of the listener, who may then feel free to sit comfortably. Such a relaxed state creates an openness for the listener's mind to accept suggestions for change.

Bateson (1991) described the goal of packaging as the recognition of an analogy between a client's old and new situations. This analogy allows for the transfer of learning and the application of skills. Once an individual recognizes that he has met a specific problem in the past, he can transfer skills to solving it in the present: "That recognition is critical to the transfer of learning."

There is no guarantee, however, that once delivered, the packaged metaphor will be opened and utilized, as this story told by the Dubner Maggid, Jacob Kranz, illustrates:

A physician prescribed for a boy... some pills coated with sugar. The patient failed to show any improvement, and the physician resolved to investigate the cause. By carefully watching the boy the doctor noticed that the foolish lad licked off the sweet coating with his tongue but spat out the pill itself. He then took the proper measures to remedy this unsatisfactory situation.

From this we learn: many a member of an audience... will swallow appreciatively the stories and anecdotes, but will refuse to heed the bitter truths which the preacher seeks to impress upon the congregation. (Newman, 1962)

Reframing

The chances of the metaphor being accepted and acted on are increased when the therapist presents the problem at hand in a way that will "change the conceptual and/or emotional setting or viewpoint in relation to which a situation is experienced and to place it in another frame which fits the 'facts' of the same concrete situation equally well or even better, and thereby changes its entire meaning" (Watzlawick, Weakland & Fisch, 1974).

Watzlawick, Weakland, and Fisch (1974), Grinder and Bandler (1981), and devotees of neurolinguistic programming term such a transformation of an experience and its reorientation toward the future *reframing*. In fact, Watzlawick and colleagues (1974), who developed the concept, define the essence of brief therapy as *the gentle art of reframing*. Erickson also formulated change in terms of reframing. The objective should be to help:

people break out of their learned limitations so they can then reframe their life experience from a broader perspective...our current-day emphasis on expanding awareness and heightening consciousness is essentially this process of breaking out of our limiting preconception to a broader understanding of our human possibilities. (Erickson & Rossi, 1981)

Communication theorists have long maintained that context determines the meaning of communication. Yapko (1990) illustrates how shifting contexts change the significance of a message:

Stealing money from a blind beggar is an act no one would condone. Stealing a serum that will cure your mother's terminal cancer from a greedy neighbor who wants a million dollars you don't have for the cure is the same act of stealing—yet it stimulates empathy in most people, not anger and a desire to punish the offender. Lying by the government to the public is considered a betrayal—unless it's for "national security." A man who acts strangely is "crazy" if he's poor—but "eccentric" if he's wealthy.

Another example Yapko used is that of the woman who complained to her friend about her husband's snoring. The friend, whose husband had died, told the first woman that she longed to hear her dead husband's snoring even though it, too, had bothered her when he was alive. This response enabled the first woman to appreciate, perhaps for the first time, her husband's snoring because it now provided clear evidence that her husband was alive and well: "The snoring behavior was the same; only the woman's attitude was changed—a successful reframe."

This shifting of an experience from one context to another is the underlying premise of reframing. Watzlawick (1978) collected illustrations of reframing, including a number from literature and history:

The Gordian knot tied together the yoke and shaft of the chariot of the king of Phrygia. Tradition maintained that it would only be undone by the future leader of Asia. Alexander the Great saw the complexity of this knot from a different perspective. He reframed the situation when he separated the yoke and chariot by cutting the knot (Watzlawick, 1978).

King Christian X of Denmark found himself in the unenviable position of having to comply with the 1943 Nazi order to identify and segregate all Danish Jews by having each of them wear a yellow Star of David. The king reframed the situation by saying there were no such distinctions among Danes. Henceforth, all citizens were to follow his lead and wear such stars, thus forcing the Germans to rescind the order (Watzlawick, Weakland, & Fisch, 1974).

Watzlawick (1976) provided additional examples of how a simple, well-chosen statement can reframe or even disrupt a belief in the outcome of a situation.

He noted that a clever bank teller may foil a bank holdup by offering a response for which the robber is unprepared. The confusion produced by an unexpected response neutralizes the threat. Watzlawick cites humorous responses reported by columnist Herb Caen (1973): "I'm going to lunch now; please step to the next window"; "I don't have a bag, I'll have to get one"; "I'm sorry, I'm a trainee and not allowed to handle cash—you'll have to wait for a regular teller." Some tellers might simply faint. Others might offer this zany response: "I'm sorry, our bank went broke this morning."

Watzlawick (1978) spoke of the alternatives for dealing with a confrontation by an armed robber. Ordinarily, two such options exist: Give in or resist. However, he reframed this situation in the following way:

> ... let us imagine that the victim has nerves of steel and manages to give a totally new meaning to the situation by telling the thug: "I have been looking for somebody like you for a long time. You can now either take my wallet—it contains twenty dollars. Or, you can earn twenty-thousand by putting my wife's lover out of commission. If you are interested, come see me tomorrow and we can work out the details." Through this simple, albeit not absolutely foolproof method the victim has extricated himself from an apparently untenable position and gained the upper hand by offering two completely different alternatives. And yet, the scenario as such has remained unchanged: A victim who seems to have money; a *desperado* who has none and who seems to have no qualms about a human life. But instead of the alternative: "Your wallet or your life (and your wallet)," the choice is now: "Twenty or twenty-thousand dollars."

Rosen (1982a) cited Erickson's use of reframing with an eight-year-old child who hated the way she looked because her freckles made her the object of teasing by her classmates. Erickson accused her of being a thief and proved it when she challenged him to do so: "You were reaching up to the cookie jar, containing cinnamon cookies, cinnamon buns, cinnamon rolls—and you spilled some cinnamon on your face—you're a Cinnamon Face." The child enjoyed the humor as well as the new name Erickson had given her. The reframing of her situation suspended the child's belief system long enough for her to consider and adopt an alternative viewpoint.

Erickson's masterful use of metaphor often resulted in remarkable transformation for his patients. He reported his intervention with a hospital medical technician who "had the largest fanny I have ever seen on a woman."

Erickson had noted how this woman tended to small children who accompanied visitors to the hospital, even giving up her day off to babysit for them. From this behavior, Erickson surmised that she longed for children of her own and posited that her shape would make it difficult for her to view herself as attractive as a potential mate and mother. One day she suddenly developed uncontrollable hiccups, which her superiors believed to be psychosomatic in origin. She flatly refused to see Erickson for treatment. Her superior presented her with the alternatives of either losing her job or undergoing a consultation with Erickson. She chose the latter. Erickson relates his encounter:

> I held up my hand and said, "Keep your mouth shut, don't say anything (Erickson gestures with his left hand as if to stop traffic), until you have heard what I have to say. Your trouble is that you haven't read the Song of Solomon. It's in the Bible beside your table, but you haven't read it. That is your problem. Now since you haven't read the Song of Solomon, I'll explain it to you. I've watched you for about a year, taking care of other women's little children, giving up your days off to do that… So I know that you like children. And you think because you've got such a great big fanny, no man will ever look at you. You would know better if you had read the Song of Solomon."
> …Then I explained, "The man who will want to marry you, the man who will fall in love with you, will look at that great big, fat fanny of yours and see only a cradle for children. He will be a man who wants to father a lot of children. And he will see a beautiful cradle for children."

Erickson then dealt with the hiccups and directed the woman to read the Song of Solomon after he left. He reported success in eliminating the symptoms. When the technician appeared a few months later, it was with an engagement ring, a fiancé, and plans for building a home with a lot of bedrooms and a big nursery (Zeig, 1980).

Admittedly, this example, as well as the one that follows, presents a gender bias on the part of the therapist. In addition, it would seem to overemphasize the importance of a client's perceptions of her body features to her self-image. Although these attitudes are inconsistent with contemporary thought, the illustrations are included because they demonstrate, in their exaggerated way, how Erickson exploited the powerful mind–body connection.

Erickson also employed the message of the Song of Solomon to help a young woman reframe the way she viewed her relatively small breasts in relation to her unsatisfactory social relationships. The result of his intervention caused her to read the Song of Solomon weekly, return to college, break up with her alcoholic boyfriend, and become engaged to a more worthwhile man (Erickson, 1960/1980).

Patients react to effective reframing with surprise and enthusiasm. Both the perception and the affect associated with the perception change as a result, thereby allowing individuals to become unstuck from previously held positions and behaviors. "The therapeutic implications of reframing are quite powerful—independent of the theory of therapy in which the reframing is used" (Bergman, 1985).

When a therapist determines that the client must see himself and his problem in a new way, reframing is the means by which this is most effectively accomplished. Because metaphor enables individuals to briefly suspend their conviction and provides a vehicle by which clients may reframe their situations, it may play a forceful role in the alteration of attitude.

Isomorphism

A number of therapists limit and restrict the type of metaphor they apply to therapeutic situations. They suggest constructing metaphors that narrowly mirror the client's problems and concerns. Lankton and Lankton (1983) use the term *matching metaphor* to offer "a dramatic theme parallel to the client's presenting problem." Erickson was fond of saying: "If you want a person to talk about his brother, all you need to do is tell him or her a story about your own brother" (Zeig, 1980). Gordon (1978) recommended that "the characters in the metaphor share many of the same logical (and even linguistic) relationships as do the actual family members." Such explicit metaphors often inspire the patient to consider new choices and solutions to problems. He further recommended using narrative that is either fictional or true. In both cases, the narrative may be tailored to the client's needs or situation.

Gordon (1978) termed the customizing of a metaphor *isomorphism*, a one-to-one relationship between the presenting problem and the created narrative. This allows both the narrative's characters and its events to parallel the client's situation. He conceived of isomorphism as "the metaphorical preservation of the relationships occurring in the actual problem situation." According to this methodology, isomorphism is "the sharing of similar form or structure of two otherwise unrelated things." Gordon provided examples of the isomorphic relationship of a basketball and the earth, a car running out of gas and a starving person. In the latter example, gasoline and food are isomorphic because they both provide energy.

These metaphors are designed to be blatantly obvious, as is a metaphor Gordon created to demonstrate the relationship between a family and a ship. In this (gender-biased) illustration, the father became the captain, the mother the first mate, a child the cabin boy. The connection was made by comparing the son's getting into trouble with the cabin boy's setting the sails incorrectly.

Douglas Hofstadter (1979) based his definition of isomorphism on the overlapping creative patterns found in Gödel's incompleteness theorem, Escher's drawings, and Bach's self-regenerating musical structures:

The word isomorphism applies when two complex structures can be mapped onto each other, in such a way that to each part of one structure there is a corresponding part in the other structure, where "corresponding" means that the two parts play similar roles in their respective structures.

To some, this may appear too obvious or simplistic. Gilligan (1987) favored material that does not directly make reference to the object of therapeutic work because "it is difficult to consciously 'resist' them, but their relevance encourages the automatic activation of similar experiences." The use of more allegorical material may allow for an easier bypass of the conscious mind.

Conversely, Yapko (1990) did not advocate mirroring the client's issues with an isomorphic metaphor in order for it to be therapeutically effective. In fact, he suggested that when clients hear interesting stories, they can feel safe and allow the unconscious to respond to the metaphor. Yapko varies the degree to which a metaphor is removed from the clients' problems. He further suggests that narratives are more useful when they are sufficiently removed from isomorphic similarities because they become less threatening when not easily recognized. In addition, they are more bewildering and confusing, "sending the client into a search, at some level, for the 'real' meaning."

Creating New Metaphors

The degree to which isomorphic metaphors are applied is a function both of the therapist's skill and of his or her determination of the client's receptivity to isomorphic or allegorical metaphors. Regardless of the degree to which the metaphor mirrors the client's situation, it is important to consider whether each metaphor should be newly created and tailored to meet specific client needs.

Thompson (1988) demonstrated an unusual facility for utilizing metaphoric material. A great deal about the use of metaphor can be learned from listening to her lectures and demonstrations of hypnotic inductions. She developed metaphors from common experiences of life, including plumbing, plants growing, forms of transportation, locks and keys, and series of related words. Her metaphor about sailing, for example, includes analogies such as: sailing through life, having to do a lot of tacking, finding safe harbors, being at the mercy of wind and rain, floods, currents, undercurrents, undertows, and so on. Her use of language, word choice, and word play is artful. A master of the metaphoric technique, she would often say to a client: "If you're going to have to sit here and listen to me, you may as well hear what you are interested in hearing about." She then asks the client to suggest a metaphor. Although she confides, "I hope I can pick something out," few have her unusual talent and experience to develop a metaphor on the spot or to quickly reference a metaphor from her large pool of available material.

Mills and Crowley (1986) also believed that the construction of personally designed metaphors is paradigmatic. The creation of tailor-made narratives is based on the "personal, idiosyncratic qualities" of the individual rather than on the sociocultural traditions which form the basis for classical narratives.

It is not necessary and is probably impossible to develop a unique narrative for each client. Thompson (1985) suggested that there are limits to the ability of individual therapists to create new metaphors, but there are no limits to the individualization, by either patient or therapist, of already existing metaphors. This knowledge liberates therapists from the need to continually individualize narrative. A story, appropriately modified, can provide a multiplicity of meanings.

Thompson further pointed out that therapists who believe that the creation of new metaphors is the only satisfactory approach "often become bogged down in looking for stories when they should be working with the patient."

Rosen (1980) included himself among the therapists who do not have the sophistication that the creation of new metaphors requires. To illustrate the use of already available metaphoric material, he indicated that he might even read one of Erickson's metaphors to his clients.

An analogy may be made to the use of a prayer book. Most people are capable of composing their own prayers, yet they rely on a prayer book in worship because of the difficulty of creating sublime dialogue. Slonimsky (1967) described this tension between the wish to create and the need to use powerfully composed liturgy:

> We can't all pray from our own creative resources because we are not all of us religious geniuses, and prayer and religion are as truly a form of genius, a gift from God, as poetry or music or any high endowment. We can't all write Shakespeare's poetry or Bach's music but we still make it our own: we can open our hearts to it, and enrich and expand ourselves by sharing and appropriating it. And so in prayer we must turn to the great religious geniuses, the Isaiahs and Jeremiahs and Psalmists, and make our own the visions they have seen, the communion they have established, the messages they have brought back, the words they have spoken as having been spoken for us because [they are] truly spoken for all men. And by an act of sympathetic fervor, of loving contagion, to achieve their glow, and to fan the spark which is present in all of us at the fire which they have lighted.
>
> This does not mean that all the deepest prayers and all the best poetry and all the highest music has all already been written, and that there is an end to inspiration. The future is open, there is no limitation on the wonder of insight and creation. But we each of us in our time and place have to husband the resources available and to warm our hands at the fires already lighted.

Metaphoric Content

There are three kinds of stories. "Ha ha" stories to amuse and entertain, "Ah ha" stories for discovery of ideas and education, and "Ahhh" stories, where the tales are sublime and connect the teller and listener with a golden thread.—Arthur Koestler

The content of a metaphor is of great significance for its enhancement of therapeutic intervention. This section indicates some of the components of metaphoric material and considers the genres of narrative material best suited to therapeutic use.

The therapist must consider whether it is more effective and productive to employ realistic or fantastic narrative material. The masters of metaphoric interventions are divided in their opinions.

Lankton and Lankton (1989) provided a catalog of metaphors that present credible events and that scrupulously avoid narratives that involve the fantastic. They maintain that using stories that are too childish or too unbelievable results in a loss of the client's respect and the therapist's credibility and rapport. When Lankton and Lankton utilize an animal, plant, or inanimate object, they anthropomorphosize them through the mind of a human protagonist.

Zeig (1989) stated that he rarely invents stories, preferring instead "to relate real stories, which convey more feeling of immediacy."

Others (myself included) strongly disagree with the premise that fanciful, whimsical, preposterous, and even bizarre metaphors are neither welcomed by the client nor are useful to the therapist.

For Crossan (1975), the important point is not whether metaphors are realistic as opposed to unbelievable, but that narrative's power is found in the ability of a story of whatever variety to hold interest. He sharply contrasted the elements of truth and the interest inherent in the content of a narrative by citing the philosopher Alfred North Whitehead (1969), who suggested that it is more important for a story to be interesting than to be true. By extension, Crossan refined the meaning of "interesting" by stating that narrative should open "the possibility of transcendental experience for here and now."

The notion of using metaphors that are only of a serious nature is alien to the style of Milton Erickson. He encouraged the use of childhood stories and whimsical humor to help patients reaccess the suggestibility of children, whose innocent responses reflect an openness to learning and change (Rosen, 1988). Bettelheim (1976) sharpened this argument by indicating that fanciful metaphoric material provides useful assistance in the delivery of a metaphor because the focus of the tale is "not useful information about the external world, but the inner processes taking place in an individual."

"Reality mirrors fantasy," stated Chinen (1989). He advocated the notion that "Fairy tales portray timeless paradigms of human life, and often mirror the scripts which individuals play out in their lives...."

For Bettelheim (1976), fairy tales served a similar function:

> Each fairy tale is a magic mirror which reflects some aspects of our inner world, and of the steps required by our evolution from immaturity to maturity. For those who immerse themselves in what the fairy tale has to communicate, it becomes a deep, quiet pool which at first seems to

reflect only our own image; but behind it we soon discover the inner turmoils of our soul—its depth, and ways to gain peace within ourselves and with the world, which is the reward of our struggles.

In the same tone, Gordon (1978) suggested that just because a narrative is a fairy tale, it need not be "insipid." Adults, as well as children, can relate to them. "There are few people, young or old, who have not been blessed by a Deus ex Machina, or have not met a special or bizarre person, or, for that matter, have not talked to their cars."

Röhrich (1986) commented on the power of fairy tales. This type of narrative, more than any other type of book-based memory, is ingrained in our general consciousness because it is one of the first genres of literature most individuals experience in their formative years. For the vast majority of people, "it is one of the deepest and most enduring childhood impressions."

Similarly, Lewis (1966b) wrote of both the preferences and dislikes of adults and children for this type of narrative. For him, fairy tales are inextricably linked to the individual's inner world. In an essay entitled "On Juvenile Tastes," he commented that "juvenile taste is simply human taste, going on from age to age, silly with a universal silliness or wise with a universal wisdom, regardless of modes, movements, and literary revolutions."

Zipes (1991) echoed this view and wrote of the "celebration of wonder" this kind of narrative material provides:

We want to remain curious, startled, provoked, mystified, and uplifted. We want to glare, gaze, gawk, behold, and stare. We want to be given opportunities to change, and ultimately we want to be told that we can become kings and queens, or lords of our own destinies. We remember wonder tales and fairy tales to keep our sense of wonderment alive and to nurture our hope that we can seize possibilities and opportunities to transform ourselves and our worlds.

The last word on the use of children's narrative belongs to Maurice Sendak, who once commented that, as "a former child," he felt fully entitled and empowered to write children's stories. That is how it is for all former children—the listening to and retelling of stories speaks to the child within all people, who, no matter how distant from childhood or how dormant the recollections, retreat to a time filled with the excitement and wonder of knights, princesses, and dragons—to a magic world in which all things are possible. Stories invite reflection and recollection. They encourage listeners to wonder and dream about life in a different way than they currently experience it.

In addition to the type of narrative, the therapist must determine what techniques of language use and storytelling might embellish the delivery and efficacy of the chosen metaphor.

Mills and Crowley (1986) defined six ingredients necessary for the creation of therapeutic metaphors. These ingredients, found in all classic fairy tales, include (1) the establishment of a metaphoric conflict that reflects the tensions individuals experience in their own lives; (2) the framing of inner tensions and unconscious conflicts in the form of heroes or villains; (3) the protagonist's application of a lesson learned to parallel situations; (4) application of the protagonist overcoming or resolving the crisis; (5) the development of a new and better identity as a result of the "hero's journey"; and (6) the acknowledgment and celebration of the protagonist's special worth.

Barker (1985) outlined seven categories of metaphors that might be selected for and employed in therapy including: (1) major stories designed to deal comprehensively with complex clinical situations; (2) anecdotes and short stories designed to achieve limited goals or make specific points; (3) analogies, similes, and brief metaphors to emphasize particular points in place of direct statements or ideas that a client may be reluctant to accept; (4) metaphors designed to enhance the quality of the therapeutic relationship or model behavior for a client to apply to other relationships; (5) metaphors with tasks attached to them that are mostly of a ritualistic nature; (6) objects such as a cloth puppet or an envelope with a blank piece of paper in it that can be metaphorically utilized during therapy to represent something other than what they are; (7) and artistic metaphors created with the assistance of drawings or craft materials to enable individuals to call forth inner resources for conflict resolution.

The first three categories associate the length or importance of the narrative with the severity of the problem it is designed to help. The remaining four categories apply to metaphors that need not be expressed verbally. Under this rubric, Barker also included metaphors specifically constructed for the individual therapeutic situation, but acknowledged a variety of resources for their creation. He suggested agricultural metaphors utilizing the plant and animal kingdoms as well as the role of the farmer to represent developmental problems and goals. Other metaphors can be taken from the world of sports' teams, finance, business, banking, navigation, technology, never-ending journeys, famous people, participants in an orchestra or band, and the therapist's personal anecdotes.

Bergman (1992) often employed humorous personal anecdotes. He believed that individuals' metaphors result in what Nathan Ackerman called "tickling the defenses." Bergman (1992) summarized the parallel use of such material to help clients understand that their problems are not unique, so that they need not feel overly guilty, responsible, or overwhelmed by the situation. "By sharing similar stories about your own situation, you're joining, you're normalizing, you're depathologizing, you're changing the affect. You're saying that it's O.K."

Bergman described how he applied the story of trying to convince his mother to allow him to buy her a microwave oven to help move intransigent clients from their fixed mind sets. He reported that his mother had an entire set of responses to each of the reasons he thought she should have the microwave that she wanted, including the expense; her dislike of receiving this kind of gift; the fact that her husband was dead and there was no point in using it for only one person; the feeling that she wouldn't live long enough to use it for any worthwhile period of time. To this last objection, Bergman related, he said to her:

"Ma, buy the microwave and if you like it, you can take it with you."
"What do you mean?" she asked.
"We'll measure you, we'll measure the microwave. We'll go down to the funeral home and you'll take it with you."
Bergman reported the end of the incident: "She cracked up and she says she loves me."

Edgette (1991) advocated the use of idioms and proverbs. He created metaphors from these pithy maxims because he believed he was tapping into easily recognizable material that carries powerful force when it enters both the conscious and the unconscious. In his trance work, he might ask a client to imagine the numbering of clouds "to encode" the notion of "being on cloud nine." For someone "under the weather," he might speak of rising above the clouds and seeing all the colors in the sky (to suggest being "in the pink") . He shared the metaphor of the conductor who was increasingly bothered by a dissonance in the brass section. He discovered an animal in that area, and he walked up and took a tuba away from the bull that was playing it ("taking the bull by the horns").

Rosen (1980) employed the use of puns, which he felt are popular because of their appeal to the right hemisphere of the brain.

Metaphors include the use of visual, auditory, and kinesthetic cues to enhance the effectiveness of the metaphor by increasing the degree of "relational familiarity" (Mills & Crowley, 1986).

There is a wealth of published narrative material available to which the therapist can turn. The wide variety of genres and diverse places of publication of material suitable for adaptation to therapeutic use has limited the utilization of metaphoric narrative in therapeutic settings. One purpose of this book is to provide a catalog and source book of representative narrative material for therapeutic and teaching applications, as well as to provide guidelines for its use.

► 3

Techniques for the Methodological Implementation of Metaphor

A man fell in love with a woman with unearthly power. The marriage proceeded when he promised not to look into her basket unless given permission. But curiosity overtook him and, forgetting his promise, he looked inside. Incredulous, he laughed at the sight of the empty basket. The wife discovered his deed and reprimanded him. He could not figure out why she had made such a fuss over the empty container. As a result of his misdeed, she walked out of their hut, into the sunset, and vanished, never to be seen on earth again.

She left not because of the broken promise but because the man could not see that the basket was not empty. "I kept all the beautiful things of the sky in a basket for you and me. If you had waited, I would have taught you to see," she commented before she left. (Adapted from Simms, 1983)

Although it is not the sole tool in the therapist's repertoire of creative interventions, metaphor is a useful part of a comprehensive strategic approach. Recognizing that there are limitations to every method and that the use of metaphor is not a panacea for the resolution of clients' concerns and problems, it is possible to provide some guidelines for the use of narrative in therapy.

As clients absorb the richness of a metaphor, they step back from their dilemmas, lose their myopic vision, and come to view their goals and to contemplate strategies for attaining them. As they come to understand that problems are repetitive, they realize that they need a way to break the chain of self-defeating behaviors that have heretofore kept them in the same place. Finding the inner resources to get "unstuck" is a valuable lesson to be drawn from narrative. When clients encounter characters who take charge of their lives and who seize opportunities, they absorb the notion that life need not remain the way it currently is.

Therapists who employ metaphor utilize a wide variety of approaches in constructing narrative for therapeutic work. Few provide explicit guidelines. A concise guide to the steps necessary for implementation of metaphoric narrative in therapy is provided here to clarify its content and use.

Seven considerations should be taken into account in the therapeutic use of metaphor:

1. Identification of the client's problem, its repetitive and self-defeating nature, and the focus on the expected result
2. The choice of visual, auditory, or kinesthetic modality for the delivery of the metaphor
3. The delivery of the metaphor, with special attention to cadence, tone, pauses, and details
4. Interspersal of focused words for the delivery of individualized symbolism
5. Embedded commands to focus the client's attention
6. Embedding of additional metaphoric material for multiple-level communications
7. Emphasis on delivery without explanation

IDENTIFYING THE CLIENT'S PROBLEM

The first step, before using metaphor in therapy, is the identification of the problem, how it manifests itself, and what changes must be made to ensure a better and different destiny for the client. This identification enables the therapist to select and develop a metaphor to bridge the gap between undesirable behavior and damaging beliefs, and a new and better outlook and set of behaviors.

CHOICE OF MODALITY

Definition of Modality

In appraising a client, the therapist must be mindful of the enormous variability of communication skills, interests, emotional health, and defensiveness. Narayan (1989) cautioned the clinician that "the experience of the inner landscape may be different" for each listener. Furthermore, she suggested that only when the story-teller respects the emotional state and preferred communication modality of the client and does not attempt to moralize or impose values can the story prove to be therapeutic. She provides an illustration of the technique of a *sadhu* (a good or virtuous man, a celibate devotee of an ascetic Hindu sect) who "is like a therapist because he doesn't change anything, but tells stories so people can recognize their own outlook and make their own choices."

The choice of modality for the delivery of the metaphor is critical to its success. A *modality* is a sensory preference for the receipt of metaphoric language. There are three major modalities: visual, auditory, and kinesthetic. Most people respond to sensory experiences and receive communication best via one of these modes.

Bandler and Grinder (1975) and Grinder and Bandler (1976) articulated a widely used understanding of modalities. Based on observation of Erickson's finely honed skill in approaching clients as individuals with particular frames of reference, they posited that people prefer one of these three major varieties of sensory experience. These modalities are reflected in clients' use of language and their images of themselves and their worlds.

Individuals who operate in the visual modality respond to physical and linguistic cues derived from or evocative of the sense of sight. They speak of colors and describe the spectrum of vision as *hazy, dim, blurred,* and *sparkling.* They use words like *see, observe, watch, look,* and *visualize* not only to describe how they relate to the physical world, but also how they come to terms with interpersonal relationships.

Persons functioning in the auditory modality respond to sound and the quality of sound. They use terms like *hear, speak, sound, dialogue, wordy, loud, quiet, harmony,* and *roar.*

The affective world of kinesthetic clients focuses on feelings. They speak of *grasp, touch, experiencing pain, hurt, comfort,* and so on.

How Modalities Enable Clients to Receive Messages

By determining the modality in which a person operates, it is possible to communicate in a way that is most comfortable and familiar to the client. Through consideration of clients' cues, the therapist determines the modality to which a given client most closely responds and in which he or she operates.

How to Implement Modalities

Anchoring

Lankton (1980) suggested that the therapist can take best advantage of these modalities through *anchoring.* He defined an *anchor* as "any stimulus that evokes a consistent response pattern from a person." Anchors tie metaphoric suggestion directly to the three main sensory modalities. Speaking the client's language elicits more than a mere connection to the individual's frame of operation; it evokes associations with the past. Lankton (1980) defined this relationship by suggesting that "To make sense of a given word, you must access past experience(s) and form a gestalt of sensory information…"

Cameron-Bandler (1978) defined the notion of anchoring as a process that makes "deliberate association between a stimulus and a specific experience," a feeling, sight, or sound from the past. Such a purposefully inserted stimulus can trigger an experience or feeling over and over. A readily understood example is that of a melody associated with a romantic episode. Hearing the melody in the future will be enough to trigger romantic thoughts and feelings.

Similarly, Gordon (1978) related anchoring to the common experience of uncovering and returning the individual to the forgotten past by suggesting that "Everyone has periodically had the experience of seeing, hearing, feeling, smelling, or tasting something which takes them [sic] back to some experience or event in the past."

The therapist who, through metaphor, successfully establishes an anchor for the client's feelings related to the specific problem provides the client with one of the tools for evoking those inner resources necessary to resolve the issue.

Pacing

The notion of *pacing*, whereby the therapist mirrors or matches particular aspects of the client's behavior or language use, enhances the relationship between the two.

This technique is not new to this century. In the late sixteenth century, Francis Bacon (1597/1937) wrote an essay entitled "Of Negotiating," which expressed the principles of this concept.

> If you would *Worke* any Man, you must either know his Nature, and Fashions, and so Lead him; Or his Ends, and so Perswade him; Or his Weaknesse, and Disadvantages, and so Awe him; or those that haue Interest in him, and so Gouerne him. In *Dealing* with Cunning Persons, we must euer Consider their Ends, to interpret their Speeches; And it is good, to say little to them, and that which they least look for. In all *Negociations* of Difficultie, a Man may not looke, to Sowe and Reape at once; But must Prepare Business, and so Ripen it by Degrees.

Haley (1981) suggested that Erickson made wide use of this technique. Erickson expected his students to become astute observers in order to utilize movement, posture, and language to influence clients. In therapy, he abandoned his style of language and would always speak in a fashion similar to that of his client.

In applying the notion of pacing to hypothetical therapeutic settings, the psycholinguists Lakoff and Johnson (1980) presented a list of metaphors that might be offered in response to a client who speaks easily or frequently of horticultural activities. Under the rubric of IDEAS ARE PLANTS, they offer the following examples that would mirror or pace the client's responses:

His ideas have finally come to *fruition*.
That idea *died on the vine*.
That's a *budding* theory.
It will take years for that idea to *come to full flower*.
He views chemistry as a mere *offshoot* of physics.
Mathematics has many *branches*.
The *seeds* of his great ideas were planted in his youth.
She has a *fertile* imagination.
Here's an idea that I'd like to *plant* in your mind.
He has a *barren* mind.

Similarly, Sarbin (1986) noted the expansive quality of metaphor to lead to the development of ancillary and supporting metaphors. "To identify a political figure as a puppet, for example, leads to the use of related metaphors, such as pulling strings, manipulating characters, the puppet stage, scriptwriting, and so on."

The case of Joe, mentioned previously, illustrates this technique. Erickson paced his opening conversation with Joe by relating his own formative years growing up on a farm to Joe's occupation of florist:

I know you are a florist, that you grow flowers, and I grew up on a farm in Wisconsin and I liked growing flowers. I still do.... (Erickson 1966/1980)

Through pacing, Erickson established rapport with Joe. Once Erickson had met the horticulturist on his own terms, Erickson continued and explained to Joe how he expected Joe to meet him on his ground:

Now as I talk, and I can do so *comfortably*, I wish that you will *listen to me comfortably* as I talk about a tomato plant. (Erickson 1966/1980)

Another powerful demonstration of this technique stems from the time when Erickson was confronted by a patient who told him that, although he had wanted to come to see him, "I don't like the looks of you. I don't want to be your patient!" Erickson responded simply, "But you are here." This was met with a string of profanities.

"All right," I said. "Shut up! Sit down in that chair there and go into a trance!" And the patient did.

Why did this person come all the way...to see me? Why shouldn't I recognize that the patient wanted violence when the patient started swearing at me from the threshold of my office? Why shouldn't I offer back a violence of an acceptable kind? (Erickson, 1992)

Erickson's masterful pacing, which mirrored the invective spewed at him by the reluctant patient, was so effective that the patient had no choice but to comply with the therapist's suggestions.

Pacing, a technique of rapport building, is often seen in the activities of performers and speakers as they get a "feel" for the audience during the warm-up phase of a presentation. Skilled individuals intuitively gain the sense of rhythm present among their spectators. Dilts, Grinder, Bandler, and DeLozier (1980) elucidated the methodology of communicating in the context of the client's world through a parallel unconscious process they refer to as *synchrony*. They suggest that it is akin to reading clients' minds or second-guessing their internal processes in order to reduce resistance between clients and therapist and create what they term client *irresistibility*.

Grinder and Bandler (1981) suggested that the therapist can build rapport with clients by regulating voice tempo to the clients' rates of breathing, even blinking, nodding, and rocking at the same rate as the clients. Commenting on behaviors that are observable also builds rapport. When the therapist's world matches that of the patient, the therapeutic relationship will be one that fosters communication and understanding as well as cooperation.

Wallas (1985) described the spell-like quality that rapport affords a therapist as an "open sesame" for metaphoric use. Once a metaphor is sufficiently removed from a client's problem or experience, "the new possibilities it offers become intriguing suggestions rather than commands."

Bergman (1991) applied an anthropological aspect of developing rapport through cultural identification with his clients. He has used Yiddish "to join and connect with a Jewish family." Certainly, where appropriate, tribal or national connections should be employed to facilitate pacing. Cultural affinity between therapist and client, though not a requirement, often provides certain advantages in understanding the idiosyncratic nature of the client's culture of origin and may speed the building of rapport.

Barker (1985) cautioned that pacing should be done sensitively and unobtrusively. Gilligan (1987) concluded that pacing is most easily used when it is employed "as an extremely pervasive, general, and naturalistic phenomenon." For greatest effectiveness, this technique should operate outside the client's conscious thought processes. Pacing should be subtle enough to elude conscious recognition, yet sufficiently powerful to affect the unconscious.

THE DELIVERY OF THE METAPHOR

The third step, the storytelling itself, is not spontaneous or unplanned. To be delivered successfully, the metaphor must be carefully prepared.

Telling a story involves more than just repeating the details of a narrative. Livo and Rietz (1991) wrote about the dynamic quality found in skilled storytelling. They suggest that the storyteller must know the story in such a way as to give it passion, power, and mystery. The storyteller should imbibe and share the story's profound meaning.

Livo and Rietz (1987) provided suggestions for successful storytelling, including the following:

1. Choosing a familiar story
2. Rereading it several times
3. Sequencing the events
4. Telling the story in front of a mirror, tape, or video camera
5. Practicing facial and hand expressions
6. Employing pauses at appropriate moments
7. Using voice for emotional effect such as joy or sorrow
8. Finding personal insights to add a sense of ownership to the telling of the story

Barker (1985) offered some general suggestions for the delivery of a metaphor: considered preparation, observation of what needs to be emphasized, variation of pace and style of delivery, selection of stories that the therapist personally finds interesting, and careful attention to the listener's responses.

A metaphor is not read verbatim; it is delivered orally. The written story and the oral story are received in different ways. When the narrator is bound to a written text, the effectiveness of the metaphor is greatly diminished. The narrator should practice telling the metaphor, varying the rhythm, tone, and pauses. This enables the therapist to keep the client's attention and to direct him or her to specific components of the metaphor.

The timing of the delivery is of importance. Metaphor must enter naturally into the therapeutic session so that it does not seem abrupt or contrived. Each therapist has to develop a sense of when a client will welcome a metaphor. It is seldom advisable to begin a session with a metaphor, although conceivably this might be a way to get the client to sit up and take notice. However, since metaphoric intervention is beyond the therapeutic expectations of most clients, it may be better to wait until the client's level of confidence in the therapist is such that he or she will accept and trust it. Considering that storytelling by its very nature is hypnotic, and that there are natural ninety-minute ultradian cycles of waking trances, there are times of the day that are optimal for metaphor delivery.

The delivery of the metaphor is simply a break in the expected rhythm of the therapeutic session. It is akin to the technique in drama whereby the protagonists temporarily step outside the action and inform each other, the audience, or both of something that is not obvious to the rest of the characters. Having done so, they step back into the play and resume the action.

Metaphor delivery begins with a transition to metaphoric language: "While you were telling me what happened, I was reminded of a story"; "I find that my mind is drawn to a story that will interest you"; "I am curious about what you think of this story, which may have a message of deep interest to you." Transitions like these help clients note the metaphor's significance by arousing their curiosity and interest. The transition gently urges clients to listen. It sets the metaphor in motion by integrating it into the conversation instead of presenting it in a disruptive fashion ("Now I am going to tell you a story.") that might lead the client to seek an explanation or interpretation from the therapist. Integrating the story into the flow of the conversation also reduces the risk of the client searching for a single meaning.

INTERSPERSAL OF FOCUSED WORDS

The fourth step deals with focused words, phrases, and sentences selected for the conveyance of individual symbolism. Words evoke a panoply of feelings and thoughts; they contain a myriad of labyrinthine associations, feelings, thoughts, ideas, and relationships. In context, individual words carry stories as well; they create what Silko (1991) termed "an elaborate structure of stories-within-stories."

The complexity of the unconscious learning process has a profound effect on an individual's use of words. The therapist must exercise caution in choice of words as well as choice of metaphor. The use of metaphor must be planned with considerable care. It is not a haphazard process of the free association of ideas and communications that come to mind during a therapeutic session. An example of the lengthy and fastidious care given in the preparation of an induction is found in Erickson (1944/1980).

Purposely groping for a word is a useful technique that helps draw the client into the metaphor. If the client attempts to help the therapist with word selection, his or her interest is heightened and the client becomes a part of the telling.

Metaphor, the language of delivery, and the concept of change are all carefully planned to increase the likelihood of achieving specific therapeutic results. Helping clients focus on particular words directs their attention to the symbolism attached to the words. The selection of specific words or phrases allows the story to be matched to the individual client. Erickson termed this the *interspersal approach* (Erickson, 1966/1980). To stimulate new associations, words or phrases are interspersed singly or repeatedly throughout the therapeutic conversation or in the delivery of a metaphor. Such words and phrases are often delivered after a pause, with a shift in tone or emphasis subtle enough to not distract the client. For example, in attempting to help the client build on the expectation of positive change, the therapist would employ the following kinds of phrases: "You are capable of so many changes"; "You can expect more change"; "Change is inevitable"; "You can have a change of heart"; or "You can change your mind."

EMBEDDED COMMANDS

The fifth consideration, an additional opportunity to focus the client's attention on what should be stressed, is provided by an *embedded command* created by inserting the client's name into the sentence to indicate that the command is directed to him or her (Gordon, 1978). The statement "He raced to save the game as the crowd roared," with changed emphasis, becomes, "He raced to save the game, Jay, as the crowd roared."

A shift in voice from third to second person further alerts the unconscious mind that the message is intended for the listener and contributes to a deeper embedding of the intended command (Kershaw & Wade, 1991).

EMBEDDING FOR MULTIPLE-LEVEL COMMUNICATION

Sixth, just as specific words are given additional power in context, the addition of an anecdote, quotation, or story within a story increases the force of the message by allowing communication on several different levels. Metaphors vary in size and content. They may be extended narratives or a single phrase or word that calls forth memory. These additional quotes, anecdotes, or brief stories establish multiple-level communication as the original story, brought into sharper focus, is identified more memorably and meaningfully. Some stories already have additional stories embedded within the text. Bal (1991) used the example of *The Thousand and One Nights* to illustrate the motif he terms *hypo-stories*—stories within stories. The main narrative tells of a king who kills each of his new wives on their wedding night in retaliation for his first wife's deceit. The captivating stories Scheherazade tells the king to avoid meeting the same fate are embedded narratives.

Erickson believed he could embed an idea within a metaphor via an anecdote. As a result, the client would continue to ruminate on the idea until it had grown and influenced the desired behavior. Erickson used the term *seeding* to describe embedding ideas for later use. He would emphasize these ideas at the beginning of a conversation to lay the groundwork for a response that he would later build on if the situation warranted it (Haley, 1973).

Zeig (1990) defined *seeding* "as activating an intended target by presenting an earlier hint." He pointed out the analogous terms *priming* or *cueing* in experimental psychology and *foreshadowing* in literature, theater, and music. Foreshadowing is described succinctly in this statement attributed to Chekhov: "If there is a gun on the mantle in the first act, somebody will get shot by the third act!" Zeig (1990) also supplied an analysis of the extensive use of foreshadowing found in *The Wizard of Oz,* in which each protagonist in Oz is presaged by a denizen of Kansas. Each personality is ultimately discovered to have contained the resources for creative solutions within. Zeig commented that careful use and planning for seeding can shorten the term of therapy through decreased client resistance.

Madanes (1990) applied this concept to family therapy. She suggested that a family should be skillfully prepared to enable it to later grasp and be moved by suggestions for change made in prior phases of therapy. Such advance preparation lays the groundwork for major change, motivates the clients, and makes the therapist believable.

Barker (1985) pointed to the simplicity and effectiveness of metaphor's use by breaking off a story, conversation, or other communication in the middle to turn to a number of other interventions, such as reframings, paradoxes, analogies, or other metaphors, before returning to complete the communication. Seeding is a technique whereby the introduction of a therapeutic intervention can interrupt a strategy already in place. This process is, for the two (or more) techniques so intertwined, mutually strengthening.

In short, seeding provides a powerful tool for the development of techniques that optimize patient cooperation, the gathering of enhanced treatment information and the intensification of the message on both conscious and unconscious levels. The use of this technique should be subtle enough to circumvent detection so that its power can be accessed by the unconscious and called up at the appropriate moment into consciousness.

DELIVERY WITHOUT EXPLANATION

The master expounded the law to an audience hostile toward him. They mocked him, saying, "What you say does not in any way explain the verse."

Replied the master, "Do you think that I was trying to explain the verse in the book? That needs no explanation. I was trying to explain the verse within me" (Buber, 1948).

The seventh and final step, delivery of the metaphor without explanation, requires that the therapist or narrator not be too literal, analytical, or specific. Lack of explanation allows clients to use their conscious and unconscious minds to make sense of the message and to assign personal meaning to it. This forces the listener to do what Erickson (1985) has termed an *inner search*. This is similar to Erickson's *waiting technique* applied in hypnotic induction. Gordon (1978) called the process of the client applying his experiences and evaluative skills to understanding the metaphor on both conscious and unconscious levels the *transderivational search*. By intentionally abstaining from supplying interpretation, the therapist forces clients to work harder than they might ordinarily in order to resolve the ambiguity and to provide their own interpretations.

CAVEATS ATTENDANT TO THE USE OF METAPHOR IN THERAPY

Like most interventions, metaphor can sidetrack, mislead, and even misdirect the therapeutic effort. Bateson (1989) warned that "there are few things as toxic as a bad metaphor."

This message, applied to the spectrum of therapeutic metaphors, alerts the user to employ care in selecting material for appropriate use in therapy lest clients receive the wrong message or incorrectly apply it to their life situations. O'Flaherty (1988) suggested that a myth that evokes evil or unethical behavior in the listener is pernicious.

Mills and Crowley (1988) also offered a warning. They suggested that metaphoric application creates new tasks and places new demands on the therapist. The "cleverness trap" can snare the inexperienced therapist, who may be unwittingly seduced by the manipulative quality of the technique. At the same time, clients understand and resent being manipulated by an empty technique employed by an inexperienced therapist who does not understand its function, and uses it for personal power, prestige, or control of others. Patients pick up the shallowness in such therapeutic attempts because there has been "no deepening association with the inner sources of illness and creativity that are the true quest of all healing work" (Erickson, 1983).

Lankton (1989) cautioned against hastily constructing metaphors without the benefit of a treatment plan and an assessment of the client and the client's contract. He suggested that such impulsively created metaphors lead to transference and countertransference problems because of the intense memories and emotions metaphors evoke.

Haley (1981) added a stern warning about the polarity that the use of metaphors can promote, particularly if the metaphor is not well grounded in reality. When used in fantasy, humor, and play, metaphor is rewarding; in therapeutic situations, however, where the balance of power between therapist and client is an issue, the use of metaphor can be dangerous because it arouses violent emotions. This concern evolved out of Bateson's decade-long research project on communication: "The schizophrenic individual manages to use metaphor in a way that enriches language, while he also uses it to deny, and to express the despair of one who feels helplessly caught in a restrictive struggle with an uncertain world" (Haley, 1981).

APPLYING METAPHOR TO THERAPEUTIC SITUATIONS

The following examples introduce the professional to the use of metaphor in a counseling setting. Each example has been developed in terms of the seven considerations outlined above. For each, the following typographic conventions apply:

- The modalities, the various words associated with sight, sound, and feeling, are indicated by *italics*.
- Words indicating stage directions (Cadence, tone, pauses, and details) are enclosed in square brackets ([ ]).
- Interspersal of focused words for individualized symbolism is indicated in a particular session by SMALL CAPITAL LETTERS.
- Embedded commands are names in ***boldface italics*** and are used to focus the person's attention to a specific part of the metaphor.
- Additional material embedded for multiple-level communication, representing metaphors within the metaphor, is set in **Roman boldface.**

EXAMPLE OF THE APPLICATION OF METAPHOR TO FAMILY THERAPY

Description of the Presenting Problem

Carol, aged 37, and Jerry, 40, are the parents of three children: Lynn, 14; Becky, 12; and Warren, 9. Carol and Jerry report that the fifteen years of their married life have been stormy and punctuated by numerous problems involving their marital relationship and their differing philosophies of child rearing. Jerry, a successful corporate executive, is focused on his rising career. Carol, a local realtor, regrets that she never did more with her career. Instead, she stayed at home to be with the children as much as possible, and as she put it, "to fill in the gaps left by Jerry's long hours and frequent business trips."

Of late, the children have become more independent and are involved in activities outside their home for longer portions of the day. The frequency and intensity of Carol and Jerry's fighting has increased. A large measure of their fighting centers around Warren, who is doing poorly in school and spends long periods of time in his room or in front of the television. He appears to be unconcerned with his personal cleanliness, and his room is always a "disaster." The parents agree that punishment and bribes have not worked. Both report that their girls are perfect young ladies, although they admit that Lynn has become secretive and aloof in the last year.

Jerry is concerned that Carol is restricting Warren's freedom by keeping him closer to home than Jerry thinks Warren ought to be. He complains that Warren has few friends, isn't good at and doesn't enjoy sports, plays with children younger than he, and makes friends primarily with girls in the neighborhood. Jerry blames Carol for turning Warren into a "sissy" and a "mama's boy" by encouraging him to stay at home and by not pushing Warren to participate in after-school and community sports activities. Jerry criticizes Carol by saying: "If she didn't spend so much time doing volunteer work and socializing with her friends, she could earn more money selling real estate. That would take some of the financial pressure off of my shoulders and she could devote more energy to help Warren become the man I think he should be." They have fought on and off for months over whether Warren should go to a sports camp next summer. Jerry worries that Warren seems a bit feminine and fears that he will grow up to become a homosexual.

Carol feels that Jerry is a workaholic who never spends much time with the children. Carol says that if Jerry were home more and were not always doing "office work" at home, she could devote more time to her real estate career. This would allow Jerry and Warren to spend more time doing sports and other male-oriented activities. Carol complains that Jerry and Warren's relationship is a poor one. Jerry yells at Warren and intimidates him; Warren shuts Jerry out by going off to his room or watching television. Carol wishes Jerry provided Warren with a better role model.

Identification of the Problem

Carol and Jerry have spent years fighting about the same issues. Recently, the frequency of their fights has increased. Neither feels he or she has ever had any impact on the other; that is why they are seeking help. Jerry also believes that if he doesn't do something now to change what Jerry terms Warren's feminine tendencies, it will be too late.

On some level, both parents recognize that they have a tendency to fight with each other through Warren, who is their "identified patient." Both have poor "conflict resolution" skills and are at a complete loss as to what to do about Warren, their relationship, and the future of their marriage.

Goals for the Family

The primary objective is to help Carol and Jerry to deal with their disappointments in marriage and career and to learn how to communicate more clearly with each other in order to resolve issues in a way that prevents them from constantly resurfacing. They need to learn compromise skills.

Warren should no longer be the focus of Carol's and Jerry's attention, anger, and disappointments. He should be encouraged to become more actively involved with friends in school and with extracurricular and weekend programs. He should be kept out of his parents' arguments. He should be empowered to take charge of his responsibilities for school and his room.

The parents need to pay careful attention to giving all of their children greater responsibility in their personal lives. They need to provide recognition for accomplishments and demonstrations of new skills. They need to learn to model for their children a loving relationship that demonstrates how parents solve problems and nurture each other and their children.

The Implementation of Techniques in the Delivery of the Metaphor

The observation was made that Warren and his siblings tend to operate on a visual plane. This modality is not surprising in the media age. To establish rapport and to enable Warren to accept the metaphoric message more easily, a focus on this style of communication is employed with words, such as *visualize, see, read, learn, recognize, picture,* and *radiant.* Jerry communicates best on an auditory level and constantly uses clichés like: "I hear what you are saying"; "It sounds to me"; "Tell me what you want." When speaking to Jerry, words such as *hear, word, tone, popping,* and *sound mind* are employed to facilitate the therapeutic relationship. Carol, who focuses on feelings, represents the kinesthetic modality. She frequently speaks of "being in touch" with herself and her family and of "being stuck," "turning the situation around," "moving closer," and "being blocked." *Unafraid, sense of trust, sense of power, emotions evoked, afraid, grateful, rejoice,* and *felt* are words used to foster communication between the therapist and this client.

The metaphor chosen must speak to these individuals through the modalities that they are most likely to understand and be comfortable with. A complete description of the evaluative process for making these decisions is found in Bandler and Grinder (1975) and Grinder and Bandler (1976).

Statement of the Session's Concerns

During this session, Jerry is angry about Warren's lack of compliance with Jerry's image of how a male child in his family should behave.

Source of the Metaphor

The metaphor is adapted from "Iron Hans" in *Grimm's Fairy Tales* (1972).

The Counselor Introduces the Metaphor

"*Jerry*, I can *hear* your frustration at not being able to have Warren *listen* to the *tone* you would like to establish and expect for this family. As I sit here and consider your words, I find that the story of Iron Hans keeps popping into my head. I would like you to *listen* to it carefully." *Warren*, **Lynn**, and **Becky,** see if you can *picture* this tale in your head. I don't think it's one you may have *seen* in a book or on TV. *Carol*, I know you will *sense* the same strong *emotions evoked* as you *feel* the power of this story." [pause]

Telling the Metaphoric Tale

People in a kingdom were *afraid* to go into the great forest because those who ventured in seldom returned. **Warren**, I want you to *visualize* a loyal servant who one day expressed a WILLINGNESS to investigate, at great personal risk, the danger in the forest. *Unafraid*, he VENTURED forth, DISCOVERED who was responsible for the failure of citizens to return, and CAPTURED the red-haired, wild, rusty-looking Iron Man at the bottom of a bog.

Recognize that it is EASY TO GET LOST in a bog. Walking around with wet, mud-covered feet, you get the feeling of being BOGGED DOWN, like you can never get [grope for word to solicit responses from the family] UNSTUCK, almost like BEING IN QUICKSAND [hand motion to indicate being trapped]. Well, his FORTITUDE, his STRONG WILL and DETERMINATION enabled him to SUCCEED where others had failed.

You might be interested in *hearing*, **Jerry**, that this king did not have a particularly sound mind because, instead of INVESTIGATING who Iron Man was, he had him imprisoned in a cage in the royal courtyard and forbade anyone, on pain of death, from opening it. His wife, the queen, was charged with the RESPONSIBILITY of keeping the key and *felt a new sense of trust* [strong emphasis] on the part of her husband. *Carol*, you know that being the KEEPER OF THE KEY gives a person a *sense of power*. Do you think she *welcomed* this or *felt* it to be a burden?

While the king and queen were well meaning, they were possessive parents who LONGED TO BE PROUD of their nine-year old son. One day, their son was playing in the courtyard when his golden ball rolled into Iron Man's cage. He asked for it to be returned, and Iron Man told him that he would return the ball if he opened the cage. The prince was an OBEDIENT CHILD and would not violate his father's word. He told Iron Man that he couldn't "because the king had forbidden it." Each day the scene was reenacted. Iron Man was determined to be free, and the boy wanted only to be the OBEDIENT SON.

Jerry, what happens next will *sound* interesting to you. The king went out hunting, and the boy took the key from under his mother's pillow and opened Iron Man's cage. Just *listen* to what is happening, *Jerry*. When the king is AWAY, the boy *sees* that he can ACCOMPLISH anything he wants because he has to [grope for word] RELY on himself without his father there.

When he finally took matters into his own hands and opened the cage, Iron Man returned the ball, stepped, out and hurried away. The timid boy called to him in a BOOMING voice, "Please don't go, for my father will beat me when he returns and *hears* about what I have done." Iron Man turned back, picked up the boy, and carried him off to the forest.

Carol and *Jerry*, I wonder if you have ever *read* or *heard* the words of Eric Fromm, who distinguishes the love between members of a couple and the love between a parent and child. For a husband and wife, he feels that "**two people who were separate become one.**" And this is what he says about a parent and child: "**In motherly love, two people who were one become separate. The mother must not only tolerate, she must wish and support the child's SEPA-RATION. It is only at this stage that motherly love becomes such a difficult task, that it requires UNSELFISHNESS, the ability to give everything and to want nothing but the happiness of the loved one.**"

When the king returned, he learned about the empty cage and asked the queen what she had done. She said that she did not know how it had happened, but that the key was missing. He saw that she was not [emphasis] to BLAME.

Iron Man told the boy that he would never see his parents again and that he would BE ON HIS OWN, but if he was ever in trouble, he was to call on him.

The prince never did return to his parents' kingdom but, instead, grew up as a servant in another kingdom. Some years later, when the warriors of that kingdom went off to war, the lad asked to RIDE WITH THE MEN. They told him he could follow them on whatever horse remained. All that was left in the stable was a lame horse, which he MOUNTED and RODE. The horse hobbled along until he came to the edge of the forest, where the YOUNG WARRIOR called for Iron Man. The lad asked for a STRONG STEED so that "I can fight in the wars."

Iron Man replied, "You shall have that and even more than you asked for."

Suddenly a stable boy appeared leading a FIERCE HORSE who snorted furiously and could hardly be RESTRAINED. *Warren*, I bet you can *picture* him galloping to the HEAD OF THE TROOPS. If he were *afraid*, he didn't show any fear.

You know, *Warren*, there was a man named Pythagoras who lived 2500 years ago. He was an expert in FIGURING things out. He could *see* solutions to mathematical problems that others just couldn't *see*. His name is still attached to the study of math today. Do you know what he said? He said, "**When you go abroad, DON'T TURN AROUND at the frontier.**" Just as you are getting ready for a BREAKTHROUGH, you have to have the POWER TO KEEP GOING. And that's just what happened in our story—the new warrior STAYED HIS COURSE.

No one in battle could oppose the YOUNG MAN. The young WARRIOR not only used Iron Man's ASSISTANCE, he was NOT AFRAID; he *visualized* what needed to be done and then used all of his POWER and STRENGTH to lead the people to victory. As a reward, the *grateful* king gave his daughter, the princess, in marriage to him. To his ASTONISHMENT, his own parents came to the celebration. He *rejoiced*, not only because of the *radiant* celebration, but also because he had made them PROUD of him at last.

At the wedding feast, the music stopped, the doors opened, and a very handsome king entered with a royal retinue. He went up to the groom, embraced him, and said: "I am Iron Man. I was held under a spell, but because of you, because you *called* upon me and ALLOWED ME TO HELP YOU, I am free, just as you are free. All the WEALTH I possess now belongs to you."

Each had gotten something from the other, *Jerry*. I wonder if you are familiar with Bernard Meltzer's (1982), "A Father's Prayer." In it, a parent and a child discover PART OF THEMSELVES IN EACH OTHER. It's a good note on which to end this story [slower pace]:

Last night at bedtime
My little boy confessed to me some childish wrong
And I forgave him—kissed him—and sent him off to bed.
As he lay down I heard him pray:
"Dear God," he whispered, "make me a MAN like my daddy, WISE
**   and STRONG."**
And then in peace he fell asleep.
I knelt beside my sleeping son
Shedding tears of happiness.
As I gazed on his sleeping form, I, too, prayed.
"Dear God," I whispered, "make me PURE
Like my child lying here.
Instill in me innocence and UNSELFISH LOVE like that of a child.
Make of me a better person
So that I may help make this world a better one
For my child—and for all—in this blessed land."
Amen.

Conclusion of the Session

Delivery of the metaphor was made without explanation. No further comment was offered, and the session ended.

Discussion and Analysis of the Metaphor

This session is designed to implant the notion that this family need not be bogged down in their problems and that it is possible to solve problems and change situations. At the beginning of "Iron Man," the loyal servant solves the problem of subjects who never return from their forays into the forest. The queen takes charge via her position as keeper of the keys. That allegory urges Carol to develop a life outside of the family. Finally, the transformation of the young prince, as well as that of Iron Man, adds to the force of the metaphor of transformation.

The metaphoric message of mutual problem solving is directed to the parents. It suggests that Warren have more freedom to venture forth and develop a life independent of his mother, just as the prince leaves his overprotective parents.

The Fromm quote is directed to each family member. It emphasizes that there are difficulties in and differences between loving a spouse and loving a child; one requires drawing close and the other requires pushing away.

Using his own inner resources and determination, Warren could be like the young prince who took greater responsibility for his life and became the successful warrior and winner of the princess's hand in marriage. Just as Iron Man is transformed by a magnanimous act, the entire family can change if they help each other and allow themselves to be helped.

The Meltzer poem is directed to Jerry, who had absented himself from the daily operation of the family. He needs to be drawn back into the family orbit, to become more involved with his wife and in his children's activities. This closeness will enable him to have greater input in shaping of their lives and enable him to be proud of their efforts.

EXAMPLE OF THE APPLICATION OF METAPHOR TO THERAPY WITH A COUPLE

Description of the Presenting Problem

Jane, 24, and Tim, 28, have been married for a year and a half. They describe their relationship as loving and their marriage as quite successful except for one factor: They fight continually about Jane's relationship with her mother. Jane says that her mother is her closest friend and she relies a great deal upon her. She would like to be able to rely on her mother less than she does, but feels that her relationship is like an addiction she cannot control.

Jane says that Tim is jealous of her relationship with her mother because he has distant, cold relationships with both of his parents. She says that he is intolerant of their frequent phone calls, almost daily lunches together, forthcoming joint vacation plans, and what he terms an "endless flow of gifts and food."

Tim feels as though his house is not his own. He reports that Jane's parents are constantly there. At times he feels like an outsider in his own home. When he says that he and Jane can't afford to buy something, the object always seems to arrive as a gift from Jane's parents. Jane's father keeps telling Tim to spend everything he makes. "Don't worry about anything," his father-in-law says. "There's plenty of money, and we've made provision for your future comfort in our wills." Tim says he is made to feel that he cannot provide adequately for their daughter. Tim finds it difficult to establish friendships with other young couples because they spend every weekend and many evenings with Jane's parents. Their few married friends do not seem to be very interested in their friendship.

Most recently, Jane's parents have begun to make not-too-subtle comments about wanting grandchildren and thinking that Jane and Tim should start planning for children. Tim says: "How can we even begin to think about starting a family? I don't feel like I've had the opportunity to get to know my wife yet." Most recently, Tim has taken to offering excuses to avoid going out with Jane's parents, but Jane goes anyway, without Tim.

Identification of the Problem

Jane's relationship with her parents, particularly her mother, can be termed one of overinvolvement. Her thoughts, feelings, and actions are so closely aligned with those of her mother that it is impossible for her to think, feel, or act independently of her. Family therapists term this *ego fusion,* a quality of stuck-togetherness in which neither individual can operate without the other. In some families, the solution involves an either/or situation—total overinvolvement or a complete break—with no middle ground. Ideally, both parties should feel comfortable when not in the presence of the other.

The healthier state, called *ego differentiation,* is one in which both parties spend time with each other while also leading independent lives. Tim, wittingly or unwittingly, married into this situation for a number of possible reasons. It may have suited his own needs at first. Perhaps it was reminiscent of the relationships in his own family of origin and therefore was familiar to him. He may have looked away, thinking the situation was temporary, that it would change once he and Jane settled into married life. Perhaps, Tim thought the problem would be solved through his overinvolvement with his wife replacing her overinvolvement with her mother, but this never materialized. He may have hoped the marriage would rescue Jane from a situation that both of them believed that Jane did not know how to deal with. Both are unable to find a reasonable compromise that would allow Jane to spend some time with her mother while, at the same time, allowing the couple to establish lives independent of her family of origin.

Goals for the Couple

A primary objective is to allow Jane to separate from her parents in a way that does not rupture the parent–child relationship. At the same time, Tim should not step in to fill the void that separating from them creates for her. The goal is not to substitute overdependency and fusion of husband and wife for that of parent and child.

Their conflict resolution skills, which are primitive, need to be developed in order for them to learn safe and reasonable ways to deal with this and other conflicts.

The Implementation of Techniques in the Delivery of the Metaphor

Jane relies on auditory cues. A variety of words that enable the therapist to focus on Jane's personal style of communication are employed to enable her to receive the metaphoric message more readily and easily. Looking at the section entitled "Telling the Metaphoric Tale," we see that *listen, hear,* and *say* are the auditory words the therapist employs to transmit the meaning in a modality accessible to Jane.

Tim operates in a visual mode. *Focus, see, visualize,* and *notice* are the words used to establish rapport with him.

Statement of the Session's Concerns

In this session, Jane asks what is so wrong about being close with her parents. "I thought Tim would be happy with this arrangement since he seemed so interested in having the kind of relationship with my parents that he lacked with his own," she said. She accuses Tim of being jealous of the kind of rapport he never had with his parents.

Tim counters by saying: "There is close and there is close, but this is ridiculous. The intimacy between Jane and her mother is pushing me further and further away. She might as well move in with them, because the way things are right now, it's just as if she still lived in their house."

Source of the Metaphor

The metaphor is adapted from "Yuriko" in Kawabata (1988).

The Counselor Introduces the Metaphor

Jane, I know you *hear* that Tim is at a loss to get you to ACKNOWLEDGE a problem [pause]. *Tim*, you *visualize* yourself as being PATIENT and UNDERSTANDING up to a limit, which you believe you have reached [pause]. *Listening* to you, and *seeing* that both of you feel hurt and misunderstood, *focuses* my mind on a story of another couple that was also at an IMPASSE [hand motion to indicate being up against a brick wall]. This couple needed to SEE THE CHANGES that were taking place. Had the partners *heard* the words of this quote, written by Merle Shain, they could have found a WAY OUT of their impasse.

Before I tell you the story, *Jane*, I'd like you to listen to the words, and *Tim*, *see* if you can *visualize* them in your head: **"LOVING someone means helping them to BE MORE THEMSELVES, which can be different from being what you'd like them to be, although often they turn out the same."**

Telling the Metaphoric Tale

Jane, I want you to *listen* to this tale, and *Tim*, I want you to *focus* on this story of two lovers. It begins when Yuriko was a schoolgirl. She tried to emulate the qualities of her closest friends. If one carried a certain kind of book bag, Yuriko had to have the same one, even if it were unfashionable. To look like her friends, she would have her hair cut in the same style or wear the same clothing. She would try in other ways to approximate their facial and physical characteristics. *Jane*, she was more than a mere CONFORMIST. You could *say* that she was more like a CHAMELEON who changed her physiognomy and deportment depending on the person in whose presence she stood. Sadly [drop voice], she never found it to help her develop LASTING RELATIONSHIPS. Yet she did not know any other way. She was at a loss to find a more satisfactory way to achieve TRUE FRIENDSHIP.

Tim, I am quite interested in Yuriko's marriage. It is not clear to me how Yuriko's husband could have married her without *noticing* her CHAMELEON-LIKE approach to relationships. Nevertheless, he threw caution to the wind and married Yuriko. She rewarded him by loving him beyond imagination. She was utterly DEVOTED. In her accustomed manner, Yuriko cut her hair, wore thick eyeglasses, colored the few blond hairs above her lip with black, smoked a pipe, and walked with a man's gait. *Jane*, have you ever *heard* of such ATTACHMENT that would drive one person to want TO BE SO CLOSE to another, the first desiring only to be exactly like the second?

Tim, I think you can *see* that Yuriko's husband became increasingly irritated at each step and eventually forbade her to imitate any of his characteristics or mannerisms. More than anything else, it was as if he just DIDN'T KNOW WHAT TO DO about the problem or HOW TO CHANGE the events that seemed to be BARRELING ALONG TOWARD AN UNHAPPY CONCLUSION.

This inability to BREAK OUT of established patterns is akin to **the story of the men who chartered a plane for a hunting expedition. *Picture* this: As they loaded the plane for the return home, the pilot said: "This plane won't take more than one wild buffalo. You will have to leave the other behind." The hunters told him that last year the pilot of a plane of the same size had al-**

lowed them to take two. Doubtfully, the pilot finally said, "Well, if you did it last year, I guess we can do it again."

The plane struggled upward but failed to gain enough height to clear one of the hills surrounding the airstrip. When the plane crashed, the hunters climbed out of the wreckage. One asked the other, "Where do you think we are?"

The other looked around and said, "I think we are about two miles from where we crashed last year."

That is the problem Yuriko and her husband faced. They were STUCK, and neither knew what to do to GET BEYOND the impasse. With each angry exchange, Yuriko's love began to wane as she thought her husband more and more unreasonable, and he thought her more and more impossible. It is impossible to tell whether her imitation of him or his increasing anger with her caused the rupture in their relationship.

I wish the two of them could have figured out a way of WORKING ON THE PROBLEM. *Listen*, for example, to how a boy and his father PROBLEM-SOLVE TOGETHER.

A father watched as his son tried unsuccessfully to lift a heavy stone. The father asked: "Are you using all of your strength?"

The son nodded.

"No, you are not," the father replied. "You haven't asked me to help you."

Jane, do you know what conclusion Yuriko ultimately reached? Finally, Yuriko thought, "It is so lonely when I and the person I love are different." Somehow, I think her logic was DISTORTED.

Ultimately, she fell in love with God. She wanted to be just like God and do the same things as Him. You *see*, *Jane* and *Tim*, some people just NEVER LEARN. Well, God responded: "You shall become a lily like that Japanese part of your name, Yuri. Like the lily, you shall love EVERYTHING OR NOTHING."

So Yuriko turned into a lily. I guess I'll always wonder if that is how it had to end.

Conclusion of the Session

As in the first example, these metaphors are delivered without comment or further explanation.

Discussion and Analysis of the Metaphor

This session is designed to help Jane and Tim think about several ideas. The first is to focus Jane on the appropriate closeness of a parent–child relationship. In the primary metaphor, it is clear that Yuriko got too close to everyone with whom she came into contact. This is the feeling both partners seem to have about Jane's relationship with her parents. Neither one knows what to do.

Second, the notion of loving someone by helping that person become more himself or herself is directed to Tim as well as to Jane. It is important for Jane to become her own person. It is important for Tim to understand that he can be part of that process. Conversely, it is his frustration with Jane that complicates movement toward that goal, because Jane not only needs to deal with her inappropriate closeness to her mother, but is also locked in a power struggle over who has the right to comment on and direct the destiny of that relationship.

Third, both marriage partners need to see that they do not have to continue to be bound to the same frustrating patterns. The story of the hunters is intended to reinforce this notion. The Shain quote points them to the knowledge that they both want the same thing for each other. The brief metaphor about the boy and his father stresses the need to work on the problem together. The combined metaphors should enable the couple to consider how to deal with differences and conflict. The final statement in the delivery of the metaphor, "I guess I'll always wonder if that is how it had to end," is designed to reinforce the specter that their destiny need not play itself out according to the existing pattern.

EXAMPLE OF THE APPLICATION
OF METAPHOR TO INDIVIDUAL THERAPY

Description of the Presenting Problem

Fred is a 43-year-old, middle-level executive with an employment record marked by frequent job changes. He is consistently dissatisfied with his inability to advance within the companies that have employed him. In a number of instances, this feeling has led him to seek new positions. On other occasions, his superiors have expressed displeasure with his accomplishments and have indicated that he had reached the highest level he could within the corporate structure. Fred has correctly interpreted this to mean that he should be looking for a new opportunity. In the past, Fred felt hurt and unappreciated. He recited a litany of excuses for why he did not succeed in his position, including his inability to work within a corporate environment, lack of adequate time to complete obligations, personality conflict with his supervisors, failure of his superiors to see his true worth, and self-described "superior intelligence."

Fred's wife and two children have been very understanding and supportive, although they are disheartened by the career upheavals and uprootedness engendered by moves every few years. As his children get older, Fred feels increasing financial burdens because of his inability to advance in his career.

Fred describes himself as a detail man and believes this to be one of his great strengths. He is dogged in his ability to do every job perfectly and often puts in long hours to complete every detail of the project to which he is assigned. Fred's superiors often berate him for the time it takes him to complete his work. Instead of winning their praise for all his work and overtime, Fred is criticized for "going to the ends of the earth" for every conceivable piece of information. Fred insists that this is necessary to do the proper job. But he also admits that what he views as his strength is seen by his bosses as a failure to "distinguish between the forest and the trees." He wonders how to do the job correctly while at the same time pleasing his superiors.

When Fred is working on several projects, he tends to feel overwhelmed. Often this feeling hampers his ability to get anything done, and this only exacerbates the problem. His office and home are cluttered with such enormous piles of papers, unread newspapers and magazines, and unopened mail that his progress is slowed because of the amount of time he spends looking for things and making "to do" lists. He has frequently overlooked important bills and memos as a result. He reports that his reluctance to throw anything out arises from the irreversibility of such action and his fear of missing something important. His wife complains that he is always behind in reading the mail, newspapers, and magazines, and that the piles of dated material that he claims he must read are a fire hazard. Fred insists that he will get to all the projects that need fixing around the house, but he seems to get further behind each month.

Recently, Fred has been more willing to look beyond his conception of why his accomplishments have not matched his goals. This wish for keener insight and possible behavior change is what brought Fred to seek help. He acknowledges that he must be a large part of the problem, but he just doesn't know what to do.

Identification of the Problem

Because of his wish to concentrate on everything, Fred is very unfocused and is unable to make a distinction between vital areas that require immediate attention and matters that can or should be neglected or abandoned. He has no idea how to distinguish between mail that should be thrown out unopened and items that should be acted on quickly. His sense of being overburdened despite long hours of work is due to his assigning equal weight to all obligations and tasks. He demonstrates obsessive characteristics when planning and executing projects, especially when there are numerous tasks to be accomplished. He ruminates and daydreams about how to get things done and is compulsive about redoing things until they are perfect.

Goals for the Individual

Fred needs to deal with his unrealistic notion of perfection and to learn how to live with jobs that are not as flawless as he would like but are completed on time and satisfy his superiors. Learning to distinguish between the important and unimportant portions of tasks is imperative. Prioritizing obligations and knowing how and when to finish tasks is essential. When Fred learns to determine what his superiors expect from him and not what he thinks they expect, he should be better able to focus his activity. Fred should come to understand that he cannot see and read everything and that some material should be discarded or screened by others.

The Implementation of Techniques in the Delivery of the Metaphor

Fred relies on visual cues. The list of visual words employed to help make Fred more comfortable and to aid in communication between the therapist and the client includes *recognize, search, survey, sight, focus, lose sight of, clear, see, examine,* and *draw*. The use of the modality that mirrors Fred's personal style of communication helps him to more willingly recognize the metaphoric message as well as reduces his resistance to the message.

Statement of the Session's Concerns

Fred is lamenting that he never learned to distinguish between the essential objectives of a job and those tasks that are peripheral. He says that even as a child, he was overwhelmed by schoolwork. As a result, he was habitually late or incomplete in his work. He reports that deadlines tend to be the factor that finally force him to complete a task.

Source of the Metaphor

The metaphor is adapted from "A Little Thatched Roof," in Sadeh (1989).

The Counselor Introduces the Metaphor

Fred, knowing what is IMPORTANT makes me mindful of a story I would like you to *focus* on. Sit back and *see* if you can *picture* these events [pause].

Telling the Metaphoric Tale

A king once banished his son from the kingdom because of his inability to follow his father's instruction. Local people gave him food and shelter, but eventually he wore out the welcome mat. He traveled farther and farther away from the castle until people did not *recognize* him. He took a number of jobs as a shepherd and gradually forgot his royal lineage and the pleasures of his previous life as his work became ALL CONSUMING. Life had become simply a *search* for food and shelter. What he lacked was a thatched hut to shelter him in inclement weather.

One day, his father was out *surveying* his kingdom. It was custom for anyone who had a request to write it on a piece of paper and toss it into the king's carriage. The king *recognized* the handwriting of his son, who petitioned for a thatched hut. The king was overcome with grief, because it was *clear* that his son had *lost sight* of what was [grope for phrase to solicit response from client] MOST IMPORTANT by requesting only a hut. "If only he had asked to be restored to the royal household instead of that meager request," the king thought.

The story of the prince is comparable to that of the apprentice black-smith who learned how to hold the tongs, lift the hammer, hit it against the anvil at just the right angle, and how to increase the heat with the bellows. But when he finished his apprenticeship and was offered a job, his delight turned to despair because he *saw* that he had failed to learn the most impor-tant skill, how to KINDLE A SPARK.

Fred, your *inability to see* what to do about your predicament makes me think of a favorite anecdote of mine. I don't think you know the name Charles Steinmetz. He was an electrical engineer who invented over two hundred devices during his lifetime.

Puzzled scientists at a large corporation once called Steinmetz in to try to identify the malfunctioning part of some complex machinery. He spent some time walking around the enormous machinery-filled room *examining* every-thing carefully. Finally he took out some chalk and marked an "X" on a par-ticular part. The company engineers disassembled the machine and were amazed to *see* that Steinmetz had found the precise location of the defect.

Some days later, the company received a bill for $10,000 from Stein-metz. This was in the early part of the twentieth century, when $10,000 was a fortune. Annoyed, the company requested an itemized bill, which Stein-metz obligingly sent back. Let me *draw* a copy of the bill for you to *see*:

Making one X in chalk.............................$1

Knowing where to place it $9,999

Fred, Bertrand Russell, the mathematician and philosopher, once noted that "There is much pleasure to be gained from USELESS KNOWLEDGE." Have you ever thought of the notion of enjoying useless knowledge? There is something comforting in collecting information, but the successful individual knows how to SORT IT OUT and make [strong emphasis] PURPOSEFUL USE of it. Fred, now you can *see* how the *focus* that each individual places on the RIGHT PIECE of informa-tion results in different OUTCOMES in these stories. The prince didn't know how to use an opportunity to get back the position he deserved. The blacksmith missed the most important lesson. *Fred*, can you *see* the contrast between them and Steinmetz, who knew how to get to [grope for word to solicit client response] THE HEART OF THE MATTER?

Conclusion of the Session

Once again, the metaphor is delivered without comment or further explanation.

Discussion and Analysis of the Metaphor

The key concept for Fred to recognize is that there is a difference between *knowledge* and *knowing*. Collecting knowledge—information and facts—is not the same as knowing how to make purposeful use of it. In the primary metaphor, the prince misses the point when he makes a request of his father, the king. Instead of asking to be restored to his place in the palace, he focuses on the minutiae of keeping out the inclement weather. Similarly, the young blacksmith also fails to perceive what is most important.

The Bertrand Russell quote demonstrates that some people take pleasure in focusing on useless information. Fred misses the most important information because he persists in collecting and processing extraneous material. The reason for relating this story is to provoke Fred's conscious and unconscious mind into considering his past behavior. The goal is to have him free himself of both the obsessive enjoyment and the burden of collecting extraneous information out of fear that he will miss something if he throws anything away. The embedded message of "getting to the heart of the matter" is an important one for Fred. Like Steinmetz, Fred can zero in on the correct spot to place the X. He, too, is capable of reaching for an outcome that is different from the one he and his family have come to expect.

▶ 4

Anthology of
Therapeutic Narratives

A student of a military academy, returning home after graduation, stopped at a village inn to rest his horses. In the barn he noticed numerous chalked targets on the wall of the barn, each with a bullet hole dead center. He inquired about the marksman with such extraordinary aim. A small, barefoot boy appeared to be the masterful marksman.

"How in the world did you learn such marksmanship?" inquired the military student.

"It's quite simple," replied the lad. "First I shoot at the wall and then I draw the targets."

"I do the very same thing," the Dubner Maggid replied. "Whenever I hear a clever story or a good parable, I keep it in mind, then I eventually find the right fit for a subject I want to draw a moral from."

(Adapted from Newman, 1962)

NARRATIVES DEALING WITH FAMILY ISSUES

Building Self-Esteem

In this alternative version of the Cinderella story, the girl lived with a wonderful stepmother and stepsisters who all loved her, looked up to her, and would do anything for her. In fact, they did do everything for her: cleaned her room; put the cap back on the toothpaste if she didn't do it; did her homework for her; let her eat or go to sleep whenever she wanted; excused her from helping with the laundry, dishes, and dog. They would never even let her clean the cinders out of the fireplace.

Despite this charmed life, Cinderella was often sad and frequently cried. Her stepmother, father, and siblings did not know what to do, and Cinderella couldn't tell them what was wrong. They tried to deal with her depression by doing even more things for her and buying things for her. The list of recommedations was endless: "Take a trip. Get your hair and nails done. Go to the movies or a play. Take a hot bath. Take a cold shower. Eat something. Lose a few pounds. Try not to think about anything. Take aspirin. Take vitamins." If any of these "cures" ever worked, the solution was only temporary before Cinderella would once again burst into tears.

In desperation, her stepmother bought Cinderella a beautiful gown with matching accessories and a pair of hand-blown glass slippers. She rented a golden carriage attended by two coachmen to take Cinderella to the prince's ball. When Cinderella burst into tears, her fairy godmother appeared and said that what Cinderella needed was the sense of achievement, accomplishment, and satisfaction that comes from meeting a challenge. The fairy godmother helped the family set up a list of things Cinderella would have to do before she could go to the ball. If she didn't complete the tasks, there would be no ball.

This approach was so alien to the stepmother that the fairy godmother had to reassure her that it was the right thing to do. Cinderella began to tackle all the assigned tasks and forgot about her unhappiness. For the first time in years, she even did her own homework. By this time, she was so motivated to do things for herself that the ball no longer seemed important. But she went to the ball anyway, and the prince found her attractive. She left the ball early because she had school the next day, but she left the prince her name and address in one of her glass slippers because she wanted to see him again.

There are only two lasting bequests we can hope to give our children. One of these is roots; the other, wings.—Hodding Carter

The Cinderella story, presented from her stepmother's point of view, offers another perspective on the dynamics inherent to this folktale:

Cinderella's father actively courted her stepmother and rushed her into marriage. The father was frequently absent from home. Of course, his absence did not augur well for the development of Cinderella's self-esteem. She became a spoiled brat who threw temper tantrums, taunted her stepsisters, and manipulated everyone else into giving her exactly what she wanted. If she constantly built herself up at the expense of her stepmother and stepsisters, it was because she thought so little of herself—or anyone else, for that matter. The death of her own mother, coupled with her father's coldness and unavailability, left an indelible imprint on Cinderella.

As Cinderella reached maturity and planned her marriage to the prince, she had such little regard for her family that they were not even invited to the wedding. Immediately following the ceremony, she began spreading the rumor that the prince had searched for her for a long time and found her living in a hovel as a virtual slave under the watchful eye of her wicked stepmother. (Adapted from "Cinderella: An Address Delivered to the National Association of Family Therapists by Cinderella's Stepmother," in Friedman, 1990)

Eventually, Cinderella married him and lived happily ever after, although she did cry every now and then—which is quite normal for anybody. (Adapted from "Another Cinderella" by Norman Stiles, 1987)

Codependency

A fearsome prince often rode through his kingdom, threatening brutality, tyrannizing his subjects, snarling, and casting fierce glances at everyone he passed. His princess, always at his side, was loved by the people because they believed that she calmed the prince's fierce temper and prevented him from acting on his threats. The princess would always intercede on behalf of the people. She would explain to the prince why the people couldn't help themselves, why they really weren't so bad, or why he should spare their lives. The prince always backed down in response to her urging, but, he felt robbed of his power and his manhood as a result. Thus, there was always an anger between the prince and the princess, just as there was between the prince and his subjects.

One day, the princess took ill and died. After his period of mourning, the prince began to make the rounds of his kingdom. His subjects were terrified. Now that their beloved princess was not there to restrain his wrath, the prince would surely begin acting on his demonic threats.

But that is not what happened. Although he was able to work up his anger, when he tried to make threats, the words did not come out. The prince was incredulous at the chasm between thought and deed, and he ordered the coachman back to the palace.

At home, he soon realized that he had married the princess knowing that she would control the very anger he was afraid he could not restrain. The princess en-

---

Two men renewed a friendship. The first asked the second if he had ever married. "No," answered the second.

"Why not?" the first persisted.

"I guess I was looking for the perfect woman."

"And you never found her?"

"Yes, I did. But there was one problem. She was looking for the perfect man." (Adapted from a Sufi tale)

In some exuberant rain forests of the tropics there grow a strange variety of plants known as strangler trees. Such a plant starts by seeding itself and growing like a vine on the trunk or branches of an ordinary forest tree. Climbing over its host, the strangler enfolds it in a thick mass of roots, strangles it to death, and finally stands on its own as an independent tree!

The reason for the origin of the strangler trees... is plain. In the dense tropical forest the competition for sunlight is keen. A young plant sprouting on the dark forest floor has a poor chance of survival unless it can somehow break through the canopy overhead. The stranglers have solved the problem by climbing on other trees. And the whole life history of these outlandish trees seems beautifully contrived to accomplish their objective: to seize a place in the sun in the midst of a dense tropical forest.—Theodosius Dobzhansky and João Muça-Pires, in *Scientific American,* January 1954.

I love her and she loves me and together we hate each other with a wild hatred born of love.—Edvard Munch

abled him to maintain the illusion of power that the fear he instilled in his subjects confirmed. The price he paid for this fantasy was a high one. He incurred the hatred of the people at the same time that he witnessed their devotion to and love for the princess. Furthermore, the princess delayed the prince from ever finding the truth out about himself. Only after her death did the prince realize that her pleading petitions had actually had the opposite effect: Instead of ending the prince's tyranny, they had perpetuated it.

It was some months before the prince rode through the provinces of his kingdom again. When he did, he was a changed man—sadder, wiser, and infinitely more compassionate. (Adapted from "The Warrior and the Peacekeeper," in Prosky, 1979)

Communication

A husband and wife both noticed that a sapling had worked its way through their living room floor. But neither mentioned it because each would have felt foolish. Who had ever heard of a tree growing through the living room floor?

Time passed. The tree grew in height and girth and became more and more of a nuisance. It shed its leaves all over the living room rug. Insects burrowed in its bark; birds built their nests in its branches. The living room rug was always a mess. Larger portions of each day had to be devoted to cleaning. Still, neither spouse mentioned it to the other because they had never heard of a tree growing through the living room floor.

Growing bigger still, the tree forced them to make detours around it. Eventually they had to duck under the branches to get by. But each said nothing, for neither had ever heard of a tree growing through the living room floor.

When the tree almost touched one wall, the two had to hold in their stomachs to get by it. They were thoroughly miserable with the situation, but neither mentioned it to the other.

Speech is civilization itself. The word, even the most contradictory word, preserves contact—it is silence which isolates.—Thomas Mann

A man opened a fish market and proudly hung up a sign that read FRESH FISH SOLD HERE TODAY. A friend politely advised that it was not necessary to use the word TODAY because everyone knows that it is today. The merchant eliminated the word.

Along came a customer who suggested that the word HERE was superfluous since anyone could see that the fish is sold here. Again, the man shortened the sign.

A woman happened along and asked why the sign had the word FRESH on it, since everyone knows that you only get fresh fish at a fish store. Yet another person objected to the word SOLD since that, too, is a given for a shop. That left a one-word sign: FISH.

The last critic looked up at the sign and said, "Why bother to have a sign that reads FISH? Everyone knows you sell fish. You can smell this place a mile away." (Adapted from "Poor Fish" in Ausubel, 1948)

One day, however, the man declared that there was a tree growing through the living room floor. The woman said that she, too, had noticed it and wasn't very happy because she had to spend too much of her time cleaning. The man was particularly unhappy about having to hold in his stomach to squeeze by the tree. He was tired of bumping into the branches when he forgot to duck under them. His wife didn't like having to walk around the tree.

The next day they had the tree removed, and they were overjoyed. Thereafter, whenever a tree started growing through the living room floor, they had it removed before it became a nuisance. (Adapted from Green, 1972)

Conflict Resolution

There was always anger between a husband and wife. She was annoyed that he sat outside their house doing nothing but daydream for long hours. He believed that women must obey and serve men. She countered that a worthwhile husband would get a job or, at the very least, help with the household chores. He said that tending the sheep was work. And so it went: arguments, recriminations, anger, feelings of being taken advantage of and of never feeling understood.

Feeding the family calf was a gray area of responsibility; each wanted the other to shoulder that burden. To decide the issue, they agreed that they would remain silent. The first one to speak would be in charge of the calf's care.

Much to the surprise and curiosity of the man, the woman left the house for the day to be sure that she would not err. Later, a beggar came to ask for food. The man thought this to be a trick instigated by his wife, so he did not reply. The beggar assumed that the man was a deaf-mute, and he entered the house, ate all the food, and stole all their possessions. When the man discovered the theft, he thought to yell at the thief, but decided against such hasty behavior because he was convinced that this was a trick his wife was playing to get him to speak first.

The husband allowed himself to be victimized by a string of opportunists trying to sell him an item or a service. He was convinced they all were conspiring with his wife to get him to speak first. He was steadfast in his refusal to speak, despite the fact that each took his silence as compliance with whatever he wanted to sell or do.

Late in the day, the hungry and thirsty calf broke loose and caused such a commotion in town that the wife, seeing the calf loose, ran home to berate her husband for his neglect. At once, she noticed all the missing possessions. A huge fight ensued, with each accusing the other of having gone to great lengths to get the other to speak.

The woman set off in search of the thief and was gone for many days before she recovered the stolen possessions. When she returned, she found her husband, not outside wasting the day but in the house cooking dinner, doing the laundry, and sweeping the floor. Each immediately accused the other of being stubborn.

At that moment, the calf stirred and demanded food and water. Each ran to tend the animal when, suddenly, they stopped, looked at each other, and burst out in laughter. From that day on, they both did the chores together and, at the end of the day, sat and relaxed. The husband realized how maddening he was, and the wife realized what a nag she was. (Adapted from a Persian tale, in Chinen, 1992)

Tradition dictates that a wandering Buddhist monk can find lodging in a Zen temple providing he can win an argument with an inhabitant of the temple. In one particular location, the older of two resident monks was learned and wise, while the younger was blind in one eye and unlettered.

A wandering monk arrived and formally challenged the older monk to a debate. As the old monk was quite tired, he instructed the visitor to request a "dialogue of silence" with his younger counterpart. Shortly thereafter, the visitor bid good-bye to the older monk, saying that he had been beaten by the younger one.

"Tell me exactly what happened," said the astounded monk.

The traveler explained: "First I held up one finger, representing Buddha. In response, he held up two fingers, representing Buddha and his teachings. Continuing the debate, I held up three fingers for Buddha, his teachings, and his followers. Finally, he shook his fist at me to indicate that all three come from one reality. He won, and I have no right to remain."

The old monk went to the younger monk and asked him what had occurred. He replied: "He began by insulting me by holding up one finger, pointing out my one eye. In response I held up two fingers, congratulating him for his two eyes. Then he held up three fingers, indicating that there were only three eyes between us. Finally, I lost my temper and threatened to punch him, and he ran out." (Adapted from Reps, 1961)

The king of Persia, Darius I, was proceeding with his invasion of Scythia. The Scythians sent Darius a message consisting of a mouse, a frog, a bird, and five arrows. Darius took these items to mean that his victory over the Scythians was assured. He stated that the arrows prophesied the laying down of the enemy's arms, the mouse signified the surrender of the land, the frog presaged the yielding of their waterways, and the bird symbolized the flight of the Scythians from Darius.

A key advisor of Darius did not see things in the same way. He suggested that the Scythians were warning Darius that he had better fly away like a bird, hide in water like a frog, or burrow into the ground like a mouse, or he would be slain by Scythian archers.

Darius thought better of his optimistic outlook and beat a hasty retreat, saving his forces from defeat. —Herodotus, paraphrase

Jack dragged himself to work. A co-worker noticed how tired Jack seemed. When questioned, Jack replied, "I didn't get home until morning, and just as I was undressing, my wife woke up and said, 'Aren't you getting up pretty early, dear?' So, to avoid an argument, I put on my clothes and came back to work." (Adapted from de Mello, 1989)

I had dinner with my father last night, and I made a classic Freudian slip. I meant to say, "Please pass the salt," but it came out, "You jerk, you ruined my childhood."—Jonathan Katz

Dealing with Child–Parent Problems

A college freshman wrote to her parents:

Dear Mom & Dad,
I am sorry I haven't written to you in the three months since I arrived at college. I know I was thoughtless, but I will bring you up to date on all that has been going on during this time period. You may be quite surprised, so please sit down before you read any further.

I am getting along pretty well now. The concussion that I got when I jumped out of my dormitory window when it caught fire shortly after my arrival is pretty well healed by now. I was only in the hospital for a couple of weeks and I can almost see normally now and the headaches have just about disappeared.

Fortunately, the dormitory fire was witnessed by an attendant at the gas station near the dorm. He called the fire department and the ambulance. He was so kind to visit me in the hospital and since I had nowhere to live because the dormitory was gutted by the fire, he was kind enough to invite me to share his apartment with him. It is a basement apartment but it is fixed up and quite cute. He is a wonderful human being and we have fallen deeply in love and are planning to get married. We haven't set a date yet, but we will have to get married soon, before people become aware that I am pregnant. I know this may be shocking, but I also know how much you are looking forward to becoming grandparents and that you will be able to help me take care of your grandchild after we move in with you. We are only delaying the ceremony until we complete the prescription for penicillin we are taking to clear up the infection that I carelessly caught from him and which prevents us from passing the premarital blood test.

I know you will welcome him warmly into our family. He is considerate and kind to me and although he is not educated, he is ambitious. He is also of a different race than we, but I am sure that you will express the

---

The humorist Sam Levinson wrote that his mother came to his first-grade teacher on his first day of school and said: "If my Sammy ever misbehaves, hit the kid next to him—he learns by example!"

Some of the American Plains Indian tribes were…deeply shocked when they first saw white people beat their children. In their bewilderment they could only explain such behavior as part of an overall missionary scheme—an explanation supported by the white people's method of letting their babies cry themselves blue in the face. It all must mean, so they thought, a well-calculated wish to impress white children with the idea that this world is not a good place to linger in, and that it is better to look to the other world where perfect happiness is to be had at the price of having sacrificed this world.—Erik H. Erikson in *Young Man Luther*

same tolerance toward him as you have to other ethnic groups over the years.

Now that you are updated, I want to tell you that there was no dormitory fire, I was not injured, I was not in the hospital, I am neither pregnant nor engaged, I do not have a sexually-transmitted disease and I have no boyfriend who will move in with you, nor am I planning to get married. But I did get a D in History and an F in French and I wanted to be sure you would receive this news in the proper perspective.

Your loving daughter. (Adapted from "A Letter from a College Student," in Riemer, 1992)

Deception

An unfaithful stork spent every night carousing, drinking, and chasing female storks. The stork was pleased that his wife was a plain stork who never left the nest and never caught onto his antics. No matter what hour of the night or early morning he returned, he always brought her a box of candy, along with the same hackneyed excuse: "I was out delivering babies." When she questioned why anyone needed his help to deliver a baby, he always had the same litany of rationalizations: "Humans cannot have a baby without the help of someone; human beings are helpless; they depend on animals for food, clothing, and companionship."

And so it went, night after night. The phone would ring and he would say, "Another baby on the way," and off he would go. One time, when he was out until dawn, he explained to his wife that this was a very unusual case, quintuplets—five girls. Of course, he neglected to tell her that the girls were beautiful blondes.

One day, Mrs. Stork began to doubt her husband's admonition to never leave the nest because the world was full of stork traps. So she left and discovered that men tend to brag and distort the truth and that human baby deliveries are never assisted by a stork. The greatest blow was the discovery of what her husband was doing when he was not delivering babies. But it was a greater blow to him, because the next time he returned, she inquired about the quintuplets and then smacked him over the head with a brick. (Adapted from "The Stork Who Married a Dumb Wife," in Thurber, 1939)

A portrait artist came to do the official painting of Oliver Cromwell. The artist said: "Lord Cromwell, I am always very exact. You have a number of warts on your face and I want you to know that I am going to have to show them." Cromwell replied, "I don't mind if you paint me with warts—but don't forget my face." (Source unknown)

Immediately after his daughter announced her engagement, her father inquired, "Does he have any money?"

"Gosh, you men are all alike!" declared the girl. "That's just what he asked about you."

—Honey Greer

Distance and Pursuit

Henry had no illusions about anything. As a child he learned that mothers were not always kind and fathers were not always brave or honest. Fairies, witches, and hobgoblins did not exist; rabbits did not lay eggs at Easter; Santa Claus was merely a figment of the imagination; Heaven and Hell were the domains of fools.

Henry realized that presidents and queens were people like anybody else, subject to the same foibles and petty jealousies as other mortals. Teachers, Henry discovered, did not know everything. In fact, some of them seemed to know next to nothing. He realized that the printed word often lies. As he grew to maturity, he discovered that happiness was not elusive. Rather, it was a myth; love was only a fleeting attachment.

Henry became a carpenter. But this trade did not satisfy him because he immediately began to see the decay of buildings in the graying of fresh lumber and the rust forming on bright nails. He could not tolerate seeing the deterioration of his creations as soon as they were finished. Eventually, as a result, he became a termite inspector and spent his life crawling under old houses, ferreting out bugs and searching for traces of their damage. He lived a somber life in a basement apartment whose shades he never raised.

On Sundays, Henry walked in the park and threw stale bread to the ducks. One day, he met Lorabelle, a young woman who believed in everything. She could hear fairies whispering in the forest, see bunnies laying brilliantly colored eggs at Easter. Occasionally she would doubt her illusions, but then quickly, sometimes instantly, would find something new to believe in. Lorabelle never gave up any of her illusions; she merely laid them aside for reuse later when needed.

When Lorabelle met Henry, she was filled with illusions about him. She told him that he was wise and a good man. He countered by saying that while he might be intelligent, he was quite petty and self-absorbed. They argued and differed about everything, agreed on nothing. Nevertheless, she fell in love with him. She

---

Over time it becomes clear that inside of every distancer is a pursuer, and inside every pursuer is a distancer.... The distant husband tends to move toward his wife, and pursue her as she pulls away. The pursuing wife finds that she "has no feelings" for her husband as he moves in. These different characteristics of self emerge as the context changes. (Fogarty, 1980)

On cold winter nights, porcupines huddle together to stay warm. As they draw close together, they stick each other with their quills,

so they recoil. When they recoil, they get cold once again and move closer to huddle closer together again. Repeating the scenario over and over, they alternate between being too far apart and feeling cold and being too close and in pain.—Arthur Schopenhauer

The love on both sides is equal. Partners merely take turns with who is going to insist on the love and who is going to protest against it. (Whitaker, 1989)

thought it was a miracle that they had met. He countered that he had just happened to be feeding the ducks. "If you had come down to the other side of the pond, you would be feeling this way about someone else," Henry always said.

Lorabelle wanted to wear a dress of white lace over cream satin at a church wedding. Henry insisted that the entire affair was merely "a primitive and preposterous attempt to invest copulation with dignity and permanence, to enforce responsibility for children by the authority of a myth no longer credible." But in the end, they were married in a church, over Henry's objections and very much to his chagrin. Lorabelle wore lace and Henry wore a morning coat with striped pants. As they drove off, she whispered, "I'm so happy. Now we will always be together."

Henry coolly stated, "For our age and economic bracket, we have a 47.3 percent chance of staying together for twenty years."

Lorabelle found a white house on a hill covered with orange poppies and white daisies. Blue morning glories grew on a white picket fence. She filled their lives with fragile deceptions and always found something new to focus her efforts on. There were always flowers on the table. She placed travel posters on the walls to foster the fantasy that they might one day travel. She hung starched white curtains at the windows. She made wonderful sauces and could create culinary masterpieces from a few simple ingredients. Steak was always served with fresh parsley. Candlelight filled the dining room and the bedroom.

When Lorabelle asked Henry if he loved her, he replied, "I'm fond of you; love is just an illusion." Lorabelle prayed that Henry would one day say that he loved her. She became somber and depressed. In response to every romantic thing she said, Henry provided statistics. She wound up saying that she hated "fondness," and one day she admitted to him that he was correct: "You are petty and self-absorbed. What's worse," she continued, "you have a legal mind, and there is no poetry in you. You don't give me anything, don't love me. You are dull. You were stuck in a hole when I found you, and you would still be there if I hadn't pulled you out. There is no life in you. I give you everything and it is not enough. You are waiting to die and you want to take me with you."

Although he considered himself illusionless, Henry knew that he liked Lorabelle's elegant mirages. He gradually became less gloomy.

Lorabelle pursued a series of careers and leisure activities. In each new situation, she fell in love with a boss, a co-worker, or an acquaintance. She thought that each of them in turn appreciated her visionary qualities, only to discover that her illusions had misled her. She went into therapy and fell in love with her therapist. This also proved to be a disappointment. One by one, she would substitute a new illusion for an old one. Her illusions became more reckless as the years flew by, and her pursuits impoverished the couple.

Henry would never agree to give Lorabelle a divorce. He said that he was protecting her from her own bad judgement. "You would be married six times in five years if you were free," he replied.

Between her adventures, Lorabelle often fell into a silent gloom and stayed home in bed. However, each time this happened, she would find her way back from disillusionment through some new illusion.

As the years flew by, Henry became more withdrawn, bitter, and morose. Each day he would get up, go to work, and do nothing else. In the evenings he would drink gin, but intoxicants did not nourish illusion. Lorabelle felt anger, pity, and contempt for him. However, she did admit to herself that she stayed with him not because he would not give her a divorce but because he was the stability in her life and she appreciated being able to lean on him. And Henry admitted to himself that he stayed with Lorabelle despite his unhappiness and the foolhardiness of her schemes because he rather enjoyed her witless illusions.

One day, almost out of nowhere, Henry said, "I love you, Lorabelle."

"What did you say?" she stammered. "I thought you said that love is an illusion."

"It is," Henry said, "but I love you anyway."

"Oh, Henry, you have made me so happy. That is all I ever wanted to hear."

Life finally seemed ideal. But, as Henry and Lorabelle tried to draw closer than they had been in years, something strange occurred. Their strengthened relationship was marred by a viciousness that they employed to hurt each other. They would fight, yell, and scream, then withdraw into a bitter, silent armistice. In their misguided efforts to work out their disagreements, to forgive, understand, forget, and compromise, all they succeeded in doing was to renew their battles. Strife punctuated the great tenderness that always followed their conflicts. Henry always tried to work things out because he felt there just wasn't anything else. Lorabelle was bewildered because no matter how much she tried, she still did not have what she wanted after all her years of yearning. The lifelong tension and distance remained unchanged.

With the passage of time, Lorabelle became detached and lonely. Weary from years of trying to draw closer to Henry, she no longer tried to reach out to him or to anyone else. Although she continued to live in the house on the hill surrounded by the white picket fence, she reflected on her years of failure to find satisfaction and love, and she retreated into her own world of gloomy sadness. She was no longer a visionary; finally, she no longer had illusions about anything.

Every day Henry went to work, once again building houses, always seeking a state of beauty, truth, or goodness that he knew would never exist. But instead of the words of his youth, "It's only an illusion," he said, "It is only an illusion, but there isn't anything else." He knew all this was not real, but he enjoyed it nevertheless. Despite his lack of illusions, Henry had become the visionary. (Adapted from "The Illusionless Man and the Visionary Maid," in Whellis, 1966)

Ego Fusion

A woman received a letter from her estranged husband two years after he had deserted her. He wrote from a distant land and asked his former wife not to let their child bounce a rubber ball because he could hear the sound, which "strikes at my heart." The mother took the ball away from the daughter.

A second letter, from another place, asked the woman not to send the child to school in clogs because the sound "tramples on my heart." She complied and put sandals on the girl.

Yet another letter, from a new location, asked that the child not eat from a porcelain bowl because the sound "breaks my heart." At this point the woman had had enough; she dashed the porcelain bowl against a rock in the garden. Then she threw a table against the garden wall and finally pounded the wall with her fists. She wondered: Wasn't this the sound of her husband's heart breaking?

One more letter requested that she and the daughter not make any sound at all—no doors opening, no breathing, no clocks ticking.

Tears fell as the woman whispered to the daughter and the two of them made not one sound, even the faintest one. The mother and daughter died, and the husband lay down beside them and died, too. (Adapted from "Love Suicides," in Kawabata, 1988)

There was a long line at the entrance to the gates of heaven under the sign that read: FOR MEN WHO HAVE BEEN DOMINATED BY THEIR WIVES ALL THEIR LIVES. Nearby, another passageway opened under a sign that said: FOR MEN WHO HAVE NEVER BEEN DOMINATED BY THEIR WIVES. One man stood on the line. St. Peter came over and inquired, "Why are you on this line?"

The man replied, "Who knows? My wife told me to stand here." (Source unknown)

To some extent, each of us marries to make up for his own deficiencies. As a child, no one can stand alone against his family and the community, and in all but the most extreme instances, a child is in no position to leave and to set up a life elsewhere. To survive as children, we all have had to exaggerate those aspects of ourselves that pleased those on whom we depended, and to disown those attitudes and behaviors that were unacceptable to them. As a result, to varying degrees, we have each grown into disproportionate configurations of what we could be as human beings. What we lack, we seek out and then struggle against in those whom we select as mates. We marry the other because he (or she) is different from us, and then we complain, "Why can't he (she) be more like me?" (Kopp, 1972)

Marriage is our last, best chance to grow up.
—Joseph Barth

Don't marry a man to reform him—that's what reform schools are for.—Mae West

Most women set out to try to change a man, and when they have changed him they do not like him.—Marlene Dietrich

Encouraging Personal Mastery

A prince believed his father when he told the prince that there were no such things as princesses, islands, or God. The prince thought the king must be correct, since the boy never saw any evidence for the existence of these things in the realm. One day, the prince ran away to another kingdom, where, to his amazement, he saw islands, princesses, and a man who claimed to be God.

Upon his return home, the prince told the king that he had seen islands, princesses, and even God. The king dismissed his son's sightings, saying that they were not real. The son, convinced that he could trust what he had seen, argued with his father. His father asked, "Tell me how God was dressed."

"God was wearing evening wear," said the prince.

"Were the sleeves of his black coat rolled up?" he inquired.

"Yes," he remembered.

"You have been deceived by a magician," the father concluded.

The very next day, the prince returned to the other land and confronted the magician, saying that his father had warned him that the man was a magician and that he had used illusions to beguile the prince.

The magician sternly told the boy that it was he who was deceived. "Your father is also a magician, and in his kingdom there are many islands, princesses, and God can be found there, too. Only you can't see them because you are under your father's spell."

Returning home, the prince questioned his father. "Is it true that you are really a magician and not a king?"

"Yes, I am only a magician."

"So you are a magician and the other man is a magician. Is there any truth beyond magic?" the boy demanded.

"There is no truth beyond magic," his father admitted.

The boy threatened to kill himself because of the great sadness brought on by this realization. Then his father brought forth the angel of death, who was so terrifying that the prince trembled. The prince thought of the island, the princesses, and God, and he said: "Very well, I can bear the truth."

The father studied the boy and said, "Now you can begin to be a magician." (Adapted from Fowles, 1973)

A child sees a butterfly struggling to get out of its chrysalis. He takes pity on it and uses a pen knife to free it. But the butterfly never flies, because nature intended it to develop and strengthen its wings by forcing itself out of the chrysalis. The boy made life too easy for the butterfly, therefore, it never developed its own mastery. (Source unknown)

Man's main task in life is to give birth to himself.—Erich Fromm

Letting Go versus Holding On

At the appropriate moment, Mama and Papa assisted their fledglings to the edge of the nest. Expectantly, they watched each one tremble, flutter its wings, fall a bit, flap, dip, regain altitude and fly away. None needed any coaching, just a bit of encouragement.

Late in the season, one child remained, yet to be sent on his way. The completion of this task would signal the end of their parenting and the start of their retirement to a warmer climate. As they had done with the others, they coaxed their baby to the edge of the nest and gently pushed. He fell a few feet and, instead of spreading his wings, went into an immediate nose dive. They panicked. "Flap your wings! pick up your head! look out! fly! fly!" they both screamed.

Showing no fear, moving not a muscle, he repeatedly thought, "I'll be damned if I'm going to flap my wings just because they want me to."

Frantically, Mama and Papa swooped down, caught their child, gently landed, composed themselves, and then returned him to the nest. They reassured themselves that the baby of the family was just not yet ready. They chirped words of support to bolster his confidence: "We'll try again. Tomorrow will be better." But baby just kept thinking to himself with even more determination, "I'll be damned if I'm going to flap my wings just because they want me to."

The next morning, Mama and Papa, a bit more anxious, tried again. Comforting baby, trying to raise his confidence, they reminded him of his siblings' successes and how to glide and catch the downdrafts and winds if he became fatigued. After a deep breath, they gave a not-so-gentle push. Once again, baby plummeted, beak first, toward the ground. Despite their shouts of advice, he

---

Young stones are fidgety, according to their elders. Their ambition, once held by their parents, is to move beyond the watchful eye of authority into the cool, liberating streams that sweep them away during summer storms.

Although family ties are strong, many young stones have slipped and skedaddled away from their parents in the swift and treacherous currents. They carry scars of their journeys to new homes. One day they will brag to their children that once they were adventuresome. But as they get older, more comfortable, and fatter, they develop an aversion to movement and say it is either dangerous or sinful. Nevertheless, late at night, the light of the moon waxes, wanes, dances, and pulls at them as they long for the days when they felt free and could run with the swift, cold, pulsating stream. (Adapted from "The Stones" by Shelton, 1992)

A mother is not a person to lean on but a person to make leaning unnecessary.—Dorothy C. Fisher

Let us think of men and women who cannot grow old gracefully because they cling too hard to a youth that is escaping them; of parents who cannot let their children go free to live their own lives; of people who in times of general calamity have only themselves in mind. They hold on tight, yet they must be prepared to let go. It is only with matters of the mind and heart that it is possible to accomplish this task. Use the mind in study; its sagacity is not diminished. Give the heart away; there is more love still. We are pulled in opposite directions by this paradox and tension; solving this tug of war reaffirms that the only possible way to hold is with open arms. (Adapted from Steinberg, 1951)

moved not a muscle, all the while thinking, "I'll be damned if I'm going to flap my wings just because they want me to." Not knowing what else to do, the parents raced toward their baby to break his fall and return him to the nest once more.

This scene continued for weeks. At the onset of winter, and in the twilight of their lives, the parents were at a loss about what to do with their adolescent who refused to fly. They constantly chirped at each other, fought about possible solutions, and berated themselves for their lack of success. To make matters worse, their belligerent baby refused to help himself or show any gratitude for their support. They regretted ever having become parents.

One morning, however, baby awoke and did not see his parents. He went back to bed to wait for them, hoping they would once again get angry with him or coax him out with the promise of breakfast. Finally, when they failed to return, he became resentful and furious at their abandonment. To punish them, he went straight to the nest's edge, dove out and plunged toward the ground. Halfway down, something uncontrollable occurred. His wings jerked away from his body and became fully extended, pulling him out of his nose dive. As they carried him gracefully upward, he began to raise and lower them, and he experienced an indescribably new and wonderful feeling. He began to experiment and found that he was able to maintain the proper speed to soar and cruise. Within minutes, as he luxuriated in the warmth of the sun, he was miles away. He forgot his parents, where he had lived, or why it had taken him so long to fledge. (Adapted from "Soaring," in Friedman, 1990)

Loving and Letting Go

The mother of an industrious Native American family supplemented the family's income by creating crafts from porcupine quills and birch bark. When her supply of quills ran low, she sent her son, Tony, out to find a porcupine. The previous day, he had seen one that had been hit by a car at the side of the road. It was gone—picked up, no doubt, by someone else who knew its value. Knowing that his mother needed quills, Tony decided to hunt for a porcupine, not only to bring his mother what she required, but also to prove his prowess as a hunter. Rock in hand, he headed into the brush, where he soon spotted a porcupine. He took aim, hurled the rock, and killed the animal. Thinking of how proud his mother would be, he took a rope from his pocket to retrieve his prize. As he bent over, his heart stopped, and he reeled backward upon seeing a pink baby porcupine nestled up to the dead mother. There was no question about what to do. He scooped up the helpless baby, held it close to keep it warm, and raced home. There, all the children sprang into action. One went to the store for infant formula and pabulum, another found a baby bottle, and they all took turns getting up every two or three hours for the nighttime feedings.

That year, "Porki" taught the entire family wonderful things about porcupines. He purred like a kitten and liked to cuddle up and sleep with the children on very cold nights. He turned into a prickly ball when startled and, contrary to popular belief, didn't shoot quills at anyone.

As he grew, he would venture farther and farther out into the garden to nibble on the vegetables and to explore the outdoors. The children all knew that one day Porki would go off on his own; their mother said that was how it had to be. Nevertheless, they were sad at the thought that Porki couldn't live with them forever.

A young bunny threatened to run away. His mother, with unconditional love, promised to find him. He said that he would change himself into a trout, a rock, a crocus, a bird, a sailboat, an acrobat and a little boy. To each of these transformations, his mother promised to become an appropriate object in which he could take refuge. Realizing the impossibility of escaping his mother's pervasive love, he said: "Shucks, I might just as well stay where I am and be your little bunny." And he did. (Adapted from *The Runaway Bunny*, by Brown, 1942)

True love hurts. It always has to hurt. It must be painful to love someone, painful to leave someone.—Mother Theresa

But the child must grow. It must emerge from mother's womb, from mother's breast; it must eventually become a completely separate human being. The very essence of motherly love is to care for the child's growth, and that means to want the child's separation from herself.... In motherly love, two people who were one become separate. The mother must not only tolerate, she must wish and support the child's separation. It is only at this stage that motherly love becomes such a difficult task, that it requires unselfishness, the ability to give everything and to want nothing but the happiness of the loved one.—Erich Fromm

Soon, Porki began to stay out all day and return late at night or the next day. The children were all upset when he disappeared for a few days. Their mother cautioned them and said, "If you really love someone, you'll let him go. Porki has to make his own way in the porcupine world to really grow up."

One day, Porki stopped coming home. The mother offered the children a number of possible reasons for his departure: He had heard "the call of the wild"; he had found a girl friend; or perhaps he wanted a family of his own.

There were occasional sightings of Porki. Once, the children saw a porcupine from afar and, just for fun, called, "Hey, Porki!" When the porcupine turned and waddled up to them, they knew it was their pet. Over the years, the children had many other pets, but none was as special as Porki.

Some years later, there was a scratching at the door. When they turned on the porch light, it was Porki, who had come for a visit. It was his last goodbye; they never saw him again. But the children always remembered their mother's words: "If you really love someone, you'll let him go." (Adapted from "The Porcupine," by Keeshig-Tobias, 1990)

Marriage Satisfaction

In the film *Lovers and Other Strangers,* Richie announces to his parents, Beatrice and Frank, that he is getting divorced from Joan because, among other things, Joan claims that Richie's hair no longer smells like raisins.

Frank challenges Richie by asking, "Who's happy?" He goes on in the same vein: "Do you think your mother and I are happy?" Richie is shocked by the revelation that his parents have stayed together all these years although they are not happy, but only "content."

"Don't look for happiness, Richie," Beatrice concludes ruefully. "It'll only make you miserable!"

A marriage is the union of two good forgivers.—Robert Quillen

Chains do not hold a marriage together. It is threads, hundreds of tiny threads which sew people together through the years. This is what makes a marriage last—more than passion or even sex!—Simone Signoret

A man complained to his friend that whenever his wife gets angry she becomes historical.

"You mean *hysterical*," the friend corrected him.

"No," said the husband, "I mean *historical*. Every time we have a fight, she starts listing everything I did wrong in the last twenty-seven years."—Rabbi Sidney Greenberg

Miscommunication

A colonel issued the following order to his executive officer: "Tomorrow evening at 2000 hours, Halley's comet will be visible in this area, an event that occurs only once every seventy-five years. Have the men fall out in the battalion area in fatigues and I will explain this rare phenomenon to them. In case of rain, we will not be able to see anything, so assemble the men in the theater and I will show them a film of it."

Certain he had understood exactly what the colonel wanted, the executive officer wrote the following to the company commander: "By order of the colonel, tomorrow at 2000 hours, Halley's comet will appear over the battalion area. If it rains, fall the men out in fatigues, then march to the theater where this rare phenomenon will take place, something which occurs only once every seventy-five years."

Upon receiving this order, the company commander instructed his lieutenant: "By order of the colonel in fatigues at 2000 hours tomorrow evening, the phenomenal Halley's comet will appear in the theater. In case of rain in the battalion area, the colonel will give another order, something which occurs once every seventy-five years."

Snapped the lieutenant to his sergeant: "Tomorrow at 2000 hours, the colonel will appear in the theater with Halley's comet, something which happens every seventy-five years. If it rains, the colonel will order the comet into the battalion area."

The sergeant told his squad: "When it rains tomorrow at 2000 hours, the phenomenal seventy-five-year-old General Halley, accompanied by the colonel, will drive his comet through the battalion area theater in fatigues." (Source unknown)

A boy named Eddie Shell came one afternoon to play with Frank and me, and at the hour for going home did not know how to do so. This is a malady that afflicts all children, but my mother was not sure how she should handle it in Eddie's case. She consulted us secretly as to whether he should be asked to stay for supper; we thought not, so she hinted to him that his mother might be expecting him. He was so slow in acting upon the hint that we were all in despair and began to feel guilty because we had not pressed him to stay. What I remember now is Eddie standing at last on the other side of the screen door and trying to say good-by as if he meant it. My mother said warmly: "Well, Eddie, come and see us again." Whereupon he opened the door and walked in. (Van Doren, 1958)

A man met a friend he hadn't seen in years.

"Bill Williams, it's good to see you. But, my, how you've changed. Your hair is gray and it used to be brown. And I thought you had blue eyes and it's clear that they are brown."

The man responded, "Look, I'm not Bill Williams. I'm Charles Dulgin."

"How do you like that?" the first man replied. "Why, you've even changed your name." (Source unknown)

Obedience versus Independence

Daedalus was a Greek craftsman of such repute that King Minos invited him to design a prison that would confine the half-man, half-bull monster, the Minotaur. Daedalus, accompanied by his son Icarus, accepted the offer. Daedalus built a labyrinth of such confounding complexity that the Minotaur was contained.

Minos was determined to keep Daedalus on the island because Daedalus had conspired with the king's daughter, Ariadne, to foil Minos' plan to destroy her lover. Minos locked the father and son in a high tower. To escape, Daedalus fashioned two sets of wings from feathers, string, and wax. He practiced and taught his son how to use the wings. There was one stern warning: "Don't fly too high or too low. If you fly too low, the ocean spray will make the wings too heavy, and if you fly too high, the sun will melt the wax and the wings will disintegrate."

Once airborne, Icarus was so taken by the freedom of flight that he soared higher and higher, neglecting his father's warning. As he flew nearer and nearer to the sun, the wax on his wings softened and they fell apart. He cried out to his father as he fell from the heights into the sea, where he disappeared. Daedalus flew around and around until Icarus' body surfaced. He retrieved his child, flew home, buried his son, and never flew again.

Why did the children put beans in their ears when the one thing we told the children they must not do was put beans in their ears?—Carl Sandburg

Adolescent: A teenager who acts like a baby when you don't treat him like an adult. (Source unknown)

The old believe everything, the middle-aged suspect everything, the young know everything.—Oscar Wilde

Parental Models

A man traveling on a secluded mountain trail heard a cry for help. The cry came from a man who claimed to have been attacked, beaten, and robbed by a band of thieves. The good Samaritan dressed the man's wounds, gave him a drink of cool water, and placed him on his horse to take him for medical help. The moment he was in the saddle, the victim rode off. But the Samaritan knew all the short cuts that bypassed the trails and arrived at the bottom of the mountain before the victim. The Samaritan ordered the horse to stop.

"If you want this horse, take it as a gift because I don't want you to become a thief on my account."

The victim didn't seem to care if he stole the horse or received it as a gift, saying that he intended to sell it in the next town anyway.

The Samaritan was aghast. "If you try to sell my horse in my town, the townsmen will think you murdered me and they will kill you in return."

"Why should you care if I live or die?" said the thief.

"I don't want you to be killed or have my friends become killers on my account. Let me give you a bill of sale so that you can prove that I sold the horse to you."

The thief thought the man to be crazy and asked why he was going to such lengths to help him. He replied, "If the townspeople hear how a stranger treated me, in the future they will be afraid of helping any stranger who might be in need."

The thief stared at the Samaritan and began to cry. "I come from a long line of thieves who all came to violent ends. They taught me the tricks of the trade and never cared what happened to me. If I had had a parent like you, I would have never become a thief," he said.

"It is never too late," said the Samaritan. From that day on, the thief was a changed man. (Adapted from "The Very Good Samaritan," in Kronberg & McKissack, 1990)

Nothing has a stronger influence psychologically on their environment, and especially on their children, than the unlived life of the parents.—Carl Jung

When I was young I heard a song.
One song I heard, no others.
I learned the words and sang along;
The song it was my mother's.
She never told me how to sing.
She never told my why.
She simply sang the song she'd heard
When she was young as I.
Some lines were repeated.
Some lines were repeated.
Some lines were repeated.
And some of them were wise.

They were mommy's bible
They were mommy's blueprint
They were mommy's comfort.
But some of them were lies.
I often write my own songs now.
But more than now and then,
I find a voice inside me
Singing mommy's song again.
(Author unknown)

Children: Natural mimics who act like their parents in spite of every effort to teach them good manners. (Source unknown)

Children will be more like their parents than either parent or child would like to acknowledge. (Kushner, 1991)

Power Struggles

Daily a man gave doses of cod liver oil to his large dog because he believed that it was good for the animal. However, it became increasingly difficult to administer the treatment because the dog would hide, and then struggle as the man held the dog's head between his knees, forced his jaw open, and poured the liquid down his throat.

One day the dog broke loose, and the oil spilled all over the floor. Much to the man's surprise, the dog returned to lick it up from the floor. Thus, the man discovered that it was not the oil that was the problem, but his method of dispensing it. (Adapted from de Mello, 1989)

One night, the ship's captain thought he saw the lights of another ship heading toward him on a collision course. His signalman blinked a message to the other vessel: "Change your course 10 degrees to the south."

The reply: "Change your course to the north."

Again, the captain sent a message: "I am a captain in the Navy, change your course to the south."

The second ship replied: "I am a seaman first class. Change your course north."

This infuriated the captain, and he signaled: "Dammit, I say change your course south. I'm on a battleship!"

The final response was: "And I say change your course north. I'm in a lighthouse." (Source unknown)

A policeman faced a man on a bridge. In spite of all his efforts to convince the man not to jump, the officer was unable to persuade him to come down. Finally, the policeman lost his temper, took out his gun, and shouted, "If you jump, I'll shoot you!" The shock of this statement destroyed the man's resolve to kill himself, and he came down. (Adapted from Whitaker, 1989)

Lord Henry Brougham, a British statesman, learned that his oldest son was having an affair with a French actress. The father sent a terse note to his son: "If you do not break up the relationship, I will stop your allowance."

The young man wrote back, "If you do not double it, I will marry her."—Kazlitt Arvine, paraphrase.

I have been waiting twenty years for someone to say to me, "You have to fight fire with fire," so that I could reply, "That's funny—I always use water."—Howard Gossage

Reconciliation

Just after the beginning of World War I, the kaiser attended a prayer service in Berlin. The German minister read the biblical account of how God favored Gideon in his battle against the Midianites. Then he drew a parallel to the story. He prayed: "God of Germany, give victory to Germany. God of righteousness, give the victory to the right."

On the same morning, a prayer service was held in Paris in the presence of the war ministers. The French clergyman read the biblical account of how God favored Gideon in his battle against the Midianites. Then he drew a parallel to the story, praying: "God of France, give victory to France. God of righteousness, give the victory to the right." (Adapted from Baird, 1989)

Elizabeth Barrett Browning disregarded her parents' strong disapproval of her choice of a husband. When she married Robert, they disowned her. Several times each month, she would lovingly write to her parents to ask for reconciliation, but they never replied. After ten years of continuous letter writing, Elizabeth received a large package in the mail. She was heartbroken to discover all of her letters, unopened.—Michael P. Green, in *Illustrations for Biblical Preaching*

Before a judge, two litigants disputed the ownership of a piece of land. Said the judge, "Let the earth itself render the decision." They were both shocked as the judge bent down and placed his ear to the earth. He then rose and said, "This is the decision of the earth: 'I belong to neither of you, but you belong to me. Both of you will someday lie in my bosom. In the brief time that you walk upon me, you should do so in peace.' "—Rabbi Ezekiel Landau of Prague

A woman consulted her lawyer about a divorce. He asked, "Do you have grounds?"

"About half an acre," she answered.

He said, "No, no, that's not what I meant. Do you have a grudge?"

"No, we have a carport."

The lawyer asked, "Does he beat you up?"

"No, I get up in the morning before he does."

The lawyer, exasperated at not making any headway, finally asked, "Please tell me, exactly why do you want a divorce?"

She responded, "Because he doesn't understand me." (Adapted from Riemer, 1992)

I know one husband and wife who, whatever the official reasons given to the court for the breakup of their marriage, were really divorced because the husband believed that nobody ought to read while he was talking and the wife that nobody ought to talk while she was reading.—Vera Brittain

Responsibility versus Trust

A man traveled in a wagon pulled by three horses. Throughout the entire trip, he had difficulty controlling the horses, which would not respond to his commands. The harder he tugged on the reins, the more obstinate they became. Finally, the horses just would not slow down, no matter what he tried. A farmer walking down the road, seeing the driver's difficulty, yelled, "Slacken the reins!" Since that was the only thing he hadn't tried, the driver eased up on the reins even though this action seemed contrary to logic. Nevertheless, as soon as the reins were loosened, the horses slowed down. (Adapted from Buber, 1947)

A king wished to meet Moses, who he had heard was a wise and admirable leader. But Moses, busy leading the Israelites through the desert, could not accept the king's invitation, so the king sent his painters to capture Moses' likeness. The king showed the painting to his advisors and asked them what kind of man they thought Moses to be. They reported that based on the painting, he was wicked, greedy, proud, self-seeking, and dishonest. The king, puzzled, thought that either the painters did not know how to paint or he could not trust his advisors for an accurate evaluation.

The king set out to see Moses for himself. Finding Moses exactly as he had been portrayed, the king asked Moses to explain the discrepancy. Moses replied that the king's advisors were correct. "That is what I was made of," he answered. "I fought against those characteristics and triumphed; that is how I became what I am, and that is why I have been honored throughout the world." (Adapted from a story by Israel Lifshitz in a commentary entitled *Tiferet Yisrael*)

Not often in the story of mankind does a man arrive on earth who is both steel and velvet, who is as hard as rock and soft as drifting fog, who holds in his heart and mind the paradox of terrible storm and peace unspeakable and perfect.—Carl Sandburg (on Lincoln)

Seeking Help

A father pledged not only to be a faithful parent, but also to pass on to his son all the wisdom he had received from his own parents many years before. Daily, he prayed that his son would grow up to be both wise and good. When he told his son that he hoped he would be wise and good, the son replied that he was already. He added that young people achieved these qualities sooner and faster than the children of the father's generation.

One day, the young man fell in love and went to the woman's father to ask for her hand in marriage. "I will give you my daughter," said the father, "if you bring me a piece of the wind."

The young man did not know how to pass this test. Reluctantly, he told his father what had happened. The father berated him: "You have always boasted how quickly you became wise. Why don't you apply some of that wisdom to get your bride?"

The young man thought and thought of a way to comply with the request. When he had exhausted all the possible solutions he could think of, he came back to his father and asked for his help.

The father agreed to assist the lad, and together they paid a call on the father of the bride-to-be. He offered the youth and his father something to eat and drink. The young man's father declined everything and asked only for a glass of water. He studied the glass of water for a long time. At last he said: "Why have you given me water that has not been ground and sifted?"

The bride's father asked, "Where do you do this?"

The groom's father answered, "In the same place where you get a piece of the wind."

The bride's father consented to allow the lad to marry his daughter. He said: "I knew you could not accomplish my task. But you have asked your father for help and now I know that you are wise." (Adapted from "A Piece of the Wind," in Kronberg & McKissack, 1990)

A small boy tried in vain to lift a heavy stone. His father, watching his extraordinary expenditure of time and effort, finally asked his son, "Are you using all of your strength?"

"I am!" cried the frustrated boy.

"No, you are not," responded the father, "because you haven't asked me to help." (Source unknown)

Derek Redmond devoted his life to becoming an Olympic runner. He participated in the games in Barcelona, Spain. As he was running his championship race, he pulled a hamstring muscle and fell to the ground. In spite of his pain, Derek got up and with tortured steps, hobbled toward the finish line. The crowd understood his wish to finish. Even though the race was over, they cheered for him. Derek's father, pushing aside the ushers, worked his way out of the stands toward Derek. He went down to the field, put his arm around Derek, and half-carried and half-walked him toward the finish line. The crowd roared and rose to its feet. (News item)

When I was a boy of fourteen, my father was so ignorant I could hardly stand to have the old man around. But when I got to be twenty-one, I was astonished at how much the old man had learned in seven years.—Mark Twain

Sibling Rivalry

Two brothers faithfully worked adjacent farms. Their efforts were rewarded. Each year, they harvested their wheat crops. Although they did not have an over-abundance of grain, there was always enough to take care of their needs.

One night, the older brother, married with several children, could not sleep. He began to think about his brother. "My wife and my children will care for me in my old age. But who will take care of my brother when he is old? He will need more than I have so that he can care for himself."

With that he got up, left the house, went to his storage bins, and filled a sack with wheat. In the dark of night, he walked to his brother's granary, slipped in, and poured the grain into his storehouse.

Call it coincidence or fate, but that very night, the unmarried, younger broth-er began to worry about his brother and his brother's children. "He has so many mouths to feed. How will he be able to care for all of them if the crops are not as successful as they have been? His needs are greater than mine."

As his older brother had done, he got dressed, went to his storage bins, filled a sack with wheat, stole into his brother's warehouse, and emptied the grain into his cache. The next day, the brothers were both puzzled to find that their supplies of grain were undiminished.

Each night, each brother continued his actions, determined to help the other. Each day, they were surprised to find that their reserves remained undiminished.

Finally, one moonlit night, as each made his way toward the other's farm, he saw a figure, weighed down by a huge sack, approaching in the distance. As they drew closer, they recognized each other and realized what had been happening. They stopped and embraced.

Legend maintains that the spot where these selfless brothers met and hugged was the choice for the site of Jerusalem's ancient temple. (Adapted from a legend in Ginzberg, 1946–1964)

A king who lay dying said to his two sons, "Mount your horses and travel to Jerusalem. The one whose horse arrives last will inherit my kingdom."

Off they went, at anything but breakneck speed, each determined to fall behind the other. When finally they were in sight of Jerusalem, they sat motionless in their saddles. They finally dismounted and sat on the ground for an entire day. It seemed that this impasse would continue forever, when all of a sudden each jumped up on a horse and rode toward the city as fast as he could. What had happened? At the very same moment, they both realized that the one whose horse arrived last would inherit the kingdom, so they mounted each other's horses and raced to get that horse to Jerusalem first. (Adapted from "The Riddle," in Sadeh, 1989)

A mother and father were beside themselves because of the jealousy their three-year-old son showed toward their newborn infant. A psy-chology book recommended that they use another object to get the child to express his feelings of jealousy and aggression toward his sibling. They said to him, "Take this teddy bear and show me how you feel about the baby."

The three-year-old grabbed the stuffed ani-mal and, with obvious delight, went over to the baby and hit it on the head with the bear. (Adapted from de Mello, 1988)

Stepfamilies

A young mother became ill and died. She was survived by her husband and seven young children. The children's concern over who would care for them was soon alleviated when the nanny who had cared for their mother when she had been a child came to run the house and raise them. Although she was quite old, the children were—happy to have someone who had been close to their mother care for them.

But the tasks of keeping house, shopping for food, and caring for the children proved too great for the old woman. The father hired a series of maids, who all quit because of the criticism of the old nanny.

One day, the man married a young widow who loved children. From the very start, the nanny encouraged the children to be disrespectful and disobedient to this woman by saying that she had never heard of a good stepmother. To make matters worse, she reminded the children of the stepmothers in the stories of Snow White, Cinderella, and Hansel and Gretel.

The young stepmother was kind and patient, and she did not make an issue of the children's reluctance to love her. "Everything in due time," she repeated to herself.

She decided to make a quilt from the children's mother's clothes. Each night, when the children were asleep, she cut out shapes of dolls, stars, elves, teddy bears, evergreen trees, and birds, on which she embroidered the words *hope, love,* and *faith.* At Christmas, she gave each child a gift, which was politely received. Then she unrolled the quilt made from their mother's old scarves, aprons, dresses, and handkerchiefs. It was more beautiful than anything they had ever seen, and they were the happiest they had been at any time since their mother died.

The old nanny did not relent. "Your mother is crying in heaven because you gave your love to another woman," she rebuked them.

The resulting sadness caused the stepmother to be careless and miss a step as she went upstairs. She fell down with a crash and gashed her forehead. It was only then that the children realized how much a part of their lives she had become. The children, thinking how foolish they had been, cried, "We never realized that our mother would want us to have another mother to take care of us, but she would have. She would not have wanted us to be alone or unloved." They wondered what to do to show the stepmother how much she had come to mean to them. While the stepmother slept, the children quietly crept in and covered her with the Christmas quilt. In a matter of weeks she was healed and back to her daily routine.

The Music Man opens with a song by a group of traveling salesmen testifying that the key to success is—"know the territory!" In therapy with stepfamilies you have to know what they are all about, what it feels like to be a stepparent, and what the stresses are for stepchildren attempting to deal with drastic changes in their lives. (Visher & Visher, 1981)

Seeing all the love the stepmother gave the children filled the nanny with remorse. She became withdrawn and stayed in bed for days on end. One day the stepmother came in and said, "You must not think about the sadness of losing the little girl you once knew. You loved her so much and that is why you could not allow yourself or the children to love anyone else. The children love you and need you to talk with them about their mother, and I need you to help me with the mothering."

"Faith, hope, and love abide," said the nanny, "but the greatest of these is love." (Adapted from "The Christmas Quilt," in Kronberg & McKissack, 1990)

The Struggle to Be Good

There was a boy who lived on the island of Borneo who was not a complete boy. He was only bad, and no one could find any good in him. Some said that the half-boy had lost his good half. Others were exasperated by the practical jokes he played on the unsuspecting and the mischief he continually got into. He was known for splattering mud on clean wash, throwing fruit at farm workers, and spoiling the fun other children were having. As a result, whenever he was near anyone, he was chased, cursed, and jeered. As the half-boy grew older, he became more and more lonely; his tricks became more and more annoying, disruptive, and dangerous. The villagers spoke of driving the boy out of the village to get rid of him.

One day, a beautiful woman said to him, "You are only half a person, and that half is only the bad half. Somewhere out there is your other half—the good half. Find the other half, come back with it, and I will marry you!"

For years, Jacob lived with his regrets for his selfish, hasty acts of theft. He could not erase his remorse with rationalizations of why he might have been more fit to possess Esau's blessing and birthright. The estrangement of the twin brothers was so deep that they did not see or speak to each other for many years. On several occasions, Jacob set out to find Esau to try to right the wrong, but each time something held him back.

Finally, Jacob had no choice. He received a report that Esau was coming to find him, accompanied by a large contingent of armed men. Frightened, Jacob sent peace offerings and hastily divided his community into two camps so that one might flee if the other were attacked.

The night before the fateful meeting, Jacob made a pillow of stones and slept fitfully at the shore of the Jabbok River and dreamed that he was struggling with a stranger. After an entire night of conflict, he dreamed that the day broke and the stranger begged Jacob to let him go. In exchange for releasing him, Jacob exacted a blessing from the stranger, who changed Jacob's name to Israel, meaning "he has struggled with man and God and has prevailed." Thereafter, Jacob, a changed man, walked with a limp as a result of this contest. He was repentant and forgiving and so was confident that he could ask for Esau's forgiveness. He went forth to greet Esau; the brothers met and embraced, lending their relationship a new destiny. (Adapted from Genesis 32:4–33 :11)

The best index to a person's character is how he treats people who can't do him any good, and how he treats people who can't fight back.
—Abigail Van Buren

No one had ever spoken honestly and directly to the boy before. He was so taken by surprise that he said to the woman, "You are the only person who has ever said a kind word to me. I will begin my search tomorrow, and I will not return until I have found my good half so that I can be whole."

The very next day, the boy started off on his quest. Stopping at many villages, he inquired about the whereabouts of another half-boy. Each person sent him farther and farther up the road saying that he had heard of or seen another half-boy in a distant village. After several days of travel, the boy arrived at a village where he was met with surprise. "Another half-boy," the astonished villagers said. Soon the two half-boys met. They were a perfect match: the same height, the same color hair, the same complexion. The only difference was in their eyes. One had cold, discouraged eyes; the other had soft, warm, happy eyes.

The villagers debated how to join the two halves to make a whole. The village chief told them that they would have to go off into the jungle and wrestle there for as long as necessary, until they found themselves growing together.

"It will be a quick contest," said the bad half-boy.

"Don't be so certain," stated the good half-boy. "I have the spirit of the sunrise in me."

The bad half-boy smiled and responded, "The spirit of night is in me and it is even more powerful. It can extinguish the fires of sunrise."

The two went off into a jungle clearing where they began to struggle with one another. All night long they wrestled. At sunset, the bad half-boy had the advantage. But his gain was reversed at daybreak. The boys battled until the next day. Then all was calm. The villagers saw a handsome young man coming toward them. "The two half-boys are now one," announced the village chief.

Although he was welcome to stay in the village, the whole boy announced that he would return to find the maiden who believed in him.

Upon his return, she recognized him at once and told the others that their half-boy had accepted his good half and was now a whole person like everyone else. The villagers began to like the transformed half-boy; the maiden loved him, and they were married soon after. (Adapted from a Borneo tale in Fahs & Cobb, 1980)

NARRATIVES DEALING WITH THERAPEUTIC ISSUES

Acceptance

A prince, to the chagrin of his parents, imagined that he was a rooster. He lived under the table, refused to eat "people food," and would only consume grain which he picked up from the floor.

The best physicians, philosophers, sages, and magicians could do nothing to reverse this sad state of affairs. One day, however, a wise man who had heard of the prince's plight appeared and offered to heal the prince. The king was willing to try anything and told the man to proceed. He quickly removed his clothing, crouched down under the table, and began crowing.

The suspicious prince questioned him: "Who are you? What are you doing here?" The sage answered the prince's question with the same question. Indignant, the prince-rooster replied, "It should be obvious to you, I am a rooster."

"How odd," said the man. "Can't you see that I, too, am a rooster?"

The two became friends and lived under the table eating grain until one day the sage put on a shirt. The prince exclaimed, "Are you crazy? You are wearing the clothing of a man? Don't you remember that you are a rooster?"

The wise man simply said, "Is it difficult for you to see that a rooster who dresses like a man is still a rooster?" The prince could not refute the wisdom of the sage's words, and soon they were both dressed in clothes.

Next, the sage sent for human food and began eating it. The prince protested, "What are you doing? Roosters don't eat human food."

"You are correct," said the man, "but don't think for even a moment that a rooster who eats like a person at a table ever ceases, for so much as one moment, to be a rooster."

One day, the wise man got out from under the table and sat in a chair. He asked the surprised prince, "Why should a rooster have to spend all of his time under the table? Do you think that sitting in a chair makes you less of a rooster?"

And so it went until the rooster-prince looked and acted perfectly normally, although he knew in his heart that he was still a rooster. (Adapted from a tale of Nachman of Bratslav, collected in Sadeh, 1989)

Milton E. Erickson (1965/1980) described a patient who spoke only "word salad." Erickson studied the man and learned to emulate his patterns of speech. After several days of listening to Erickson, the man said, "Talk sense, doctor."

A woman met an old friend who asked how things were. She admitted that things were terrible since her sister had become convinced that she was a chicken. She explained, "My sister won't sleep in her bed anymore; she scratches around in the dirt in the yard, refuses to speak, only cackles and crows, and eats only seeds and grain."

"Why don't you take her to a psychiatrist?" asked the friend.

"We can't afford to" was the reply.

"What do you mean?" asked the friend.

"We need the eggs." (Source unknown)

The reason people find it so hard to be happy is that they always see the past better than it was, the present worse than it is and the future finer than it will be.—M. Pagnol

Age-Appropriate Behavior

A middle-aged man, recently separated from his wife and living alone, grooms himself before he commutes to work. He trims his moustache, dries his hair, and unbuttons the first few buttons of his shirt so that the gold chains around his neck are visible. He views himself in the mirror and likes what he sees. He thinks his problem today is that he will be mistaken for a baseball player and will have to politely decline the requests for autographs.

He gets on the bus; it is quite crowded, and he has to stand. He finds himself in front of a strikingly attractive young college woman with soft skin and flowing blond hair. She is so alluring that he cannot take his eyes off of her. The entire trip he stares at her. Then she looks up and sees him staring at her. Their eyes lock. He doesn't know where it's going to lead, but he would like to find out. He gives the girl his warmest, most inviting smile. The girl nods, smiles back at him, stands up, and offers him her seat (Kushner, 1991).

The agony and ecstasy of marriage are matched by the agony and ecstasy of the child's exploring the world farther and farther away from his parents, with a ready return guaranteed whenever the exploring leads to insecurity. (Whitaker, 1989)

Anger

Two Buddhist monks were traveling together during the rainy season. The road was filled with mud. Rounding a bend in the road, they saw a beautiful young woman, wearing a magnificent silk kimono, stuck in the road. The older of the two monks offered to help. He picked the woman up and carried her to the other side of the muddy road.

Continuing on their way, the monks did not speak again until that night, when they reached their destination. No longer able to restrain himself, the younger monk said to the older, "You know that we monks are sworn not to come

---

A passenger in a dining car gave his dessert order. "I'll have fruit tarts," he commanded.

The waiter returned from the kitchen and said there were no more to be had. The man exploded. "What? No tarts? That's absurd. I am one of the largest stockholders of this railroad. A simple thing like not having enough fruit tarts is a disgrace. I will take this up with the president of the company when I see him."

The waiter told the dining car manager what had happened and they arranged to get the tarts at the next stop. Soon after, the waiter appeared with the tarts. "I am happy to inform you, sir, that the chef has made these tarts especially for you. We would like to also offer you a bottle of this sixty-year-old brandy with the compliments of the line," the waiter stated.

With that, the passenger threw his napkin down, pounded on the table with his fist, and shouted, "To hell with the tarts! I'd rather be angry!" (Adapted from de Mello, 1989)

In this world there are only two tragedies. One is not getting what one wants, and the other is getting it.—Oscar Wilde

into contact with women. It is dangerous, especially if they are as lovely as the one you helped today. Why did you take such a risk?"

"I put the girl down on the other side of the road two hours ago," said the older monk. "Why are you still carrying her?" (Adapted from "Muddy Road," in Reps, 1961)

Being Direct

Three men, a shoemaker, a tailor, and a butcher, set off in search of work. The longer they traveled, the more discouraged, hungry, and tired they became until finally they felt they could go no farther. They needed lodging and food but had no money, so they devised a plan.

They decided to go to the next town and let it be known that they were traveling with a great healer who could heal the sick with a touch or a few words. They hoped to offer the services of this sage in exchange for food and lodging. To determine who would play the role of the great healer, they drew lots. The job fell to the tailor.

Though quite uncomfortable with this ruse, the tailor went along with the plan. They came to a town and stopped at the local tavern, where they told the innkeeper about the magical talents of their healer. The innkeeper was overjoyed, since his son had an obsession with tearing paper. Consultations with doctors, sages, and miracle workers had been to no avail. The innkeeper told the tailor-turned-sage that if he would only have a look at the young man, the innkeeper would gladly give him and his companions a meal and lodging for the night. The tailor went into the boy's room, sized up the boy who was seated amid mounds of torn paper, took the boy aside, and whispered in his ear. The tailor told his father he was cured. The next day, the men continued on their journey.

As luck would have it, they returned from their job search only to pass through the same town again. This time the innkeeper came out to greet them. He thanked the healer because, in the days since he had left, the boy was cured of his paper-tearing activities. The innkeeper invited them to eat and stay at the inn again. He said, "I do have one request, however."

He turned to the tailor and asked, "I would like to know what you said to the boy on that fateful day."

"Say to the boy?" he mimicked. "Why I bent down and whispered in his ear, 'Tommy, don't tear paper.' " (Adapted from "The Imposter Rebbe," a story of S. Halberstamm in Mintz, 1968, and a Mel Brooks comedy routine)

The woman whose behavior indicates that she will make a scene if she is told the truth asks to be deceived.—Elizabeth Jenkins

John Fitzgerald Kennedy was asked how he became a hero. He replied, "It was involuntary. They sank my boat." —Miriam Ringo, paraphrase

Being Spontaneous

Three children, their aunt, and a gentleman rode in a railway car. The aunt constantly reprimanded the children and reminded them to behave: "Don't do this," "Don't do that."

"Come, look out the window," the aunt would say to distract the children for a few moments. But the silly questions they asked about what they saw only drove her to further distraction. The gentleman couldn't stand the inane conversation or the aunt's attempts to keep the children quiet.

The aunt offered to tell them a story, but they knew that she could not tell them anything that would hold their interest. Her attempt was, in fact, quite uninteresting. It was a story about a little girl who was good, made friends with everyone, and was saved from a mad bull by people who admired her outstanding moral character.

"It's the stupidest story I've ever heard," said one niece with conviction.

The gentleman commented to the woman that she did not seem to be much of a success as a storyteller. The aunt bristled and replied that it is difficult to tell children stories they can understand and appreciate.

The man disagreed with her observation and offered to tell the children a story.

"Yes, tell us a story," demanded one of them.

He began: "Once upon a time there was a little girl named Bertha who was extraordinarily good." The children's interest waned as they heard a beginning as predictable as their aunt's.

"The girl was perfect in every way. In fact, she was horribly good." The use of the word *horrible* in connection with the girl introduced a sense of novelty that was absent from the aunt's stories.

If I had to live my life over, I would dare to make more mistakes next time. I would relax. I would be sillier, I would take fewer things seriously... I would eat more ice cream and less beans. I would, perhaps, have more actual troubles but fewer imaginary ones. You see, I'm one of those people who lived seriously and sanely hour after hour, day after day. I've been one of those persons who never went any place without a thermometer, a hot water bottle, and raincoat, and a parachute. If I had it to do over again, I'd travel lighter.—An 85-year-old Kentucky hill-country woman (Source unknown)

Cantinflas, the Mexican actor known for his role as Passepartout, Phileas Fogg's devoted valet in the 1956 film *Around the World in Eighty Days*, was noted for his comic routine featuring a combination of gibberish, double-talk, mispronunciation, wild exaggeration, and pantomime. His name has entered the Spanish language, where the verb *cantinflar* means "to talk a lot and say little." His innovative style was the result of being forced, as a teenager, to substitute for the missing master of ceremonies in a traveling road show. Once in the spotlight, he suffered overwhelming stage fright. As a result, everything he said came out garbled. The audience laughed so hysterically at his spontaneity that he began working this mishap into his routine. (Obituary in the *New York Times*, April 22, 1993)

"She was so good," he continued, "that she won three medals: for obedience, punctuality, and goodness. She always wore them pinned to her dress. They clinked as she walked along. As a reward for her good behavior, she was permitted to walk in the magnificent town park where no other children were ever allowed to walk. Bertha was surprised to find lots of little pigs running through the park. But she noticed that there were no flowers because the pigs ate them. There were also gold and green fish in the park's ponds and hummingbirds that hummed popular tunes.

Bertha walked up and down the park, enjoying the sights and the knowledge that if she had not been so good, she would never have been allowed in the park. Her three medals clinked as she walked along, reminding her how very good she really was.

Suddenly, an enormous, ferocious wolf appeared, hoping to catch a pig for its supper. But the first thing the wolf saw was Bertha in her spotless white dress. Bertha began to run, with the wolf in pursuit. She hid in some myrtle bushes, where the wolf could not find her because the myrtle fragrance masked her scent. Bertha was terribly frightened and her heart raced. She thought that if she had not been so extraordinarily good, she would never have been in this difficult situation.

The wolf had all but given up on Bertha and turned his attention to the pigs when Bertha trembled so much that her medal for obedience clinked against the one for good conduct. The wolf followed the sound of the clinking medals, dashed into the brush, and dragged Bertha out. Ferociously, he devoured her, leaving only her shoes, bits of clothing, and the three medals."

All three children agreed that this was the most beautiful story they had ever heard, despite its weak beginning. The aunt commented that it was an improper story to tell to children, one that would undermine the effects of years of discipline and teaching.

The man replied that at least he had been able to keep them quiet for ten minutes—more than she was able to do. He thought about what an unhappy woman she was and then smiled as he realized that the children would nag her for the next six months to hear another improper story. (Adapted from "The Story-teller," in Munro, 1982)

Being Stuck

A man in search of wisdom studied a wide variety of disciplines, including yoga, metaphysics, and various social and natural sciences. When he studied psychology, he was intrigued by the ability of rats to learn to negotiate mazes, the speed with which rats learn from trial and error, their ability to utilize that learning in new situations, and the rate at which labyrinth-running behavior can be extinguished. Ultimately, the man abandoned his study of psychology. He concluded that rats are smarter than people. Rats eventually lose interest in running mazes when they finally realize that cheese can no longer be found at the end of the maze. But human beings continually return to the spot where the cheese had been, thinking that since cheese had once been there, it would be there again. Or they think that since their parents said that they had once had cheese, it would be there for them, too. Or they learn in school that it would be there, so they loiter in the complex network of tunnels and blind alleys until it finally appears. Rats go for the cheese only when it is there, but human beings relive and find sustenance in their stories of cheese and often become locked into patterns of search that might last for generations. (Adapted from Hudson & O'Hanlon, 1991)

A group of hunters chartered a plane to fly them to a clearing in the thick jungle. Following their instructions, the pilot returned two weeks later to retrieve them. He looked at the animals they had killed and said, "This plane can only carry the weight of one buffalo. You will have to leave the other behind."

"But last year the pilot let us take two in a plane exactly this size," they protested.

Under duress, the pilot relented and said, "If you did it last year, I guess we can do it again this year."

The plane took off with the hunters and the two buffaloes, but the small plane was unable to gain altitude and crashed into a low-lying hill. Miraculously, the men were safe.

When they climbed out to survey the situation, one hunter asked, "Where do you think we are?"

The other looked around and said, "I think we're about two miles to the left of where we crashed last year." (Adapted from de Mello, 1988)

Mark Twain was once asked if he ever lost his confidence in his writing ability. "Yes," said Twain. "Once, after I had been writing for nearly fifteen years, it suddenly struck me that I did not possess the slightest talent for writing."

"What did you do? Did you give up writing?" he was asked.

"How could I?" was the reply. "By then I was already famous." (Source unknown)

Never let yesterday use up tomorrow. (Source unknown)

Conspiracy of Silence

Nikita Khrushchev addressed the Soviet Communist party and revealed, for the first time, the full scope of Stalin's atrocities. A voice from the gathering heckled him: "You were one of his colleagues, why didn't you stop him?"

"Who said that?" roared Khrushchev. There was silence in the room. No one moved or spoke.

In a quiet voice, Khrushchev said, "Now you know why."—Kenneth Edwards, paraphrase

---

A physician who was dying of cancer didn't want to make his friends and family suffer through his illness with him. He thought he was keeping his illness a secret, but they all were able to figure out its severity. He kept his imminent death a secret; his friends and family never let on that they knew. Finally, he died and everyone spoke of how brave he had been to bear his suffering in silence and not to tell anybody. Privately, his family and friends said how angry they were that he excluded them from his dying, that he didn't need them and didn't trust their ability to handle such sadness. But what hurt the most was that both he and they never had the chance to say how much they loved each other or to say good-bye. (Source unknown)

When a person is born, we rejoice, and when they're married, we jubilate, but when they die we try to pretend nothing happened.—Margaret Mead

Trouble is a part of your life, and if you don't share it, you don't give the person who loves you enough chance to love you enough.—Dinah Shore

Silence makes me nervous 'cause he doesn't come or go. He just hangs around with his hands in his pockets.—J.R. Slaughter

Dealing with Disappointment

One day, a princess heard a knock on the castle door. Slowly opening the door, she found the sort of slimy, wart-covered, green frog that frequently makes an appearance in fairy tales. After screaming a few times, she overcame her revulsion, became intrigued with the idea of a talking frog, and agreed to accompany him for a walk and a picnic along the banks of a wooded stream.

The princess had a wonderful time with the frog, despite that fact that while she ate wild frais-du-bois, he kept snapping up flies with his long tongue. At least he had the good sense not to offer any to her. She overlooked his disgusting eating habits and shortcomings, for she could sense that this frog was not at all like other frogs. He was special; there had to be more to this frog than her eyes led her to believe. "Perhaps there is a prince hidden somewhere under his green skin," she wondered.

Suddenly, the heavens opened up and torrents of rain poured down, accompanied by bolts of lightning and the rumble of thunder. The deluge overpowered the normally quiet, meandering stream and swept the princess away.

The frog heard her cries for help and saw her being carried off. Skilled swimmer that he was, he dove in, did the Australian crawl with all his might to catch up with the imperiled princess, and pulled her to safety. The rain stopped, and the sun shone through the dripping trees. The rays of light on the drops of rain created a crystal-like cathedral in the woods. Overcome by the beauty of the moment and full of gratitude to the frog for saving her life, the princess picked him up and planted a great big kiss on his mouth.

What happened next? Nothing! The frog remained a frog, and the princess was filled with sadness that her fairy tale did not end like the others. (Source unknown)

The King and I are more than satisfied;
It's turned out better than we ever hoped.
He's good to her, she made a lovely bride.
And think how we'd have felt, if they'd
   eloped!
We're quite aware of what his motives were:
He wanted money, and an easy life,
But in the end we had to humor her,
And all she wanted was to be his wife.
As for that fairy tale she likes to tell
About the Frog who scrambled from the well
And gave her back her ball, all dripping wet,
Then turned into a Prince (that's how they
   met),
We know he's not a Prince—the point is this:
Our poor romantic daughter thinks he is.
(Hay, 1982)

According to the theory of aerodynamics, and as may be readily demonstrated through laboratory and wind tunnel experiments, the bumblebee is unable to fly. The size, weight, and shape of its body in relationship to its total wingspread make flying impossible.

The bumblebee, however, ignorant of these profound scientific truths, goes ahead and flies anyway—and manages to make a little honey at the same time. (Source unknown)

Perfect love means to love the one through whom one became unhappy.
—Sören Kierkegaard

Depression

The citizens lived in fear of a cruel despot with a terrible temper. On a whim he would order innocent people maimed and killed. One day, he threatened to murder an unusually large number of his citizens. To further torture his intended victims, he offered them this challenge to spare their lives: "All you have to do is find something that would make me happy when I am sad and something that would make me sad when I am happy."

All night long, the people consulted with all the sages of the kingdom. The next day, they brought the king a ring. The king snarled and laughed, amused to see that the people thought that a ring of any kind could meet his challenge. But he had overlooked the inscription on the inside. When it was pointed out to him, he read: "This, too, shall pass." (Adapted from Dass, 1990)

A man came to Rabbi Stephen S. Wise to seek his advice. The man had lost his fortune in the 1929 stock market crash and was planning suicide to provide the life insurance money for his family. Wise thought for a moment and recommended to the man that he hold a family meeting and ask them what to do.

"If they argue against your taking your life," the rabbi said, "you'll know they would rather have you alive than get the insurance money. If they approve of your suicide, however, I would go on living just to spite them." (Adapted from Epstein, 1989)

Everyone is like a moon, and has a dark side which he never shows to anybody.—Mark Twain

Although the world is very full of suffering, it is also full of the overcoming of it.—Helen Keller

We're all in this alone.—Lily Tomlin

Have the courage to live. Anyone can die. —Robert Cody

Dying

A Navajo grandmother announced that when the rug she was weaving was taken from the loom, she would return to Mother Earth. Her granddaughter, Annie, was upset at the prospect of losing her grandmother because there was a strong bond between them. Annie thought of their long walks and how she loved to listen to the grandmother's stories of her past. When she asked her mother how her grandmother knew she would soon die, her mother replied, "Many old ones know more than many others will ever learn."

Annie wondered why her grandmother continued to weave on the loom. If the completion of the project would mean her grandmother's death, then the thing to do would be to weave no more. Annie tried misbehaving to keep everyone away from the loom, but her efforts failed. Finally, she crawled out of bed in the middle of the night and began pulling the strands of yarn out of the loom one by one. This continued for several nights and her mother was puzzled by what was happening.

Grandmother was not fooled. She tenderly took Annie aside and said, "You have tried to hold back time. It can't be done." Annie responded that she was finally ready to learn to weave, although she knew that every strand of yarn added to the tapestry would bring her grandmother closer and closer to death. (Adapted from Miles, 1971)

A man was being pursued by a ferocious tiger. Chased to the edge of a cliff, he noticed a thick root growing out from the side of the precipice. He grabbed hold of the root and lowered himself down over the edge. The tiger caught his scent just as the man noticed that far below him was another tiger waiting for him to fall. He held onto the root for his life, but then he observed two mice gnawing at the base of the root. At that very moment he spied a luscious strawberry growing in the side of the cliff. He gazed at it for a moment, picked it and ate it. It was the most delicious strawberry he had ever tasted. (Adapted from "A Parable," in Reps, 1961)

Let this moment last, it is so good.—Goethe, *Faust*.

A man named Rava visited his dying friend, Nachman, who asked Rava to appear to him in a dream after his death. When Nachman did so, Rava asked him if he had suffered pain when he died. Nachman replied that the pain of dying is analogous to the effort involved in taking a hair from a glass of milk. "But if I were given the opportunity to come back to life, I would not because the fear of dying is more overwhelming than actual death." (Adapted from the Talmud)

A young servant on an errand for the sultan saw Death in the Baghdad marketplace. Frightened by this image, he ran home trembling. "Master," he said, "I saw Death in the marketplace today. He made a threatening gesture and then walked away. Please give me your fastest steed so that I may flee to Samarra. I must lose no time in escaping him."

The sultan gave the boy a horse. Later that day, the king, too, saw Death in the marketplace. He reprimanded Death and asked why he had made a threatening gesture at his servant. "I did not threaten him," Death said. "My gesture was that of surprise. I did not expect to see him in Baghdad today, because tonight I have an appointment with him in Samarra." (Adapted from Maugham, 1931)

Dreadful is the mysterious power of fate; there is no deliverance from it by wealth or by war, by walled city or dark, seabeaten ships.
—Sophocles

In a box in a corner, a very dark corner of the mind of each of us, is a voice. The voice says, "I am going to die. One day, I am going to die."

We tend not to venture near that corner. We rarely listen to that voice. Sometimes it speaks to us so clearly and emphatically that we have to listen. When we're sick, when we narrowly escape harm, when someone we know dies, we hear it speaking to us. We hear it more frequently as we age, as our bodies fail, as our cumulative experience of death increases.... How we react to this voice, how we try to block it out, determines how we live our lives.—Fred Wistow

Facing Problems

A man was fed up with his life and decided to run away. In the morning, he got up and dressed, had breakfast with his wife and children, kissed them good-bye, and set off. He walked for the entire day. As dusk overtook the daylight, he took his shoes off, pointed them in the direction that he was headed, and went to sleep in the forest. Some boys, having witnessed this ritual, played a prank on him by turning his shoes in the opposite direction.

The next morning the man got up, put on his shoes, and continued his journey in the direction his shoes were pointed. As the day wore on, he noticed how familiar everything looked. Finally, he came to a small town in a clearing. Somehow, he imagined that it would look different, but the house to which he was mysteriously drawn looked exactly like the house he had left. In fact, every other house looked strikingly like those in his village. He could even imagine what the inhabitants of each house must look like. Even the wife and children at the house he stopped at bore a striking resemblance to his own. The woman invited him in, using the same nagging tone that his wife always used. He sat down, had dinner, and realized that there was no point in running away—things were the same everywhere.

The next morning, the man resolved to go back home. He traveled for a day, took his shoes off, pointed them in the direction of his journey, and went to sleep. Again, the pranksters saw what he was doing; again, they turned his shoes around. The next morning, he continued his journey in the direction his shoes pointed. When he finally returned, he was so overjoyed to be home that he swore that he would never run away again. It really didn't matter anyway, he thought, because everything is the same everywhere else. (Adapted from a Sholom Aleichem story, retold in Wiesel, 1971)

At a low point in the life of the composer George Handel, his right side was paralyzed and he was penniless. He was seized by creditors who threatened him with imprisonment. Though the temptation to give up must have been great, Handel did not. Instead, he rebounded and composed the *Messiah*, one of the greatest musical compositions of all time. (Source unknown)

During a journey of several months in the far north, the film director Robert Flaherty shot over 70,000 feet of film. Although he believed none of it to be worthwhile, others encouraged him to edit the film into a documentary. At one point, after weeks of labor, Flaherty lit a cigarette and dropped the match on the floor near the highly flammable film. The match promptly ignited the film, completely destroyed it, and badly burned Flaherty. His reaction—return to the far north to make an unforgettable documentary about native Eskimo life. The result was *Nanook of the North*, regarded as one of the most extraordinary documentary films ever created. (Adapted from *The New Yorker*, June 11, 1949)

Take your life into your own hands and what happens? A terrible thing: no one to blame.
—Erica Jong

The curious paradox is that when I accept myself just as I am, then I can change.—Carl Rogers

We know what happens to people who stay in the middle of the road: they get run over.
—Aneurin Bevan

Failure

Two performing Alaskan Kodiak bears were the featured act of a small traveling circus. Their agility in pulling a small cart, doing acrobatics, walking upright, and dancing arm-in-arm delighted patrons. The circus' last tour took it down the length of the west coast of North and South America to their final destination, Tierra del Fuego, the island at the southernmost tip of South America. There catastrophe struck. A jaguar attacked a performer and killed his trainer. The shocked crowd ran in all directions, and, in the confusion, most of the animals escaped. The prized bears wandered off into the thick undergrowth of the island. The climate provided a sanctuary in which they flourished and procreated, filling the surrounding islands with their progeny. Some seventy years later, the bears were discovered and intensely studied by researchers, who were amazed, not only to discover Alaskan Kodiak bears at the tip of South America, but also to find that all the bears performed sensational circus tricks. (Adapted from "Brilliant Silence," by Holst, 1992)

A fox, hungry and thirsty, spied a luscious bunch of grapes hanging from the arbor. He repeatedly jumped at the fruit, which was just out of his reach. Defeated in his efforts, he commented, "Oh, those grapes were probably sour anyway."—Aesop

Certain tropical monkeys are trapped by carefully securing to the ground a gourd with an opening just large enough for a monkey's hand to fit inside. When one of these monkeys discovers a coveted piece of fruit within the gourd, he inserts his hand and is then faced with a paradox: Withdraw his hand and lose the fruit, or release the fruit and gain his freedom. His own avarice does not allow him to let go. However, his self-imposed imprisonment and subsequent capture by hunters force him to release the fruit after all. (Adapted from Watzlawick, 1978)

Asked if he had ever gotten lost in the wilderness, Daniel Boone replied, "No. Often I didn't know where I was, but that's different."
—Chester Harding, paraphrase

Baseball teaches us...how to deal with failure. We learn at a very young age that failure is the norm in baseball and, precisely because we have failed, we hold in high regard those who fail less often—those who hit safely in one out of three chances and become star players. I also find it fascinating that baseball, alone in sport, considers errors to be part of the game, part of its rigorous truth.—Francis T. Vincent, Jr.

Finding the Child Within

A woman collected moments from her life to save for later use. She stockpiled a day from childhood, an hour from infancy, a few days from the age of six, a night here and an occasion there. So it went until she had assembled a lifetime of special moments, each stored in a small box labeled with its contents.

Late in life, the woman decided it was time to use some of the moments she had accumulated. First, she opened a box that contained a day when she was eight years old. She became giddy and silly, played practical jokes, ran to the park where she rolled in the grass and swang on the swings. She ate ice cream and candy. By day's end, she was exhausted, but happy nevertheless.

When she opened the box marked "age ten," she became irresponsible and left her room a mess, but she had fun. Her friends not only noticed the changes that had come over her, but also observed that she neglected her chores of dusting, cooking, opening the mail, paying her bills, pulling the weeds, and even walking the dog.

A day from age fourteen made her shy and self-conscious, aware of every blemish on her face. She cried inconsolably when she relived the day a grandparent died. But she relived the joy she felt on the day she fell in love for the first time. Then, one day, when she had used up all her life savings of days, she promptly died.

After a period of mourning, some of her friends cleaned out her office desk. They found one remaining box of the woman's savings that she had neglected to open. When her friends opened the box from age four, peculiar things began to happen: One made a chain of paper clips and played with the telephone; another raced up and down the stairs; a third played under the desk.

Now that the woman was dead, the last remaining day of her life had no reason to come to an end. It is still floating around, attaching itself to unsuspecting people who have only the life savings of the woman to blame. (Adapted from "Life Savings," in Ahlberg & Ahlberg, 1987)

An angry reader, waving the day's paper, stormed into a newspaper office and asked to see the editor of the obituary column. The reader showed the editor his name in the obituary listing. "You see," he said, "I am very much alive. I demand a retraction!"

The editor replied, "I never retract a story. But I'll tell you what I'll do; I'll put you in the birth column and give you a fresh start."
—Rabbi Saul Teplitz, paraphrase

If there is anything that we wish to change in the child, we should first examine it and see whether it is not something that could better be changed in ourselves.—Carl Jung

When childhood dies, its corpses are called adults.—Brian Aldiss

When you return to your boyhood town, you find it wasn't the town you longed for—it was your boyhood.—Earl Wilson

Every child is an artist. The problem is how to remain an artist once he grows up.
—Pablo Picasso

Holistic Healing

The Velveteen Rabbit was a sight to behold, with thick brown-and-white fur, thread whiskers, and pink-satin-lined ears. In the rush of holiday gift opening, the Boy loved the new rabbit briefly, then left him in a toy cupboard where he was forgotten among the wind-up toys, boats, and wooden playthings. There the rabbit was befriended by the Skin Horse, the longest lived resident of the nursery. He was so old that his seams showed and his coat was bald in spots. He had outlived a long succession of toys of every size and type.

One day, when the Skin Horse and the Velveteen Rabbit were packed up close together, the rabbit asked the horse what "real" is. The horse took a deep breath and carefully explained that

real isn't how you are made, but rather something that happens to you. When a child loves you, really loves you, knows that you are more than something to play with, then you become real. It happens magically and gradually, bit by bit, which is why it only happens to those who are very well made and not too delicate. By the time it happens, you are frayed around the edges and threadbare because your hair gets loved off, your eyes come loose, your stuffing hangs out and you become quite grimy and tattered. But it doesn't matter how you look, because when you are real, you stay real forever and you are always beautiful. You can only be ugly to those who can't see what is real.

The Velveteen Rabbit longed to be real but was saddened at the thought of growing old and worn. If only he could become real without losing his shiny eyes and his plush fur.

Eventually, the Velveteen Rabbit became a favorite of the Boy. Every night the Boy snuggled with him in bed and made tunnels under the blankets for him to burrow in as real rabbits do. Although he missed his chats with the Skin Horse, and being held tightly took some getting used to, the rabbit came to love the way the Boy talked to him, played secret games, and snuggled his warm chin into his

---

The modest Finnish army of only nine divisions managed to hold off the forty-five-division Soviet army for 105 days in the winter of 1939–1940. When they finally were crushed by these overwhelming odds, Finnish President Kallio was forced to sign a treaty dictated by Moscow. As he picked up the pen to sign, he uttered, "Let the hand wither that signs this monstrous treaty!" Several months later he suffered a paralysis of that arm.—Aini Ranjanen, paraphrase

The witch doctor succeeds for the same reason all the rest of us succeed. Each patient carries his own doctor inside him. They come to us not knowing that truth. We are at our best when we give the doctor who resides within each patient a chance to go to work.—Albert Schweitzer

Our Creator has given us five senses to help us survive threats from the external world, and a sixth sense, our healing system, to help us survive internal threats.—Bernie S. Siegel

fur. The rabbit never noticed that his fur had become matted and thin, that his pink nose was scraped off where the Boy kissed him, or that his seam had come undone. His whiskers were loved off, and his pink ears turned gray. But the rabbit went everywhere with the Boy, whose nanny reprimanded him for being unwilling to go to bed without it.

"Such a fuss over just a toy," she said.

And the Boy answered, "You must not say he's just a toy. He is real."

When the Velveteen Rabbit heard that, he was overjoyed. Now he knew that what the Skin Horse had said was true. Now he was real! (Adapted from *The Velveteen Rabbit,* Williams, 1926)

Hope

On a whim, the king sentenced a man to die. The condemned man appealed to the monarch. "Your Majesty," said the man, "give me a year to teach your dog to talk, and if I don't succeed, then you may kill me."

The potentate was so taken aback and intrigued by this proposition that he smiled and agreed.

When the man came home, his friends asked him if he were crazy. "How do you expect to teach a dog to speak?"

"A year is a long time," replied the man. "In a year the king may die. And if he doesn't, the dog may. And if neither of them does, who knows? Perhaps I really will be able to teach it to speak." (Adapted from a fable of Aesop, in Sadeh, 1989)

Upon being told that a friend, once unhappily married, had remarried, the English journalist and lexicographer Samuel Johnson observed that this was a case of "the triumph of hope over experience."—James Boswell, paraphrase

In the midst of winter, I discovered that there was within me an invincible summer.
—Albert Camus

Hopelessness: Feeling Unable to Make a Difference

In 1485, King Richard III was preparing for the battle against the army of Henry, Earl of Richmond, to decide which of them would rule England. On the morning before the conflict, Richard's groom took his horse to the blacksmith. The blacksmith was short one nail to complete the job of reshoeing Richard's horse. Rather than wait, the groom left, hoping that the shoe would hold without the last nail.

Once in battle, Richard galloped toward his retreating soldiers to encourage them to fight, but his horse's shoe flew off, the horse stumbled, and Richard was thrown to the ground. Seeing his troops beating a retreat, Richard waved his sword and shouted the lines immortalized by Shakespeare: "A horse! A horse! My kingdom for a horse." (*Richard III* V, iv, 7) Moments later Richard was dead. That fateful day is remembered in these lines from a nursery rhyme:

> For want of a nail, a shoe was lost,
> For want of a shoe, a horse was lost,
> For want of a horse, a battle was lost,
> For want of a battle, a kingdom was lost,
> And all for the want of a horseshoe nail.
> ("Jacula Prudentum," by George Herbert, 1593–1633)

Three men were on a deserted island. A genie appeared and granted each man one wish. The first one wished to be home, and in an instant he was. The second man also wished to be at home. He, too, was whisked away. The third man said: "Gee, I miss those guys. I wish they were back here." (Source unknown)

Abraham Lincoln, having followed a fiery, two-hour address by the clergyman-turned-politician Edward Everett, believed his brief remarks at Gettysburg were a failure. (Source unknown)

Integrity

A rich man gave all his money to the poor. He joined a religious order of hermits who worshipped God in the desert. One day, the man was sent to town with another hermit to sell two old donkeys that could no longer carry any weight.

In the marketplace, a man stopped and asked if the donkeys were worth buying. The man replied, "If they were worth buying, do you think I would be selling them?"

Another potential buyer asked why their tails were so ragged and their backs so scarred. This time, the man replied that they had to be thrashed and their tails had to be pulled to get them to move.

With no buyers for the donkeys, the two returned to the desert, where the companion reported on the comments of the newest member of the group. The others angrily asked why he had discouraged the buyers. He answered, "Do you think that I gave up my home and all of my wealth in order to make a liar out of myself for two jack-asses?" (Adapted from a seventeenth-century Italian tale of Rabbi Yehudah Aryeh of Modina, collected in Sadeh, 1989)

When Abraham Lincoln campaigned for the presidency, his strongest opponent was Edwin Stanton. Stanton used every opportunity to degrade and embarrass Lincoln in public. Despite Stanton's bitter diatribes and cruel comments about Lincoln's appearance, Lincoln was elected. Lincoln immediately appointed Stanton to fill the important post of secretary of war. When Lincoln's advisors reminded him of the things Stanton had said about him, Lincoln answered by saying, "I find he is the best man for the job."

After Lincoln was assassinated, Stanton referred to Lincoln as one of the greatest men ever to have lived. (Source unknown)

A great teacher always attracted large crowds of people who sought his advice and listened to his lessons. Each time he spoke, the same heckler in the audience would contradict him and question everything he said, much to the dismay of everyone else. One day, the adversary died, and everyone sighed with relief. But the master was plunged into deep grief. When questioned about his melancholy, he said that the man had been his only true friend. As he burst into tears, he said, "He was the only one who challenged me." (Adapted from a report of the adversarial relationship between Resh Lakish and Rabbi Yohanan in the Talmud)

I don't have a warm personal enemy left. They've all died off. I miss them terribly because they helped define me.—Clare Boothe Luce

The greatest use of life is to spend it for something that will outlast it.—William James

Living for Others/Yourself

A chicken and a pig were walking along when they met a stranger who solicited from them the ingredients for bacon and eggs. The chicken wholeheartedly agreed to fullfil the request, while the pig broke out into a sweat and refused to participate. When the chicken asked why, the pig replied: "From you he only wants a contribution. From me he expects a total commitment." (Source unknown)

A cow and a pig were walking along. The pig lamented to the cow about how unpopular he was. "People are always speaking about your gentleness and your kind eyes," said the pig to the cow. "But all that people get from you is milk. I give far more. I give bacon, ham, bristles for brushes, leather, chitlins, and some people even pickle my feet. Why don't people love me as much as they love you?"

The cow replied, "It is because whatever I give, I give while I am alive. It is true that you may give more, but they get it all from you only after you're dead!" (Source unknown)

The Swedish chemist Alfred Nobel made a fortune by licensing his formula for powerful explosives to weapons makers. When Nobel's brother died, one newspaper mistakenly printed the obituary notice for Alfred instead of his brother. The obituary identified Alfred, the inventor of dynamite, as the man who had made a fortune enabling armies to achieve more terrible and efficient means of mass destruction. Nobel was taken aback by this grim depiction of his accomplishments. He was horrified to think that he would be recalled as a merchant of death and destruction.

As a result of having had the rare opportunity to read his own obituary, Nobel devoted his fortune to establishing awards for accomplishments in fields that would benefit humanity. It is for these awards, the Nobel prizes, that he is remembered today. (Source unknown)

I would rather be ashes than dust. I would rather that my spark should burn out in a brilliant blaze than it should be stifled by dry rot.

I would rather be a superb meteor, every item of me in magnificent glow, than a sleepy and permanent planet.

The proper function of man is to live, not to exist. I shall not waste my days in trying to prolong time. I shall use my time.—Jack London, in the *San Francisco Examiner*, 1916

Loneliness

There was a seamstress who, despite a life of poverty, possessed a spirit of generosity and great inner strength. She showed her wealthy customers bolts of rich fabric, which she fashioned into extraordinarily beautiful garments. But she found her greatest purpose in life by taking remnants of fabric and fashioning them into clothes that, each year at Thanksgiving, she gave to the children in the local orphanage.

Many years after the seamstress had died and the orphanage was closed, a newspaper reporter remembered that a wealthy businessman had grown up in the orphanage. The reporter interviewed the businessman and asked him the secret of his success.

In a deliberate, matter-of-fact fashion, the businessman replied, "When I was in the orphanage, the loneliness seemed endless. The longing for my dead parents was more than I could bear. In spite of the kindness of the staff and the friendship of the other children, I felt very alone. Every year I waited for Thanksgiving for one reason. At this season each child was given a new set of clothes. For me, what was even more wonderful than receiving a brand new set of clothes was the special secret they held. Every year I would find a small note in one of the pockets. It was a message I savored throughout the year. It contained the reassurance that I would not forever be alone, that there would be an end to my loneliness."

"What was written on the notes?" interrupted the reporter. "What message could have made it possible for you to overcome such difficult odds?"

"That is unimportant," he replied. "Someone, and I never learned who, sent those messages just to me. They made me feel special and that made all the difference." (Adapted from a story by Rabbi Sue Elwell, in Umansky & Ashton, 1992)

How sad would be November if we had no knowledge of spring!—Edwin Teale

We don't see things as they are, we see things as we are.—Anaïs Nin

Making a Difference

A grandfather planted a turnip. By harvest time, it was gigantic—so large that he wasn't able to pull it up—so he asked his wife to help. Still it would not budge, so they enlisted the help of a child. One child's help was not enough to loosen it; they went and got a second child, then a third child, then three grandchildren. All of them still could not pull it out. Finally, they enlisted the help of a beetle. That little bit of extra help enabled them to dislodge the root. (Adapted from "The Turnip," in Afanas'ev, 1945)

A man walked along the seashore with his grandson. As they passed beached starfish, the boy picked them up and tossed them back into the ocean. The old man protested, "The beach goes on for miles, and there are millions of starfish. What you are doing won't make any difference."

The boy looked at the starfish in his hand, gently threw it into the ocean, and said, "It will make a difference to this one."—George Bush

A man must sit in a chair with his mouth open for a very long time before a roast duck will fly in. —Chinese proverb

Mourning and Grief

A grief-stricken mother went to a holy man to ask for prayers and incantations to bring her dead son back to life. He told her to fetch a mustard seed from a home that had never known sorrow. He said, "We will use it to drive the sorrow out of your life."

The mother came to a beautiful mansion, knocked on the door, and asked the woman who answered the door if this were a home that had never known sorrow. The woman told her that she had come to the wrong house and began to describe the series of tragedies that had befallen her.

I associated pain with what I like to call the cycle of human eternity; where there is life, there is pain, for there can be no life without pain. Where there is pain, there is love. Where there is love, there is healing. Where there is healing, there is hope; and where there is hope, there is life. Much of our earthly career is enveloped by this cycle. —Rabbi George Lieberman

A broken hand works, but not a broken heart. (Source unknown)

All human life has its seasons, and no one's personal chaos can be permanent: Winter, after all, does not last forever, does it? There is summer, too, and spring, though sometimes when branches stay dark and the earth cracks with ice, one thinks they will never come, that spring, that summer, but they do, and always. —Truman Capote

It's a kind of test…and it's the only kind that amounts to anything. When something rotten like this happens, then you have your choice. You start to really be alive, or you start to die. That's all.—James Agee

These words were in the captain's heart. He shaped them soundlessly with his trembling lips, as he had not breath to spare for a whisper: "I am lost." And, having given up life, the captain suddenly began to live.—Carson McCullers

The mourner said to herself, "Who is better able to help this poor, bereft woman than I who have had a misfortune of my own?" She stayed to comfort the woman and then went on to other places, only to find that each home had its own sadness and misfortune. The woman became so involved in helping others deal with their grief that she was able to forget about her own grief for long periods of time—so much so that she forgot about her own quest for the magical mustard seed, which had, indeed, driven sorrow out of her life. (Adapted from *Buddhist Parables,* 1922)

Narcissism

In an ancient kingdom, the people would elect a new king in an unusual way. When the king died, a rare bird known as the Bird of Happiness was sent forth, and the person on whose head the bird alighted was proclaimed king.

A slave in this land was a court jester. He wore a cap of chicken feathers and a belt of lamb's hooves and he carried a little drum and a mirror. The people he entertained laughed at his antics, but his face was always sad. One day, as he was preparing for an appearance in the royal court, the jester noticed that some seeds were stuck to his shoes. He gathered them up and examined them closely. Then, not knowing what to do, he tossed them into the center of his hat and ran off to his performance.

The sad-faced slave realized immediately that something was wrong. The king had died. Since the people were in no mood to laugh, the clown lay down behind the royal throne and fell asleep.

He awakened to the noise of a bird fluttering in the room. The royal bird had been released and was flying about. It made several passes over the head of the slave and finally landed on his hat and pecked at the seeds.

It was not the image of his own face that transfixed him as he bent down over the pool. Narcissus had seen that face often before: in mirrors, in a thousand photographs, in women's eyes. It was an undistinguished face, but handsome enough, with its long eyelashes, full lips, and stately nose sloping to a curious plateau near the tip.

No, it was something else now that rooted him to the spot. Kneeling there, gazing into the so taken-for-granted form, he grew more and more poignantly aware that it was mere surface. When the water was calm, *it* was calm; when the water rippled at the touch of a leaf or a fish, it too rippled; or broke apart when he churned the water with his hand. More and more fascinated, he kept staring through the image of his face into the depths beneath, filled with a multitude of other, moving, shadowy forms. He knew that if he stayed there long and patiently enough, he would be able to see straight through to the bottom. And at that moment, he knew, the image would disappear. (Mitchell, 1990)

He fell in love with himself at first sight and it is a passion to which he has always remained faithful. Self-love seems so often unrequited. —Anthony Powell

Narcissism: When one grows too old to believe in one's uniqueness, one falls in love with one's complexity.—John Fowles

The slave was trying to shoo the bird away when he heard the crowd roar, "Long live the king." Then the slave was lifted high and paraded about by the people.

The slave tried to make sense of what he was experiencing. "But I am only a slave," he thought.

The prime minister spoke: "The only thing we ask of you is that you never forget that you are the king."

The new king agreed. His first order of business was to ask that a simple hut with no windows and only one door be built in the royal courtyard. When it was complete, the new king entered it. Then, after only a few minutes, he left and locked the door with a sturdy lock.

Every year, the king issued new laws. He ordained that slaves should be set free after six years of servitude. Then he ordered that a slave could buy his freedom. One day, he decreed that no person had the right to own another human being. The changes in the kingdom were so gradual that the people of the kingdom hardly noticed them, just as they did not notice the change that came over his face as the king gradually lost his sadness.

Every year, on the anniversary of his election to kingship, the king would unbolt the door of the hut, enter, stay a few minutes, and then leave and lock the door behind him. Once, the prime minister asked the king what he was guarding so carefully in the little hut.

The king answered, "Those are my prized possessions." He opened the door and invited the minister in. When the minister emerged, he said, "I saw only a feather cap, a belt of lamb's hooves, a drum, and a mirror."

"Those are my prized possessions," said the king. "When I promised you that I would never forget that I was king, I also promised myself to remember that I was once a slave. Each year I go into the hut, wear the hat and the belt, and gaze at myself in the mirror to fulfill that pledge." (Adapted from Afghani and Iraqi folk tales in Sadeh, 1989, and Noy, 1963, and expanded by Cone, 1965)

Overcoming Fears

In ancient Egypt, there lived a boy who was thought to be a coward. Even his name, Moibi, meant "frightened one." To intimidate him, villagers told him stories about monsters that lived in the forest. The boy believed them. Fearing that one of the monsters might jump out and harm him, Moibi always raced through the forest to get home as quickly as possible.

One day Moibi heard the cries of an animal. Following the sound, he saw a rabbit caught in a tangle of brambles. He released the hare, who told him how frightened he was. "You must be very brave to come alone into the forest," said the rabbit.

"Oh no, I am not at all brave. I only came here because I heard your call. In my village I am called a coward," said the boy. "I am frightened of crocodiles, snakes, spiders, anything that moves or rustles in the underbrush. Now that you know the truth about me, you will not find me to be much protection."

Said the rabbit, "I should like to give you something in return for the kindness and courage you have shown me by overcoming your fears."

"I would like the one thing that no one can give me—courage," Moibi said.

"It is true that I cannot give you courage, but I can tell you what road to follow to find it," said the hare.

The very next day, Moibi set out on his journey. Almost from the start, he felt different. At the river, he looked at the menacing crocodiles and said: "Just try to attack me and you will be killed." He almost couldn't believe his own ears when he listened to his words. He safely forded the river, and the frightened croc-

---

When Lord Louis Mountbatten was a child, he was told to go to bed in the dark. He told his father that he wasn't afraid of the dark; rather, it was the wolves he was fearful of. His father smiled at his child's imagination and ingenuity and replied, "There are no wolves in this house."

The frightened child replied, "I know there aren't, but I think there are."—Alden Hatch, paraphrase

A man walking on a deserted street noticed a group of men walking toward him. His imagination got the better of him, and he feared that they would harm him. He became so panicked that he jumped over a fence and fell over on the other side. The men saw what he had done and went to investigate what had happened. They found the man lying on the ground, frozen with fear. One of the group asked if he could be of help. Thinking rationally about his miscalculation, the man said: "It is more complicated than you might assume. You see, I am here because of you; and you are here because of me." (Adapted from a Sufi tale)

If anyone tells you "I achieved something without struggling at it" do not believe him. But if he tells you "I struggled and achieved something," you then may believe him.
—Talmud

Unhappiness is not inevitable. Even when we are angry, judgmental and miserable, we have the best of intentions. We have been systematically trained to use unhappiness as a strategy to take care of ourselves. We can un-teach ourselves...and begin again.
—Barry Neil Kaufman

odiles stayed away from him. Each new and successful encounter with forest creatures fortified the boy's courage.

Soon he arrived at a village in which people were crying and wailing. Moibi asked the chief why everyone was so unhappy. The chief told Moibi about the threat from the fire-breathing monster that would soon devour their village. No one was willing to go up the mountain to fight the fierce beast. The boy volunteered, surprising himself as the words came out of his mouth.

Moibi climbed the mountain and saw the monster basking in the sun outside his cave. The closer he came, the smaller the beast got. The enormous beast saw him, and snorted fire, and the singed Moibi retreated. But Moibi was puzzled by the fact that the monster grew in size as he got further away. He thought that if he got close enough, the monster would be a small enough to kill. He steeled himself and looked in a different direction as he ran up the mountain to the monster's cave. When he arrived, he discovered that the monster was actually the size of a frog. He picked it up and scratched its back, and it made a sound that was a cross between a purr and a simmering pot. Moibi carried it off as a pet.

Back in the village he was acclaimed a mighty hunter, and nobody would believe that he hadn't killed the monster until he showed them how the little monster's size increased as they walked further away from him. "What is his name?" they asked Moibi. Before he could answer, the little monster said, "Most people call me 'What-Might-Happen.' " (Adapted from *The Monster That Grew Small,* by Grant, 1987.)

Paranoia

A hen was scratching about in the barnyard when all of a sudden something fell from the skies and hit her on the head. "The sky is falling," cried the little chicken. Whether she felt obligated to warn others or was just being a busybody is uncertain. She was next seen running wildly throughout the farm, screeching that the heavens were caving in. The other farm animals, unmoved by her dire observation, continued doing what they were doing, taking time to ask teasingly: "What did you say?"

"The sky is falling, the sky is falling, a piece hit me right on the head." The turkeys, ducks, and roosters smiled smugly and said, "Sure it is, my dear. It has happened to us many times."

When the hen would not allow the matter to rest, one feathered fellow offered the suggestion that perhaps a berry or a nut from a tree had whacked her on the head. They were all amused by her persistent certainty, especially in the face of the indisputable logic they offered to explain the incident.

Then something unbelievable happened. Slowly at first, and then with increasing intensity and size, chunks of ice crystals and huge slabs of ice-blue sky began raining down. Very quickly everyone was killed, because the heavens really were falling. (Adapted from "The Hen and the Heavens," in Thurber, 1939)

A man driving down a country road got a flat tire. Because he had no jack with which to change the tire, he decided to walk to the nearest farmhouse to see if he could borrow a jack. As he walked down the road, a question occurred to him: "What if the farmer doesn't want to lend me a jack?"

He continued on his way and resolved to pay the farmer for the use of the jack, if necessary. "After all," he reasoned, "how much could he want for a jack? Ten dollars?"

Farther along, he wondered if the farmer might try to take advantage of him and ask fifty dollars for the jack. At the thought of this, he became quite annoyed. He walked up to the door of the farm house and knocked. When the farmer opened the door, the man exclaimed,

"Who needs your damn jack? You can take it and shove it!" (Source unknown)

A young woman was experiencing great stress. Her therapist prescribed tranquilizers and asked her to come back in a few weeks. When he next saw her, he asked if she noticed any difference in herself. "No," she said, "I don't. But I have observed that other people seem a lot more relaxed." (Adapted from de Mello, 1989)

I told my psychiatrist that everyone hates me. He said I was being ridiculous—everyone hasn't met me yet.—Rodney Dangerfield

Life is a rock. And a hard place.—Juli Duncan

Pessimism

Scientists were eager to discover the effect of the environment on the behavior of twins. They constructed an elaborate laboratory in the form of a room with a one-way mirror that allowed them to study the activity going on in it. The room was filled with manure. The scientists opened the door, put the first child in, sat back, and watched through the one-way mirror to see what he would do in this situation. The child began crying, screaming, and pounding on the door. He yelled: "Get me out of here! I can't stand the smell! This place is disgusting!"

The scientists removed him and placed his twin brother in the same room full of manure. This child's behavior was quite different. As they watched, he played in the manure, dug in it, threw it up in the air, laughed, and appeared to be having a wonderful time. They opened the door, but he was oblivious to the fact that they were now standing there. Finally, they asked, "What are you doing?"

The child replied, "With all this manure in this room, there must be a pony in here somewhere." (Source unknown)

Two frogs fell into a can of cream,
Or so I've heard it told.
The sides of the can were shiny and steep,
The cream was deep and cold.
"O, what's the use," croaked number one,
"Tis fate; no help's around.
Good-bye my friend! Good-bye, sad world"—
And weeping still, he drowned.
But number two of sterner stuff,
Dog-paddled in surprise,
The while he wiped his milky face
And dried his milky eyes.
"I'll swim awhile at least," he said—
Or so I've heard he said.
"It really wouldn't help the world
If one more frog were dead."
An hour or two he kicked and swam,
Not once he stopped to mutter
But kicked and kicked and swam and kicked
Then hopped out, via butter.—Author unknown

It's hard to see a halo when you're looking for horns.—Cullen Hightower

After the sixth day of creation, God rested. He turned to one of his angels and asked, "Well, what do you think? Are you optimistic or pessimistic?"

The angel hesitated, frowned, shook his head, and finally responded, "Lord, I'm optimistic."

In surprise, God asked, "Well, if you are optimistic, why are you frowning?"

The angel answered, "I'm frowning because I believe my optimism is unjustified." (Source unknown)

Problem Solving

Some years ago, when the British government was considering building a tunnel to connect England with the Continent, the budget office advertised for bids for the work. One bid, submitted by the firm of Cohen and Goldberg, was so extraordinarily low that a government representative was dispatched to see if the firm could do the work for the modest sum claimed. The office was on the fifth floor of a less-than-magnificent building in one of London's poorer neighborhoods.

When asked if they could build a tunnel of such magnitude for such a small sum, Cohen replied, "We certainly can."

"But how can you afford to buy the equipment and hire the workers for so little money?" the representative inquired.

"What workers, what equipment? All we need is two shovels."

Taken aback by this response, the government man asked, "How can you do it with just two shovels?"

Goldberg answered: "It's simple. I'll stand here and start digging; Cohen will stand on the Continent and start digging. When we meet, you'll have your tunnel."

"But what happens if you never meet?" the official insisted.

"Well, then, you'll have two tunnels!"—Leonard Fein, paraphrase

---

The Esterházy family of Hungary was the patron of the Austrian composer Franz Joseph Haydn. One year, the court musicians complained to Haydn that they had not been home to see their families in a very long time. Not wanting to offend his patron, but still hoping to get the message to Prince Esterházy, Haydn wrote his Symphony no. 45. In the last movement, each performer, upon completing his part, blew out his candle and slipped away from the orchestra. The prince understood the message of Haydn's Farewell Symphony and instructed Haydn to send the musicians home.
—Will and Ariel Durant, paraphrase

The British novelist G. K. Chesterton was once asked what books he would like to have if he were stranded on a desert island. Without thinking, he replied, "Thomas's *Guide to Practical Shipbuilding.*"

Every problem contains the seeds of its own solution.—Stanley Arnold

A man whose marriage was failing sought advice of a wise man. The sage advised, "Go home and listen to your wife more carefully than you ever have before."

Several days later, he returned home and reported that though he had listened to every word his wife spoke, nothing changed. In response, the sage offered this insight and advice: "Now go home and listen to everything that your wife didn't say." (Source unknown)

The reverse side also has a reverse side.
—Japanese proverb

The problem is not that there are problems. The problem is...thinking that having problems is a problem.—Theodore Rubin

Reaching for the Good

Once there was a golden palace that contained everything a child could ever want. Entry could be achieved only through the performance of good deeds. One child, hoping to be admitted, gave some coins to a beggar and was confident that she would gain admission. However, the doorkeeper shook his head and encouraged her to try again. On her way home, she saw a lame woman toiling under the weight of a heavy bundle. Seizing the opportunity, the child carried the bundle for the grateful woman. This deed, too, was not sufficient to gain entry, and the guard urged her to try again.

Discouraged, the child decided to abandon the struggle; the key seemed beyond her reach. Walking past a forest, she heard a faint cry. As she entered a thicket, she saw a dog with its paw caught in a hunter's trap. She knelt, pulled at the heavy spring to free the animal until her fingers were raw and bleeding. She used the hem of her skirt to bandage the dog's injured paw. The dog licked her hand and whimpered thankfully.

Suddenly, the old doorkeeper stood before her and handed her the key to the golden palace. She said in astonishment: "I did not help the dog for the key. I had forgotten all about it."

The guard replied, "It is clear that you helped without any expectation of reward. This key is for those who forget themselves in the performance of good for others." (Source unknown)

An American journalist tracked Marie and Pierre Curie, the discoverers of radium, to their vacation cottage. Sitting outside was an unassuming woman. The reporter, not knowing that this in fact was Madame Curie, asked her if she were the housekeeper. Madame Curie said that she was. She told the reporter that Madame Curie was not in and would not be back anytime soon. Trying to salvage his long trip, he asked the woman if she could tell him something confidential about the scientist. Curie replied: "Madame Curie has only one message that she likes to give to reporters. That is: Be less curious about people and more curious about ideas." —Henry and Dana Lee Thomas, paraphrase

A farmer who always succeeded in raising prize-winning corn had the peculiar habit of sharing his hybrid seed with all of the neighboring farmers. When asked why he was so generous, he said: "It is a matter of self-interest. The wind carries pollen from field to field. If my neighbors grow inferior corn, the cross-pollination lowers the quality of my crop. That is why I want them to plant only the very best." (Adapted from de Mello, 1989)

…giving is a very good criterion, in a way, of a person's mental health. Generous people are rarely mentally ill people.—Karl Menninger

Reaction versus Response

A horticulturist took special care of an American holly tree. He sheltered it from harsh weather, fed, watered, and fertilized it. Soon the need arose to transplant it to a spot that offered more room. He carefully dug the roots, watered, and fertilized the holly in its new location.

Despite the great care showered on the tree, the disturbance to its system was too great. It began to shed leaves. Its growth was stunted. No books or advice seemed to provide a cure for the tree's precipitous deterioration. Entire branches shriveled up and turned brown. Unable to deal with this failure, the horticulturist terminated his active care. Nevertheless, the sight of the bare branches and withered leaves tormented him. Springtime brought no improvement in the tree's condition. He made one last effort to save the tree with more fertilizer, thick mulch, cautious pruning. It was no use; there was no renewal.

Just before his summer vacation, the gardener made one last pass with a pruning shears, testing each branch for life before cutting it back. His disappoint-

---

A king, traveling through the wilderness with his favorite hawk, searched for a spring at which to slake his thirst. He saw a trickle of water coming down over the edge of a rock. He held a cup to it and, drop by drop, the water filled the cup. As he was about to drink, the hawk swooped down and knocked the cup from his hand. The king picked up the empty cup and again collected the drops of water. As he raised the half-full cup to his lips, the hawk again caused him to spill the precious liquid. Becoming increasingly angry, the man threatened the bird with death. Again, he filled the cup and this time drew his sword. As the hawk flew close to the cup, the king struck the bird and killed it.

The king was unable to retrieve his cup, which had fallen between the rocks, so he climbed to drink directly from the source of the spring. At the source, he was shocked to see a dead, poisonous snake in the pool of water.

The hawk had saved his life, and the king had repaid him with death. From that day on, he resolved never to do anything in anger. (Adapted from "The King and His Hawk," a legend about Genghis Kahn, in Bennett, 1993)

Upon his return from the discovery of the New World, Christopher Columbus was honored at a banquet. A jealous acquaintance rudely asserted that had Columbus not discovered the New World, someone else would have.

Columbus did not immediately acknowledge the impertinent remark. Instead, he invited the guests to take an egg and try to make it stand on one end. The guests tried in vain, whereupon Columbus took an egg, cracked it against the table, and set it standing on the crushed end. In this way, he demonstrated to all that once people are shown the way, anyone else can follow. —Benzoni, Historiadel Mondo Nuevo, paraphrase

Once a word has been allowed to escape, it cannot be recalled.—Horace

It is easy to fly into a passion—anybody can do that—but to be angry with the right person to the right extent and at the right time and with the right object and in the right way—that is not easy, and it is not everyone who can do it. —Aristotle

Anger is never without a reason, but seldom with a good one.—Benjamin Franklin

When a kettle boils, it spills hot water down its side.—Midrash

Take calculated risks. That is quite different from being rash.—George S. Patton

ment in the tree and his inability to remedy this sorry situation turned to ruthless anger. He began indiscriminately cutting all the branches, leaving only a denuded trunk where once the graceful holly had stood. He left for a long vacation thinking that he would dig out the stump when he returned. But when he revisited the scene of his brutality, he could see the trunk sending forth an array of healthy green shoots from every cut and wound he had inflicted. (Adapted from "An American Holly," in Friedman, 1990)

Reality Testing

One day a horse ran away from its owner, a man skilled at interpreting the hidden meaning of events. When people tried to console him for his terrible loss, he asked, "Why are you so certain that this is a disaster and not some kind of blessing?"

After some time, his horse returned with a magnificent stallion following behind. His friends offered their congratulations, but the man was circumspect and asked, "How can you be so certain that this is not a calamity?"

The man's son loved to ride the stallion. One day the horse threw the boy, who fell and broke his hip. Everyone offered solace and comfort at the terrible misfortune that had befallen the lad and his father. The father replied, "We shall see if this is such a catastrophe."

Some time later, a band of marauding nomads invaded the region. All able-bodied men took up arms and went to fight against the threat. The lame son was unable to join in the battle, in which many lives were lost. Thus, he was able to care for his father in his old age. (Adapted from "The Lost Horse," in Roberts, 1979)

Mama and Papa Duck had seven ducklings. Six were ordinary, but the seventh was an unbelievably ugly duckling. People continually made nasty comments about just how ugly he was. However, he didn't let their remarks get to him because in his heart of hearts, he knew that one day he would probably become a really beautiful swan whom everyone would admire. Unfortunately, he was wrong. The ugly duckling turned out to be a really ugly duck. (Adapted from "The Really Ugly Duckling," in Scieszka & Smith, 1992)

The old monk advised a novice that the most dangerous thing in the world is a woman. "Never touch or talk to one. A woman is as dangerous as a tiger," he warned.

One day, as the novice went to fetch water, he stumbled and fell. A young woman found him and bandaged his injuries. This pleasant encounter led the novice to assume, "If a woman is like a tiger, then a tiger must be quite like a woman."

Later, when the young monk came across a tiger, he tried to befriend it, and the tiger attacked him. He barely escaped and realized that the old monk was wrong. (Adapted from Gao Wang, in Wren, 1990)

If your train's on the wrong track, every station you come to is the wrong station.—Bernard Malamud

Even if you're on the right track, you'll get run over if you just sit there.—Will Rogers

Redeeming Failed Efforts

A king owned the largest, purest, most magnificent diamond in the world. It was a stone that had no equal. Daily, he would admire and examine the gem. One day, he carelessly dropped it, creating a large flaw in the stone. Distraught, he called for the most skilled craftsmen in the kingdom and offered great riches to anyone who could erase the imperfection. But it was impossible to fix the stone.

One day, a craftsman who had heard about the scratched gem and the reward announced that he could make the stone more beautiful than before. Realizing that he had nothing to lose, the king set the man up in a workshop and had him begin work. For days, the craftsman diligently sat at his bench and worked on the diamond. Finally, he emerged from his seclusion and handed the diamond to the king. He had kept his word; it was now the most beautiful diamond imaginable. Instead of trying to remove the scratch, he had carved a graceful rosebud around the imperfection and used the scratch as its stem. (Adapted from an eighteenth-century story, "The Blemished Diamond," by the Maggid of Dubno, collected in Ausubel, 1948)

Abraham Lincoln was once rebuked by a woman for speaking forgivingly about the rebellious Southerners. Annoyed, she suggested that instead he ought to be thinking about destroying them.

Lincoln replied, "Why, madam, do I not destroy my enemies when I make them my friends?"
—Carl Sandburg, paraphrase

The precious diamond must be cut in order to show its luster. The sweet incense must be burned in order to inhale its fragrance. Adversity is like the periods of rain—cold, comfortless, unfriendly, yet from such seasons the flower and their fruit leave their birth. Stars may be seen from the bottom of a deep well when they cannot be discerned from the top of a mountain....Adversity has the effect of exciting talents which prosperity would permit to lie dormant. Prosperity is a great teacher, adversity is a greater one. Possession pampers the mind, privation trains and strengthens it.
—Rabbi Joseph Krauskopf

Redirecting Life

A college student in a premedical program did his best to get the highest grades and was admitted into the medical school of his choice. As a reward, his parents sent him to Japan for the summer. There he met a guru who told him that his sense of values was warped. The guru said, "Your greatest pleasure in life has been to overshadow your classmates. Getting an A so that your classmate gets a B in order for you to get a prized place in medical school is what gives you satisfaction. You will choose a mate and get married not because of love but because you will want to win the woman that everyone else wants. Your whole life is defined by competition, rivalry, and getting ahead. Come stay here in the ashram. You will see that it is different here: we all share; no one competes; everyone is happy."

Convinced of the need to change the way he lived his life, the young man called his parents and informed them that he was dropping out, despite their objections.

Six months later, the student wrote to his parents to tell them how ecstatic he was. He wrote: "I know you weren't delighted about the decision I made, but I must tell you how happy I am. For the first time in my life, I am at peace. There is no strife, no dissension among the members of the ashram and no dissonance in my soul. We all share equally. We all love each other. The way of life is so much in harmony with the inner essence of my soul that in only six months I have become the #2 disciple in the ashram and I think I can be #1 by June." (Adapted from Kushner, 1991)

A Polish Jew was unhappy living in Poland and applied for a visa to emigrate to Israel. He went to Israel but concluded that he couldn't adjust; he was unhappy there as well. He got permission to travel back to Poland. Alas, it didn't work out this time, either. Once again, he traveled back to Israel.

When the second trip to Israel didn't prove satisfying, the man requested permission to return to Poland. The exasperated Israeli immigration officer said, "You are not happy in Poland so you travel to Israel. You are not happy in Israel so you travel to Poland. So when are you happy?"

The man smiled and said, "That's easy. When I am traveling!" (Adapted from Israel, 1993)

Mickey Mantle, star player of the New York Yankees, was once in a hitting slump. Each time he struck out, he walked into the dugout and kicked the water cooler. After watching this behavior several times, Casey Stengel, manager of the team, went over to Mantle and said,

"Mickey, it ain't that water cooler that's gettin' you out." (Source unknown)

Before you study Zen, a bowl is a bowl and tea is tea. While you are studying Zen, a bowl is no longer a bowl and tea is no longer tea. After you've studied Zen, a bowl is again a bowl and tea is tea.—Zen proverb

We are not creatures of circumstance, we are creators of circumstance.—Benjamin Disraeli

People often say that this or that person has not yet found himself. But the self is not something that one finds. It is something that one creates.—Thomas Szasz

Even for the neurotic executive—as for everyone else—work has great therapeutic value; it is generally his last refuge, and deterioration there marks the final collapse of the man, his marriage, his social life, and the outside interests—all have suffered beforehand.—Richard A. Smith

Reframing

A king had twin sons, one a pessimist, the other an optimist. When he died, one of the twins would be the new king. A panel of judges would designate as leader whichever son won the debate over whether the kingdom was good or bad.

The pessimist pointed to the starving peasants as proof that the kingdom was bad. The optimist said that their starvation made them into better people because they learned the value of patience.

Upon seeing a blind man, the pessimist observed that a world in which God allows people to go blind is a terrible place. The optimist's rejoinder was that blindness strengthened the blind man's other senses.

Finally, the twins came upon a man who was dying alone in the street. The pessimist stated that the world was a terrible place because no one stopped to help the dying. The optimist countered, "Everyone dies sooner or later. Death is not an enemy, but a friend."

The judges announced that they were in favor of the optimist but would allow the pessimist one more opportunity to state his case. The pessimist asked the

---

A lady was concerned about her cat Ginger's ability to stay cooped up on a train for a two-day trip. She asked the veterinarian to give Ginger some tranquilizers to prevent the animal from getting too upset.

Once on board the train, the medicated Ginger went berserk, broke out of her cage, and, with bulging eyes and hair standing on edge, leapt about the lady's compartment hissing, yowling, clawing everything, and terrorizing the other passengers. A second dose of the pills provided no relief.

The veterinarian discovered that he had inadvertently prescribed amphetamines instead of tranquilizers. With dismay and trepidation, he called the woman and inquired how the trip had gone.

"I appreciate your call, doctor," she said. "Ginger was dreadful on the train. I cannot imagine how much worse she would have been without the pills. I am grateful to you for your help." With modesty, the doctor accepted her thanks.—David Treadway, paraphrase

Procrustes, one of six bandits encountered by Theseus on the road to Athens, terrorized travelers by means of his iron bed. Weary travelers were offered a place to sleep, but the offer was not risk-free. If the traveler was too short for the bed, he would be stretched; if he was too tall, his extremities were amputated.

A shoe company wanted to expand its sales into Africa. It sent one salesman to East Africa and a second to West Africa. The salesman in the east sent a cable, "Forget about doing business here—no one wears shoes."

The salesman in the west responded, "Great place to do business—no one wears shoes."—Andy Zipser

Thomas Edison failed over and over before he finally perfected the storage battery. When asked how it felt to have failed innumerable times in his experiments, the great inventor replied, "I have not failed even once, because now I know several thousand things that don't work." —Edmund Fuller, paraphrase

You will not grow if you sit in a beautiful flower garden, but you will grow if you are sick, if you are in pain, if you experience losses, and if you do not put your head in the sand, but take the pain and learn to accept it, not as a curse or punishment but as a gift to you with a very, very specific purpose.—Elisabeth Kübler-Ross

judges if they thought the blind man was better off because he was blind. In unison they answered, "Yes." He requested that they close their eyes and asked if patience was better than food. Again, they answered, "Yes!"

He asked that they all keep their eyes closed until he commanded them to open them. Then he drew his sword and slaughtered his brother. When he asked them to open their eyes, they were aghast to see the optimistic brother dead.

"I have won the debate," the pessimistic brother exclaimed. "Your blindness impeded you from preventing this murder; being patient prevented you from opening your eyes. Thus, neither is good. Furthermore, if people are better off dead, then my brother is better off. Therefore, you must proclaim me king." And they did. (Adapted from "The Optimist and the Pessimist: A Fable," by Flood, 1990)

Resistance to Change

She was the fourth in line in her family to be called Anna. Like her mother, grandmother, and great-grandmother, she lived in the old family farmhouse filled with the treasured possessions of those who had lived before her. She slept under a quilt sewn by her great-grandmother, in a bed built by her great-grandfather. The dishes in the cupboards were those of another great-grandmother, and the walls were covered with pictures of aunts and uncles and other family members long gone.

Anna did things in the ways her family had done for generations. Her garden was in the same place that her parents had had their garden. The morning glory continued to entwine the white picket fence that encircled the yard. New plants were always grown with seeds saved from the previous summer.

When Rabbi Hayyim Halberstram of Zans was young, his ambition was to preach to everyone in his country in order to get them to change their ways. But when he reached the age of thirty and evil was still all about him, he thought that perhaps he had been too ambitious, and thereafter limited his labor to his own region of the country. By age forty, no more successful than before, he decided to limit his activities to his own community. When his community had not changed by the time he was fifty, he decided to focus his attention on his family. But his family had grown and moved away, leaving him by himself. This made him realize that he should have begun with himself in the first place. For the rest of his life, he concentrated on improving himself. (Adapted from "Begin with Yourself," in Buber, 1948)

It came to me that reform should begin at home, and since that day I have not had time to remake the world.—Will Durant

Consider how hard it is to change yourself, and you'll understand what little chance you have of trying to change someone else.—Jacob M. Braude

The reasonable man adapts himself to the world; the unreasonable one persists in trying to adapt the world to himself. Therefore, all progress depends on the unreasonable man.—George Bernard Shaw

Plus ça change, plus c'est la même chose.
The more things change, the more they remain the same.—French proverb

Some things did change, however. Anna kept her car in the barn where her grandfather had sheltered his cows. She froze produce from her garden, whereas her grandmother had canned fruits and vegetables and her great-grandmother had set things out to dry in the sun. The retired washboard hung near her washer and dryer. Although the sense of the past was comforting, Anna would freely admit that at times it was stifling.

In the far corner of Anna's yard was a strange and beautiful tree. According to family legend, the seeds for the tree had been a gift to her great-great-great-grandfather from a gypsy king in return for some unremembered kindness. That was why everyone called it the "gypsy king's tree." It was a very tall tree with no branches near the ground. The leaves were of a unique shape that Anna had never seen anywhere else. When the tree flowered in late May, the blossoms perfumed the air for miles around.

Family legend held that when the gypsy king had given the seeds to Anna's great-great-great-grandfather, he promised that the tree's fruit was magic. He said, "Anyone who eats the fruit will have an exciting life filled with adventure and opportunity."

This promise was not easily realized. Although the tree bloomed profusely every year, it only bore fruit every five years. Even then, it produced only about a dozen fruits of a bright golden color with a rose blush on one side. Moreover, when these fruits fell from the tree, they would seem to disintegrate instantly. Thus, to eat a piece of the tree's fruit, a person actually had to catch it as it fell.

Because the tree was tall without low branches, it was impossible to climb without a long ladder. Therefore, it was not a surprise that no one from Anna's family had ever eaten one of the fruits, except Anna's grandmother's brother, Frank, who simply left one day and was never heard from again. He was the only family member who had not stayed near the family homestead. No one knew whether or not he had actually eaten the fruit, but her grandmother told Anna that he had spent a lot of time sitting under the tree waiting for the fruit to fall.

One year, in the fall, Anna watched the fruit from her bedroom window. There were eleven fruits that year: five the size of softballs, one very large one, and the rest the size of small green apples. The yellow ones were ripe and were ready to fall at any time. Watching them and thinking about their taste prevented Anna from getting much done. She spent a lot of time under the tree daydreaming. She even slept under its branches for a couple of nights.

Of course, Anna never believed the story. How could a piece of fruit provide adventure and opportunity? Thinking that the fruit would taste wonderful, she studied a way to get to the top of the tree. She thought she might get some boards, nail them to the trunk, and climb up this improvised ladder. Or she could throw a rope with a rock tied to one end up to one of the high branches and climb to the top. Perhaps she could entice the fire department to do her work. After all, it occasionally got cats out of trees. Why wouldn't it come to harvest one piece of fruit?

Then again, Anna thought the fruit probably was not worth all that bother. Most likely it was bitter, perhaps even poisonous. She might get scratched up or break her neck. At the very least, the neighbors would think that she was crazy. She really didn't think she believed the story. And even if she did, who in her right mind would want to change a safe, comfortable life for adventure? She could not imagine what that might be like. "Not as nice as staying put," she concluded.

The next day, she thought she would call in sick to work because the biggest fruit looked as though it might fall at any minute. It had been wobbling in the wind the previous night, and she thought she would sit there, just in case. (Adapted from "The Gypsy King's Tree," by A. Klassen, in Jorgensen, 1992)

Restraining the Workaholic

A hard-working peasant could never get ahead because he did not own any land. Hearing that a neighboring widow planned to sell her land, he and his wife sold most of their possessions, borrowed what they could, and managed to scrape together enough to buy a small piece of that land. Within a year, the peasant's hard work had paid off. He was free of debt and had become somewhat prosperous.

One day, the peasant heard that fertile land in a more remote area could be acquired cheaply. He sold his land, packed up his family, and bought a larger farm in the interior of the country. Soon he was ten times better off than he had been before.

He heard that by going into an even more remote area of the country and making friends with the rulers who controlled the area, he would be able to buy much land for a few rubles an acre. Thinking of how much land he could acquire and the wealth he could amass, the peasant left his family to manage his farm and headed off to acquire an even larger spread of land.

One day, a poor woman with many children found an egg. She told her children that they would not eat the egg but ask a neighbor to put it under one of his hens. She continued, "When it hatches we will not eat the chicken, it will produce more eggs, which will hatch into more chicks. Then we will buy a cow. We will not eat the cow, but wait until it has calves. With the proceeds from the sale of the calves, we will buy a field. Then we will have chickens, cows, and a field, and we won't want for anything anymore."

While she spoke in this reverie, the egg fell out of her hands and broke! (Adapted from a story of Rabbi Hayyim Halberstram of Zans, collected in Agnon, 1948)

You never know what is enough unless you know what is more than enough.
—William Blake

I never met anyone who said, "I should have spent more time at the office."—J. Zink

Andrew Carnegie, at one time the wealthiest man in the world, amassed his tremendous fortune by making steel. When asked why he didn't stop working long after he had more wealth than he could possibly ever need, he replied, "I didn't know how to stop." (Source unknown)

He who knows that enough is enough will always have enough.—Lao-tzu

After befriending the chiefs of that land and giving them generous gifts, the peasant received permission to acquire whatever land he wished. The price was the same as it was for anybody else: one thousand rubles a day.

The peasant was puzzled. A thousand rubles a day? What kind of measure was that for a land purchase?

The chief clarified the conditions. "For that price, you can have as much land as you can walk around in one day. The only condition," he added, "is that you must return to the spot where you started on that day."

All night, the peasant began planning how he would use the land and how he would sell a portion of it to recover his cost. Delighted at the prospect of good fortune, he began early the next day, marking all the land he intended to acquire. He walked quickly and took no time to rest. As he hurried along, he would admire additional acreage and make a brief detour to include it as well. As his greed got the better of him, he realized he might not have enough time to return to the starting point. Winded, with his heart pounding, he raced back toward his starting point. Thinking he would be a fool to stop, he continued toward the goal as the sun began to drop below the horizon. With his remaining strength, he lunged at the mark and fell forward just at the moment when the sun dropped below the horizon.

"You have gained much land," said a chief with a sense of irony, for when they tried to help the peasant up, blood streamed from his mouth, and he died. They dug a grave on that very spot in a six-foot swath of land, just large enough for him to be buried in. (Adapted from "How Much Land Does a Man Need?," in Tolstoy, 1886/1983)

Satisfaction versus Discontent

A man decided to give up his worldly possessions and live a monastic life. The abbot advised him that he would be allowed to utter only two words every five years.

At the end of five years, the novice was summoned to the abbot. With bowed head, he uttered his allotted words: "Bed hard."

After another five years of silence, once again he stood before the abbot, who asked, "What have you got to say for yourself?" The man replied: "Food lousy."

At the end of the fifteenth year, the scene was repeated. The man said: "Miss friends."

When twenty years had passed, the man was eligible to become a full-fledged member of the order. The abbot asked him what he would like to say with his two words. The man said: "Going home." The abbot replied: "Quite frankly, I'm not surprised. All you've done is complain from the minute you set foot in this place." (Source unknown)

When I was young and free and my imagination had no limits, I dreamed of changing the world. As I grew older and wiser, I discovered the world would not change, so I shortened my sights somewhat and decided to change only my country.

But it, too, seemed immovable.

As I grew into my twilight years, in one last desperate attempt, I settled for changing only my family, those closest to me, but alas, they would have none of it.

And now as I lie on my deathbed, I suddenly realize: *If I had only changed my self first*, then by example I would have changed my family.

From their inspiration and encouragement, I would then have been able to better my country and, who knows, I may have even changed the world. (Tomb inscription in Westminster Abbey from the year 1100, in Canfield and Hansen, 1993)

Most of the shadows of this life are caused by standing in one's own sunshine.—Ralph Waldo Emerson

Spirituality

Princess Eleanor always got whatever she wanted. Every one of her whims was fulfilled by order of her father, the king. Consequently, Eleanor never cried. One day she said to her father, "I want to see God."

"God? But no one has ever seen God," her father said.

"That is exactly why I want to see God," Eleanor replied with a sweet smile.

"If that is what you want, that is what you shall get," he told her.

The king asked his chief judge to show God to Eleanor. The judge led Eleanor to the royal library where the Great Book of Law was kept. "This book contains all the laws in the kingdom. It is as good as God," he stated.

Eleanor was not impressed. She stamped her foot and insisted that the book was not God.

Next, the king called on the royal treasurer and asked him to show God to Eleanor. "Very well," he replied as he led the princess off to the royal treasury.

The treasurer unlocked the lock, swung open the thick iron doors, and showed Eleanor all the glistening gold. "But I want to see God, not just a pile of gold," she bellowed.

The king wondered how to fulfill Eleanor's wish. Then, while taking a walk, he noticed an old man planting a tree. "Do you expect to live long enough to enjoy the fruit from that tree, old man?" the king asked.

"No, but I hope my grandchildren will enjoy it, God willing," he answered.

"God willing?" the king repeated. Then he asked the old man, "Do you know where to find God?"

The old man answered with a question: "Don't you?"

"I am not sure," the king replied. "My daughter wants to see God. Could you show God to her?"

The old man agreed. When Eleanor arrived, she demanded to see God and threatened the man with all kinds of dire consequences if he did not fulfill his promise. "Not so fast," said the old man. "First you must come with me."

They walked to a ramshackle hut at the far end of town. The old man knocked on the door and told the princess to go in. She pushed the door open. She had never seen such poverty before. Sitting at a table was a little girl dressed in old, mended, worn clothing. Eleanor ordered the girl to rise in the presence of the princess. But the girl was crippled and unable to stand.

God granted a man one wish, to do good without knowing it. God thought that this was such a splendid idea that the wish was granted to all human beings.—Sufi tale

The higher goal of spiritual living is not to amass a wealth of information, but to face sacred moments.—Abraham Joshua Heschel

The disciples of Menachem Mendl of Kotzk asked him where God is to be found. He replied, "Wherever people are willing to let him in." (Buber, 1948)

The longest journey is the journey inward. —Dag Hammarskjöld

Eleanor's head began to spin as she backed out of the hut and closed the door behind her. Silently, the two returned to the palace. The princess had completely forgotten about herself and her demand to see God. Seeing this, the old man smiled and said, "Now you are ready."

He handed the princess a mirror and asked her to look deep inside her soul. For the first time in her life, the princess who never cried had tears rolling down her cheeks. The old man asked Princess Eleanor why she was crying.

"All my life I have been selfish and have thought only of myself. I never realized how selfish I was! Do you think it would help if I brought that girl some food and some warm clothes to wear?" she asked.

The old man put the mirror away and said, "Now you have seen God." (Adapted from "The Princess Who Wanted to See God," in Cone, 1965)

Symptom Prescription

A dying woman warned her husband that because she loved him so much, she would come back to haunt him if he ever took another wife. He promised that he would remain faithful to her even after she was dead.

When she died, he heeded her precaution for several months, but the loneliness was more than he could bear. He met and fell in love with another woman and proposed marriage.

From that moment on, the ghost of his dead wife appeared nightly. She berated him for not keeping his promise. The ghost had a frightening ability to describe in detail everything that had taken place between him and his fiancée. She could even repeat their conversations word for word.

A princess refused to talk, much to the chagrin of her father. The king posted signs throughout the kingdom proclaiming that anyone who could get the girl to talk could take her for a wife. The only danger was that failure meant certain death. Many tried and many died.

One day, however, a young man who came from poor peasant stock requested an opportunity to try. When he was put in the room with the princess, he said nothing to her and did not even acknowledge her presence. They both sat in different corners of the room in complete silence until the fellow picked up a candlestick and began to talk to it.

"What do you think you are doing?" the princess demanded. "Are you crazy? You can't talk to a candlestick."

"Mind your own business," he replied. "Nobody asked your opinion."

She thought for a moment and said, "If you are talking to a candlestick, you must be crazy."

The palace guards overheard the conversation and reported the events to the monarch, and so the young man won the woman for his wife. (Adapted from "The Princess Who Refused to Talk," in Sadeh, 1989)

As a child, businessman William H. Danforth was frail and sick. His teacher's challenge changed his life: "I dare you to become the strongest boy in this class." Danforth not only succeeded, but lived a life of tireless energy. Through his book, *I Dare You*, he inspired thousands of others to achieve their best, both physically and spiritually.

You can become strongest in your weakest place. (Source unknown)

Despairing that he would be visited forever, the man sought the advice of a Zen master. The Zen master commented on the cleverness of the wife's ghost. He suggested that the man flatter the ghost and tell her how impressed he was that she knew everything. Then he suggested that the man strike a bargain with her: If she would answer a single question, the man would break his engagement and remain single.

He advised the man to take a handful of beans and ask her exactly how many he had in his hand. If she was unable to answer the question, she was a figment of his imagination and would disappear. And that is exactly what happened. (Adapted from "The Subjugation of a Ghost," in Reps, 1961)

Taking Risks

Two brothers journeyed through a forest, where they found a stone with this inscription on it: "The finder of this stone must go deeper into the forest at sunrise, swim to the other side of a river, capture two bear cubs, run up a mountain with them until he comes to a house. In the house he will find happiness."

The younger of the two tried to convince his older brother to set off with him, but the older brother had a litany of excuses why he could not: They could not be sure that the message was true; they might never find the river; even if they found the river, it might be too difficult to ford; the mother bear might attack when her cubs were taken; and they had no idea what kind of happiness they would find.

Convinced of the validity of the stone's message, the younger brother set off on his quest. He accomplished each of the tasks described on the stone. When he reached the house on the mountain, people came out to greet him and declared him king.

In the late 1800s, a bishop visited a college and stayed at the home of its president, a professor of physics and chemistry. The bishop was convinced that humankind was close to the millennium because everything in nature had been discovered and all possible inventions had been invented.

The president politely disagreed and predicted that within the next fifty years people would learn to fly.

The bishop broke out into laughter. "Rubbish, my dear man!" he exclaimed. "If God had intended us to fly, he would have provided us with wings. Flight is reserved for the birds and the angels."

Accordingly, Bishop Wright never invented the airplane, but his sons, Wilbur and Orville, did. (Source unknown)

In ancient times there lived a man who, above all things, prized his heart. It was his most valued possession and noblest motive of his life. Concerned that it might become bruised and calloused accompanying him on his daily rounds, he determined a method for its safekeeping. Tenderly, he placed it in a cushioned vault, protected by layers of steel, away from the jars and bruises of life. He rejoiced in this happy decision; had he not protected the most sublime aspect of his being?

The long-awaited day of reconciliation finally arrived. Trembling with anticipation, he reached into the open vault.

But the heart no longer fit. He was too old, and his heart was too young. They had not grown together. (Adapted from Matz, 1959)

The newly elected king ruled for only five years when another king defeated him and he was forced to flee and wander. One day, he happened upon his brother's village. The two embraced and told all that had befallen them. The older brother was just as he had been when the younger brother left. The younger brother spoke of his great adventure and of losing his kingdom. Thereupon, the older brother insisted that he had been right all along. But the brother who had served as king did not regret what had happened one bit. He responded, "I have nothing now, but I will always remember what happened to me. You, however, have no memories at all." (Adapted from "The Two Brothers," in Tolstoy, 1962)

Transcending the Past

A poor, unsuccessful fisherman, after fishing junk out of the sea, finally hauled in a copper bottle. When he opened the bottle, a puff of smoke and a genie emerged. The genie threatened to kill the fisherman. Despite all the fisherman's pleas, the genie would not relent. The fisherman taunted the genie by thinking aloud that he did not believe he ever could have fit into such a small jar. To prove that he was incorrect, the genie returned to the bottle, and the fisherman replaced the top and threw him back into the ocean. (Adapted from "The Fisherman and the Jinny," in Mathers, 1980)

Film director Robert Mitchum was asked how he had succeeded in marriage for thirty years when so many of his show-business colleagues had failed miserably. He responded, "Mutual forbearance. We have each continued to believe that the other will do better tomorrow." (Adapted from Fadiman, 1985)

The situation reached the height of the ludicrous when I suddenly realized one day that of everything I had written about the man I could just as well have said the opposite. I had indubitably reached that dead end which lies so artfully hidden in the phrase "the meaning of meaning."—Henry Miller

The Unexpected Nature of Change

A church was in decline. Worshippers no longer came to pray; gifts and contributions were no longer received; the monastery was decrepit; novices no longer applied for training and admission into the order; only four brothers remained in residence. All were at a loss to know how to recover from these problems or how to reverse the decline. The brothers became cruel and unkind to one another and would speak to each other only when necessary.

Near the monastery was a rundown shack used by the local rabbi for study and prayer. The brothers, desperate about their situation, went to the rabbi. He commiserated with them and acknowledged that they were all living in an age of little faith. He said that he was having the same kind of problems with his own community and that there was nothing he could suggest to improve their situation. As the dejected brothers were about to leave, the rabbi added that although he could not tell them how to solve the problem, there was one thing he could tell them. He said, "One of you four is the Messiah."

From that day forward, nothing at the monastery was ever the same. Now the brothers were as polite as could be, treating each other with dignity and respect. Their kindness did not go unnoticed in the surrounding town, as individuals began to make pilgrimages to pray and to speak with the kind brothers. People began to bring gifts and help restore the dilapidated building. Soon the monastery looked quite successful. The brothers never understood that it was the rabbi's simple statement that had set this chain of events in motion. (Adapted from "The Rabbi's Gift," in Peck, 1987)

Nothing in life is more exciting and rewarding than the sudden flash of insight that leaves you a changed person—not only changed, but for the better.—Arthur Gordon

Meteorologist Edward Lorenz explicated the concept of the compound effect of minute changes on complex systems. A single, imperceptible factor can have a profound influence on systems of all kinds. Changes magnify and intensify as they move from their points of origin. For example, two cars traveling in the same direction at 59- and 60-miles per hour, respectively, will, at the end of a complete day, have a distance between them of twenty-four miles. The notion suggests that imperceptible events can have meaning beyond that which is immediately apparent. He coined the term *butterfly effect* to suggest that a butterfly that flapped its wings in Brazil might produce a tornado in Texas. (Stewart, 1992)

How true it is that our destinies are decided by nothings and that a small imprudence helped by some insignificant accident, as an acorn is fertilized by a drop of rain, may raise the trees on which perhaps we and others shall be crucified.—Henri Frederic Amiel

The Uses of Paradox

A king suffering from an unknown malady offered half his kingdom for a cure. Only one sage accepted the offer. He advised, "Find a happy man, put his shirt on the king, and he will be healed." The king's envoys searched in vain. No one could be found who was truly happy. If a man was rich, he hoped for greater wealth; the healthy person was poor; the destitute were jealous of their neighbors. The list of complaints about children, spouses, in-laws, careers, and wealth seemed endless.

One night, the king's son overheard a poor man thanking God because the day had gone well. He prayed, "My work is done. I had enough to feed my family. I am truly happy!"

The king's son ordered that the man be given whatever he wanted for his shirt, but when his agent went to collect the prized garment, he discovered that the man had no shirt. (Adapted from "The King and the Shirt," in Tolstoy, 1962)

Despite months of scrimping and saving, Della had so little money for a Christmas gift for Jim that she despaired of ever being able to get him the watch fob for the pocket watch which had been handed down from his grandfather to his father to Jim. Della sobbed at the thought of not being able to purchase the gift she knew would give him joy.

Pensively, she looked at herself in the mirror, focused on her cascade of knee-length brown hair, quickly put on her jacket, and went out. At a shop with a sign that read "Hair Goods of All Kinds," Della hurriedly entered and asked the proprietor to buy her hair. The woman studied Della's hair and offered her twenty dollars for it. On her way home, Della purchased a gold chain to replace Jim's worn, leather fob.

When Jim arrived home, he seemed stunned at what Della had done. Della told Jim that she had cut and sold her hair because she could not live through Christmas without giving him a gift. Pensively, Jim removed a package from his coat pocket and said to Della, "There is no way that a haircut could make me love you any less. But if you unwrap this package, you will see why I was so startled."

Della's delicate fingers tore at the string and paper. When she saw the contents, she let out a scream of joy, which was followed by streams of tears. There on the table was the set of bejeweled, tortoise-shell hair combs she had hoped for. She comforted Jim by saying that her hair would soon grow in. Then Della gave Jim his gift and asked that he take out his watch so that she could show him how beautiful the gold chain would look. Jim tried to change the subject. When Della insisted, he suggested that they put their gifts away. Finally Jim told Della that he had sold his watch to buy her the hair combs. (Adapted from "The Gift of the Magi," by O. Henry, in Porter 1907)

The young samurai warrior stood respectfully before the aged Zen master and, in a voice accustomed to instant obedience ordered, "Master, teach me about heaven and hell." With a look of disgust, the master said: "Teach you about heaven and hell? I couldn't teach you about anything. You are dirty. You smell. Your sword is rusty. You are an ignorant fool who is a disgrace to the samurai class! How dare you suppose that you could understand anything that I might have to say!"

The old man went on and on, becoming even more insulting and abusive, while the young swordsman's surprise turned first to confusion and then to hot anger. Master or no master, who could insult a samurai and live? With teeth clenched and in a fury, the warrior blindly drew his sword, and prepared to end the old man's sharp tongue and life in one quick motion. The master looked straight into his eyes and quietly said, "That's hell."

The samurai realized that the master had hounded him into a living hell, driven by uncontrolled anger and ego. The young man, profoundly humbled, sheathed his sword and bowed low to this great spiritual teacher. Looking up into the wise man's time-worn face, he felt love and compassion for the man. At that moment the master raised a finger and said, "And that's heaven." (Adapted from Dass & Gorman, 1988)

The Chinese word *maodun*, meaning "contradiction," is written by combining the characters for *spear* and *shield*. It originated in a folktale of an arms seller who bragged that his spears were so sharp that they could penetrate anything and his shields were so sturdy that they would repel anything. A suspicious customer asked what would be the result of using his spears against his shields. The seller could not answer. (Adapted from Wren, 1990)

An old man, listening to the pitter-patter of rain, thought of both the melancholy and joyous sounds of the storm. He thought of the inconvenience of traveling in inclement weather and the life-giving moisture the rain brings. He remembered that, to some, this is a source of annoyance; but it is essential for all growing things. As his mind flowed to these confluences of sound and thought, he recalled something his father had told him as a child. "There is sadness in beauty," the father said. "When you understand that, you will no longer be a boy." (Source unknown)

The test of a first-rate intelligence is the ability to hold two opposed ideas in mind at the same time, and still retain the ability to function. —F. Scott Fitzgerald, in *The Crack Up*

Every psychological extreme secretly contains its own opposite, or stands in some sort of intimate and essential relation to it.—Carl Jung

Waiting for a Miracle: Resistance to Help

As the flood waters began to rise, the man took great comfort in his faith that God would not allow any harm to befall him. A group of emergency workers knocked on his door and tried to persuade him to evacuate. He responded to their offer of help by saying that they need not worry because God would protect him.

The waters continued to rise, and the man retreated to the second story of his home. A rescue team came by boat to his window and urged him to come with them. Still steadfast in his faith, he declined their offer, saying, "I have faith that God will save me."

Finally, the rising water forced the man to seek sanctuary on the roof of his home. Shortly thereafter, a helicopter hovered over him and let down a ladder. The rescue worker shouted for him to climb up to safety. Again, he waved the help away.

The waters continued to rise. Finally the man was swept away by the raging waters and died. When he appeared before God, he was quite angry. "God," he asked, "how could you have allowed this to happen to me? I had faith that you would preserve me from harm. Why didn't you save me?"

"Save you?" God incredulously replied. "I tried to. I sent a rescue team, a boat, and a helicopter." (Source unknown)

Pray as if everything depends on God. Act as if everything depends on you.—Gates of Prayer (Stern, 1975)

It is a funny thing about life; if you refuse to accept anything but the best, you very often get it.—W. Somerset Maugham

Don't wait for your ship to come in; swim out to meet it. (Source unknown)

Glossary

Analogic communication   The communication that occurs when individual components of information are amassed to create a complex, context-specific message. Analogic communications contain multiple referents. Analogic communication occurs in and corresponds to the structures and functions of the right hemisphere of the brain.

Anchoring   The process by which the therapist utilizes a sensory stimulus, because of its relationship to past experiences, feelings, sights, or sounds, to evoke consistent responses.

Archetypes   A Jungian concept of universal motifs found in the unconscious, which may reflect, influence, or explain all behavior.

Ashram   A dwelling, often secluded, of a Hindu or other Eastern sage, in which disciples receive instruction and may also live in a communal setting.

Baal Shem Tov   The Hebrew term *baal shem*, literally "master of the name," was frequently given to mystical figures who were believed to possess secret knowledge of God. Israel ben Eliezer (1700–1760), the founder of the Hasidic movement, was thought to possess such remarkable powers and theological insights that the word *tov*, meaning "good," was added to the title *baal shem*. The resulting title, "master of the good name," indicated unusual status.

Baptism   Although the ritual practice differs from church to church, this ceremony initiates an individual into the history and community of Christian faith, thus enabling full participation in ritual and worship.

Bicameral   Describing the existence of two hemispheres of the brain.

Canalization   Term used by Jung to describe the process by which psychic energy becomes channeled, converted, and transformed to help ensure the fulfillment of desired goals.

Charter myths   Stories that validate aspects of a society's cultural norms.

Collective unconscious   A Jungian concept maintaining that all peoples, regardless of their cultural origins, manifest one corpus of aboriginal mythological associations.

Conversational trance   An altered state of consciousness, akin to daydreaming, also referred to as a "light" or "everyday" trance. In this state, an individual is keenly aware of inner mental and sensory experiences as well as of external stimuli.

Digital communication   Communication that occurs when individual components of information are processed as discrete units, each with a specific referent. Digital communication occurs in and corresponds to the structures and functions of the left hemisphere of the brain.

Dubner Maggid   Title given to the eighteenth-century Jewish preacher Jacob Kranz. *Maggid* means "storyteller." Kranz was from the eastern European city of Dubno(w).

Embedded message/command   Term describing a technique for providing emphasis and client direction in the delivery of a metaphor by the insertion of a word, name, or phrase into a sentence. This may provide multiple-level communication. Also referred to as "seeding," it is analogous to the terms *priming* or *cueing* used in experimental psychology, or to "foreshadowing" in literature.

Eucharist   A Christian ritual in which celebrants consume wine and a wafer that is believed by the faithful to have been transubstantiated into the blood and body of Jesus.

Functionalism   Term used by Malinowski to indicate that all of society is interdependent and that all cultural material serves to assure the survival of the cultural institutions.

Haggadah   Prayer book used at the Passover celebration, called a *seder*. The book, which relates the story of the Exodus of the Israelites from Egypt, has its origin in the Roman period.

Hasidic movement, Hasidism   An eighteenth-century Jewish faction founded in Poland by the *Baal Shem Tov*, based on the notion that God could be found not only through traditional forms of worship, but also by means of song, story, dance, and ecstatic prayer. The movement spread rapidly through eastern Europe because it proved to be an antidote to the oppressive conditions under which Jews were living.

Interspersal   A technique of metaphor delivery that includes the use of focused words, phrases, and sentences selected for the symbolism they evoke in the individual to whom they are directed.

Isomorphic   Characteristic of a metaphor that closely mirrors or parallels another situation, experience, or problem.

Left hemisphere of the brain   The center of order, logic, and clearly defined rules, often associated with digital communication.

Maggid   An itinerant storyteller who traveled through the Jewish communities of Eastern Europe in the eighteenth and nineteenth centuries.

Matzah   Flat, unleavened bread consumed during the festival of Passover. Called the "bread of affliction," it is said to have originated when the Israelites left Egypt in such haste that they did not have sufficient time to allow their bread to rise.

Midrash   Term meaning "to expound," and referring to the numerous collections of Jewish law and lore. These collections include sermonic material designed to elucidate a fine point of law or to expand material found in the Bible.

Modality   An individual's preferred communication style, either visual, auditory, or kinesthetic (emotional).

Neurolinguistic programming   A therapeutic approach that applies the client's favored sensory modality of information reception toward the reframing, transformation, and reorientation of experiences and problems.

Pacing   A technique whereby a therapist emulates some aspect of the client's language or behavior to enhance the therapeutic relationship between them.

Packaging   The indirect presentation of an idea through delivery of an appropriate metaphor may enable the therapist to bypass a client's resistance.

Passover   Jewish religious festival that commemorates the deliverance of the Israelites from Egyptian slavery almost four millennia ago. Modern-day observance is largely home-centered, although synagogue worship is a component of the observance as well.

Qur'an   The holy book of Islam.

Reframing   The shifting of an experience from one conceptual or emotional context to another, thereby changing the entire meaning of the experience or problem.

Right hemisphere of the brain   The center of emotion, symbol, imagery, and narrative, often associated with analogic communication.

Seeding   See *Embedded message/command.*

Talmud   The great rabbinic compendium of Jewish law, custom, and practice, written over a period of several hundred years. Two distinct editions were written, one in Babylonia and one in Jerusalem. A reference to the Talmud generally refers to the Babylonian edition, which is far more extensive than the Jerusalem edition.

Transderivational search   Also termed "inner search," this process encourages patients to use both their conscious and unconscious mind to make sense of a message or metaphor.

Ultradian cycle   A ninety-minute, recurring sequence of body rhythms during which an individual may enter a light trance.

Bibliography

Aarne, A., & Thompson, S. (1964). *The types of the folktale: A classification and bibliography, rev. ed.* Folklore Fellows Communications No. 184. Helsinki: Suomalainen Tiedeakatemia.

Abusch, T. (1993). Gilgamesh's request and Siduri's denial: Part II: An analysis and interpretation of an Old Babylonian fragment about mourning and celebration. *Journal of the Ancient Near Eastern Society of Columbia University, 22,* 3–17.

Afanas'ev, A. (1945). *Russian fairy tales.* Translated by N. Guterman. New York: Pantheon Books.

Agnon, S. (1948). *Days of awe: A treasury of traditions, legends, and learned commentaries concerning Rosh Hashanah, Yom Kippur and the days between.* New York: Schocken Books.

Ahlberg, J., & Ahlberg, A. (1987). *The clothes horse and other stories.* New York: Viking Kestral, Penguin.

Anderson, W. (1951). *Ein volkskundliches experiment.* Helsinki: FF Communications.

Aristotle. (1972). *Poetics.* Translated by M. Hubbard. In D. Russell & M. Winterbottom (Eds.), *Ancient literary criticism.* Oxford: Oxford University Press.

Ausubel, N. (1948). *Treasury of Jewish folklore: The stories, traditions, legends, humor, wisdom and folk songs of the Jewish people.* New York: Crown.

Bacon, F. (1597/1937). *The essays or councels, civill and morall of Francis Lo. Vervlam, Viscount St. Alban: newly written.* London: Oxford University Press.

Baird, R. (1989, Fall). Picturing God. *Journal of Religion and Health, 28*(3), 223–239.

Bal, M. (1991). *On story-telling: essays in narratology.* Sonoma, CA: Polebridge Press.

Bandler, R., & Grinder, J. (1975). *The structure of magic, Vol. 1.* Palo Alto: Science and Behavior.

Bandler, R., & Grinder, J. (1979). *Frogs into princes: Neurolinguistic programming.* Moab, UT: Real People Press.

Barker, P. (1985). *Using metaphors in psychotherapy.* New York: Brunner/Mazel.

Bateson, G. (1979). *Mind and nature: A necessary unity.* New York: Dutton.

Bateson, G., & Bateson, M. (1987). *Angels fear: Towards an epistemology of the sacred.* New York: Macmillan.

Bateson, M. (1989). Mary Catherine Bateson, anthropologist. In B. Moyers, *A world of ideas: Conversations with thoughtful men and women about American life today and the ideas shaping our future.* (Ed. B. Flowers). New York: Doubleday.

Bateson, M. (1991). *Composing a life.* Audiotape. Washington, DC: Common Boundary.

Beck, B., Claus, P., Goswami, P., & Handoo, J. (1987). *Folktales of India.* Chicago: University of Chicago Press.

Bennett, W. (Ed.). (1993). *The book of virtues: A treasury of great moral stories.* New York: Simon & Schuster.

Bergman, J. (1985). *Fishing for barracuda: Pragmatics of brief systemic therapy.* New York: W. W. Norton.

Bergman, J. (1991). *Treating families that seem too much like your own family.* Audiotape. Washington, DC: American Association for Marriage and Family Therapy.

Bergman, J. (1992). *Affect, humor and metaphor in family therapy.* Audiotape. Washington, DC: American Association for Marriage and Family Therapy.

Berry, T. (1988). *The dream of the earth.* San Francisco: Sierra Club.

Bettelheim, B. (1976). *The uses of enchantment: The meaning and importance of fairy tales.* New York: Knopf.

Blanchard, T. (1994). Sacred scars: How storytelling heals and restores. *Sh'ma: A journal of Jewish responsibility, 25*(479), 1–3.

Booth, W. (1978). Metaphor as rhetoric: The problem of evaluation. In S. Sacks (Ed.), *On metaphor.* Chicago: University of Chicago Press.

Bronstein, H. (1974). *A Passover haggadah: The new union haggadah.* New York: Central Conference of American Rabbis.

Brown, M. (1942). *The runaway bunny.* New York: Harper & Row.

Bruner, E. (1986a). Ethnography as narrative. In V. Turner & E. Bruner (Eds.), *The anthropology of experience.* Urbana: University of Illinois Press.

Bruner, E. (1986b). Experience and its expressions. In V. Turner & E. Bruner (Eds.), *The anthropology of experience.* Urbana: University of Illinois Press.

Bruner, J. (1979). *On knowing: Essays for the left hand, expanded edition.* Cambridge, MA: Belknap Press, Harvard University Press.

Bruner, J. (1986). *Actual minds, possible worlds.* Cambridge, MA: Harvard University Press.

Buber, M. (1947). *Tales of the Hasidim: The early masters.* New York: Schocken Books.

Buber, M. (1948). *Tales of the Hasidim: The late masters.* New York: Schocken Books.

Buber, M. (1955). *The legend of the Baal-Shem.* New York: Harper & Row.

Buckley, A. (1985). *Yoruba medicine.* Oxford: Clarendon Press.

Buddhist parables. (1922). Translated by E. Burlingame. New Haven: Yale University Press.

Caen, H. (1973, February 2). Herb Caen. *San Francisco Chronicle, 109*(33), 25.

Cameron-Bandler, L. (1978). *They lived happily ever after: A book about achieving happy endings in coupling.* Cupertino, CA: Meta Publications.

Canfield, J., & Hansen, V. (1993). *Chicken soup for the soul: 101 stories to open the heart and rekindle the spirit.* Deerfield Beach, FL: Health Communications.

Capra, F. (1988). *Uncommon wisdom: Conversations with remarkable people.* New York: Simon & Schuster.

Chaplin, D. (1930). *Some aspects of Hindu medical treatment.* London: Luzac & Co.

Chinen, A. (1989). *In the ever after: Fairy tales and the second half of life.* Wilmette, IL: Chiron Publications.

Chinen, A. (1992). *Once upon a midlife: Classic stories and mythic tales to illuminate the middle years.* Los Angeles: Jeremy P. Tarcher.

Church Hymnal Corporation. (1979). *Book of common prayer.* New York: Church Hymnal Corporation and the Seabury Press.

Clinton, J. (1986). Madness and cure in the thousand and one nights. In R. Bottigheimer (Ed.), *Fairy tales and society: Illusion, allusion, and paradigm.* Philadelphia: University of Pennsylvania Press.

Coles, R. (1989). *The call of stories: Teaching and the moral imagination.* Boston: Houghton Mifflin.

Combs, G., & Freedman, J. (1990). *Symbol, story & ceremony: Using metaphor in individual and family therapy.* New York: W. W. Norton.

Cone, M. (1965). *Who knows ten? Children's tales of the Ten Commandments.* New York: Union of American Hebrew Congregations.

Crossan, J. (1975). *The dark interval: Towards a theology of story.* Niles, IL: Argus Communications.

Dalley, S. (1989). *Myths from Mesopotamia: Creation, the flood, Gilgamesh, and others.* Oxford: Oxford University Press.

Dass, R. (1990). *Journey of awakening: A meditator's guidebook.* New York: Bantam Books.

Dass, R., & Gorman, P. (1988). *How can I help?: Stories and reflections on service.* New York: Knopf.

Davidson, D. (1978). What metaphors mean. In S. Sacks (Ed.), *On metaphor.* Chicago: University of Chicago Press.

de Mello, A. (1988). *Taking flight: A book of story-meditations.* New York: Doubleday.

de Mello, A. (1989). *The heart of the enlightened: A book of story-meditations.* New York: Doubleday.

de Shazer, S. (1985). *Keys to solution in brief therapy.* New York: W. W. Norton.

Dégh, L. (1981). Conduit-théorie. In K. Ranke et al. (Eds.), *Enzyklopädie des Märchens,* Vol. 3. Berlin and New York: Walter de Gruyter.

Dieckmann, H. (1986). *Twice-told tales: The psychological use of fairy tales.* Wilmette, IL: Chiron Publications.

Dilts, R., Grinder, J., Bandler, R., & DeLozier, J. (1980). *Neuro-linguistic programming,* Vol. 1. Cupertino, CA: Meta Publications.

Döblin, A. (1984). *Tales of a long night.* Translated by R. Kimber & R. Kimber. New York: Fromm International Publishing.

Duhl, B. (1983). *From the inside out and other metaphors: Creative and integrative approaches to training in systems thinking.* New York: Brunner/Mazel.

Edgette, J. (1991). *Using idioms and proverbs in family-oriented hypnotherapy.* Audiotape. Washington, DC: American Association for Marriage and Family Therapy.

Epstein, L. (1989). *A treasury of Jewish anecdotes.* Northvale, NJ: Jason Aronson.

Erickson, M. (1927/1980). Facilitating a new cosmetic frame of reference. In E. Rossi (Ed.), *The collected papers of Milton H. Erickson on hypnosis: Vol. 4. Innovative hypnotherapy* (pp. 465–469). New York: Irvington.

Erickson, M. (1944/1980). The method employed to formulate a complex story for the induction of an experimental neurosis in a hypnotic subject. In E. Rossi (Ed.), *The col-*

lected papers of Milton H. Erickson on hypnosis: Vol. 3. Hypnotic investigations of psychodynamic processes (pp. 336–355). New York: Irvington.

Erickson, M. (1960/1980). Breast development possibly influenced by hypnosis: Two instances and the psychotherapeutic results. In E. Rossi (Ed.), *The collected papers of Milton H. Erickson on hypnosis: Vol. 2. Hypnotic alteration of sensory, perceptual and psychophysiological process* (pp. 203–206). New York: Irvington.

Erickson, M. (1965/1980). The use of symptoms as an integral part of hypnotherapy. In E. Rossi (Ed.), *The collected papers of Milton H. Erickson on hypnosis: Vol. 4. Innovative hypnotherapy* (pp. 212–223). New York: Irvington.

Erickson, M. (1966/1980). The interspersal hypnotic technique for symptom correction and pain control. In E. Rossi (Ed.), *The collected papers of Milton H. Erickson on hypnosis. Vol. 4. Innovative hypnotherapy* (pp. 212–223). New York: Irvington.

Erickson, M. (1983). *Healing in hypnosis: The seminars, workshops, and lectures of Milton H. Erickson, Vol. 1.* Edited by E. Rossi, M. Ryan, & F. Sharp. New York: Irvington.

Erickson, M. (1985). *Life reframing in hypnosis: The seminars, workshops, and lectures of Milton H. Erickson, Vol. 2.* Edited by E. Rossi & M. Ryan. New York: Irvington.

Erickson, M. (1986). *Mind–body communication in hypnosis: The seminars, workshops, and lectures of Milton H. Erickson, Vol. 3.* Edited by E. Rossi & M. Ryan. New York: Irvington.

Erickson, M. (1992). *Creative choice in hypnosis: The seminars, workshops, and lectures of Milton H. Erickson, Vol. 4.* Edited by E. Rossi & M. Ryan. New York: Irvington.

Erickson, M., & Rossi, E. (1976/1980). Two-level communication and the microdynamics of trance and suggestion. In E. Rossi (Ed.), *The collected papers of Milton H. Erickson on hypnosis: Vol. 1. The nature of hypnosis and suggestion* (pp. 430–451). New York: Irvington.

Erickson, M., & Rossi, E. (1976-1978/1980). Indirect forms of suggestion in hand levitation. In E. Rossi (Ed.), *The collected papers of Milton H. Erickson on hypnosis: Vol. 1. The nature of hypnosis and suggestion* (pp. 478–490). New York: Irvington.

Erickson, M., & Rossi, E. (1979). *Hypnotherapy: An exploratory casebook.* New York: Irvington.

Erickson, M., & Rossi, E. (1981). *Experiencing hypnosis: Therapeutic approaches to altered states.* New York: Irvington.

Erickson, M., & Rossi, E. (1989). *The February man: Evolving consciousness and identity in hypnotherapy.* New York: Brunner/Mazel.

Erickson-Elliot, B., Erickson, K., Erickson, L., & Erickson, R. (1986). *How Milton Erickson encouraged his children to develop individuality.* Audiotape. Phoenix: Milton H. Erickson Foundation.

Fadiman, C. (Ed.). (1985). *The Little, Brown book of anecdotes.* Boston: Little, Brown.

Fahs, S., & Cobb, A. (1980). *Old tales for a new day: Early answers to life's eternal questions.* Buffalo, NY: Prometheus Books.

Fellner, C. (1976). The use of teaching stories in conjoint family therapy. *Family Process, 15*(4), 427–431.

Flood, R. (1990). The optimist and the pessimist: A fable. In J. Kincher, *Psychology for kids.* Minneapolis: Free Spirit.

Fogarty, T. (1980). The distancer and the pursuer. *The Family, 7*(1), 11–16.

Fowles, J. (1973). *The magus.* New York: Dell.

Frankel, E. (1989). *The classic tales: Four thousand years of Jewish lore.* Northvale, NJ: Jason Aronson.

Franzke, E. (1985). *Fairy tales in psychotherapy: The creative use of old and new tales.* Toronto: Hogrefe & Huber.

Friedman, E. (1990). *Friedman's fables.* New York: Guilford Press.

Fromm, E. (1951). *The forgotten language: An introduction to the understanding of dreams, fairy tales, and myths.* New York: Holt, Rinehart & Winston.

Frye, N. (1993). Literature as therapy. In R. Denham (Ed.), *Northrop Frye: The eternal act of creation.* Bloomington: Indiana University Press.

Frykman, J. (1985). Use of indirect suggestion in brief therapy. In J. Zeig (Ed.), *Ericksonian psychotherapy. Proceedings of the Second International Congress on Approaches to Ericksonian Hypnosis and Psychotherapy: Vol. II. Clinical applications.* New York: Brunner/Mazel.

Funk, R. (1966). *Language, hermeneutic and the word of God.* New York: Harper & Row.

Funk, R. (1988). Forward. In J. Crossan, *The dark interval: Towards a theology of story.* Sonoma, CA: Polebridge Press.

Gardner, R. (1971). *Therapeutic communication with children: The mutual-storytelling technique.* New York: Science House.

Gaster, T. (1928). Sacrifice (Jewish). In J. Hastings (Ed.), *Encyclopedia of religion and ethics,* Vol. 11. New York: Charles Scribner's Sons.

Gilligan, S. (1987). *Therapeutic trances: The cooperation principle in Ericksonian hypnotherapy.* New York: Brunner/Mazel.

Ginzberg, L. (1946–1964). *The legends of the Jews,* Vols. 1–7. Philadelphia: Jewish Publication Society.

Gold, J. (1990). *Read for your life: Literature as a life support system.* Markham, Ontario: Fitzhenry & Whiteside.

Gordon, D. (1978). *Therapeutic metaphors.* Cupertino, CA: Meta Publications.

Gordon, D. (1982). Ericksonian anecdotal therapy. In J. Zeig (Ed.), *Ericksonian approaches to hypnosis and psychotherapy. The Proceedings of the First International Congress on Approaches to Ericksonian Hypnosis and Psychotherapy.* New York: Brunner/Mazel.

Gordon, D. (1988). *Stories that change people.* Audiotape. Boulder, CO: NLP Comprehensive.

Gordon, D., & Meyers-Anderson, M. (1981). *Phoenix: Therapeutic patterns of Milton H. Erickson.* Cupertino, CA: Meta Publications.

Grant, J. (1987). *The monster that grew small: An Egyptian folktale.* New York: Lothrop, Lee & Shepard.

Green, B. (1972). The tree that grew through the living room floor. *Journal of Contemporary Psychotherapy, 4*(2), 95–96.

Grimm's fairy tales. (1972). Translated by M. Hunt. New York: Pantheon Books.

Grinder, J., & Bandler, R. (1976). *The structure of magic,* Vol. 2. Palo Alto, CA: Science and Behavior.

Grinder, J., & Bandler, R. (1981). *Trance-formations: Neuro-linguistic programming and the structure of hypnotic experience.* Moab, UT: Real People Press.

Grolnick, S. (1986). Fairy tales and psychotherapy. In R. Bottigheimer (Ed.), *Fairy tales and society: Illusion, allusion, and paradigm.* Philadelphia: University of Pennsylvania Press.

Grunwald, M. (1901–1906/1963). Bibliomancy. In I. Singer (Ed.), *The Jewish encyclopedia*, Vol. 3. New York: KTAV.

Haley, J. (1973). *Uncommon therapy:The psychiatric techniques of Milton H. Erickson, M.D.* New York: W. W. Norton.

Haley, J. (1976). *Problem-solving therapy.* San Francisco: Jossey-Bass.

Haley, J. (1981). *Reflections on therapy and other essays.* Rockville, MD: Triangle Press.

Haley, J. (1982, September–October). Behind the one-way mirror: An interview with Jay Haley, Part 1. *Family Therapy NetWorker, 6*(2), 21–29, 58–59.

Haley, J. (1985, March–April). Conversations with Erickson: Twenty-five years later, a chance to listen in on discussions that helped shape family therapy. *Family Therapy NetWorker, 9*(2), 30–43.

Haley, J. (1990). *Zen and the art of therapy.* Audiotape. Phoenix: Milton H. Erickson Foundation.

Hardy, B. (1968, Fall). Towards a poetics of fiction. *Novel, 2.*

Hay, S. (1982). *Story hour.* Fayetteville: University of Arkansas Press.

Heilbrun, C. (1990). What was Penelope unweaving? In C. Heilbrun, *Hamlet's mother and other women.* New York: Columbia University Press.

Hillman, J. (1975). *Re-visioning psychology.* New York: Harper & Row.

Hofstadter, D. (1979). *Gödel, Escher, Bach: An eternal golden braid.* New York: Basic Books.

Hoffman, J. (1986). *Law, freedom, and story: The role of narrative in therapy, society, and faith.* Waterloo, Ontario: Wilfrid Laurier University Press.

Holst, S. (1992). Brilliant silence. In J. Thomas, D. Thomas, & T. Hazuka (Eds.), *Flash fiction: Seventy-two very short stories.* New York: W. W. Norton.

Hudson, P., & O'Hanlon, W. (1991). *Rewriting love stories.* New York: W. W. Norton.

Israel, R. (1993). *The kosher pig and other curiosities of modern Jewish life.* Los Angeles: Alef Design Group.

Jaynes, J. (1976). *The origin of consciousness in the breakdown of the bicameral mind.* Boston: Houghton Mifflin.

Jorgensen, L. (1992). *Stories: Uses for resolution and wonder in therapy and literature.* Audiotape. Phoenix: Milton H. Erickson Foundation.

Jung, C. (1921/1971). Psychological types. *The collected works of C. G. Jung, Vol. 6.* Translated by R. F. C. Hull. Bollingen Series XX. Princeton: Princeton University Press.

Jung, C. (1928/1960). The structure and dynamics of the psyche. *The collected works of C. G. Jung, Vol. 8.* Translated by R. F. C. Hull. Bollingen Series XX. Princeton: Princeton University Press.

Jung, C. (1934/1959). The archetypes and the collective unconsciousness. *The collected works of C. G. Jung, Part I, Vol. 9.* Translated by R. F. C. Hull. Bollingen Series XX. Princeton: Princeton University Press.

Jung, C. (1958). *Psyche and symbol.* New York: Doubleday.

Jung, C. (1978). *Psychology and the East.* Translated by R. F. C. Hull. Princeton: Princeton University Press.

Kaplan, B. & Johnson, D. (1964). The social meaning of Navaho psychopathology and psychotherapy. In A. Kiev (Ed.), *Magic, faith, and healing: Studies in primitive psychiatry today.* New York: Free Press.

Katz, N. (1985). The hypnotic lifestyle: Integrating hypnosis into everyday life. In J. Zeig (Ed.), *Ericksonian psychotherapy. Proceedings of the Second International Congress on Approaches to Ericksonian Hypnosis and Psychotherapy: Vol. I. Structures.* New York: Brunner/Mazel.

Kawabata, Y. (1988). *Palm-of-the-hand stories.* Translated by L. Dunlop & J. Holman. San Francisco: North Point Press.

Keen, S., & Valley-Fox, A. (1973). *Telling your story: A guide to who you are and who you can be.* Garden City, NY: Doubleday.

Keeshig-Tobias, L. (1990). The porcupine. In D. Yashinsky (Ed.), *Tales for an unknown city.* Ontario: McGill–Queen's University Press.

Kermode, F. (1979). *The genesis of secrecy: On the interpretation of narrative.* Cambridge, MA: Harvard University Press.

Kershaw, C. (1992). *The couple's hypnotic dance: Creating Ericksonian strategies in marital therapy.* New York: Brunner/Mazel.

Kershaw, C., & Wade, J. (1991). *Using metaphors and stories in psychotherapy.* Audiotape. Houston: Milton Erickson Institute of Houston.

Kluckhohn, C. (1942). Myths and rituals: A general theory. *Harvard Theological Review, 35,* 45–79.

Kluckhohn, C., & Leighton, D. (1951). *The Navaho.* Cambridge, MA: Harvard University Press.

Kluckhohn, C., & Wyman, L. (1938). Navaho classification of their song ceremonials. In *Memoirs of the American Anthropological Association, 50,* 3–38.

Kopp, S. (1972). *If you meet the Buddha on the road, kill him!: The pilgrimage of psychotherapy patients.* Palo Alto, CA: Science and Behavior Books.

Kroeber, K. (1992). *Retelling/rereading: The fate of storytelling in modern times.* New Brunswick, NJ: Rutgers University Press.

Kronberg, R., & McKissack, P. (1990). *A piece of the wind and other stories to tell.* New York: Harper & Row.

Kurtz, E., & Ketcham, K. (1992). *The spirituality of imperfection: Storytelling and the journey to wholeness.* New York: Bantam Books.

Kushner, H. (1991). *How to live the rest of your life.* Address delivered at the annual meeting of the Urban Land Institute. Audiotape. Decatur, GA: The Resource Link.

Lakoff, G., & Johnson, M. (1980). *Metaphors we live by.* Chicago: University of Chicago Press.

Lakoff, G., & Turner, M. (1989). *More than cool reason: A field guide to poetic metaphor.* Chicago: University of Chicago Press.

Lankton, S. (1980). *Practical magic: A translation of basic neuro-linguistic programming into clinical psychotherapy.* Cupertino, CA: Meta Publications.

Lankton, S. (1989). *Goal-oriented metaphors and treatment planning.* Audiotape. Phoenix: Milton H. Erickson Foundation.

Lankton, C., & Lankton, S. (1983). *The answer within: A clinical framework of Ericksonian hypnotherapy.* New York: Brunner/Mazel.

Lankton, C., & Lankton S. (1986). *Enchantment and intervention in family therapy: Training in Ericksonian approaches.* New York: Brunner/Mazel.

Lankton, C., & Lankton S. (1989). *Tales of enchantment: Goal-oriented metaphors for adults and children in therapy.* New York: Brunner/Mazel.

Leary, D. (1990). Psyche's muse: The role of metaphor in the history of psychology. In D. Leary (Ed.), *Metaphors in the history of psychology* (pp. 1–86). Cambridge: Cambridge University Press.

Lewis, C. (1961). *An experiment in criticism*. Cambridge: Cambridge University Press.

Lewis, C. (1966a). *Of other worlds: Essays and stories*. Edited by W. Hooper. New York: Harcourt, Brace & World.

Lewis, C. (1966b). Sometimes fairy stories may say what's best to be said. In W. Hooper (Ed.), *Of other worlds: Essays and stories*. London: Geoffrey Bles.

Livo, N., & Reitz, S. (1987). *Storytelling activities*. Littleton, CO: Libraries Unlimited.

Livo, N., & Reitz, S. (1991). *Storytelling folklore sourcebook*. Englewood, CO: Libraries Unlimited.

MacIntyre, A. (1984). *After virtue: A study in moral theory, 2nd ed*. Notre Dame, IN: University of Notre Dame Press.

Madanes, C. (1990). *Stories of psychotherapy*. Audiotape. Phoenix: Milton H. Erickson Foundation.

Malinowski, B. (1922/1961). *Argonauts of the western Pacific*. New York: E. P. Dutton.

Malinowski, B. (1926/1954). Myth in primitive psychology. In R. Redfield (Ed.), *Magic, science and religion*. New York: Doubleday.

Malinowski, B. (1936/1962). *Sex, culture and myth*. New York: Harcourt, Brace & World.

Mathers, J. (Ed.). (1980). *The book of the thousand nights and one night*. Norwich, England: Folio Press.

Matz, M. (1959). The heart that did not grow. In S. Greenberg & A. Rothberg (Eds.), *Bar Mitzvah companion: The Jewish heritage as set down in story, legend and essay*. New York: Behrman House.

Maugham, S. (1931). Sheppey. A play in three acts. In S. Maugham, *The collected plays of Somerset Maugham, Vol. 3*. London: William Heinemann.

May, H., & Metzger, B. (Eds.). (1971). *The new Oxford annotated Bible: Revised standard version*. New York: Oxford University Press.

May, R. (1991). *The cry for myth*. New York: W. W. Norton.

Meltzer, B. (1982). *Guidance for living*. New York: Dial Press.

Meyers, R., & Sperry, R. (1953). Interocular transfer of a visual form discrimination habit in cats after section of the optic chasm and corpus callosum. *Anatomical Record, 115*, 351–352.

Miles, M. (1971). *Annie and the old one*. Boston: Little, Brown.

Mills, J., & Crowley, E. (1986). *Therapeutic metaphors for children and the child within*. New York: Brunner/Mazel.

Mills, J., & Crowley, E. (1988). A multidimensional approach to the utilization of therapeutic metaphors for children and adolescents. In J. Zweig & S. Lankton (Eds.), *Developing Ericksonian therapy: The state of the art. Proceedings of the Third International Congress on Approaches to Ericksonian Hypnosis and Psychotherapy*. New York: Brunner/Mazel.

Mintz, J. (1968). *Legends of the Hasidim*. Chicago: University of Chicago Press.

Mitchell, S. (1990). *Parables and portraits*. New York: Harper & Row.

Munro, H. (1982). *The story-teller: Thirteen tales by Saki*. Boston: David R. Godine.

Murphy, J. (1964). Psychotherapeutic aspects of Shamanism on St. Lawrence, Alaska. In A. Kiev (Ed.), *Magic, faith, and healing: Studies in primitive psychiatry today.* New York: Free Press.

Myerhoff, B. (1986). Life not death in Venice: Its second life. In V. Turner & E. Bruner (Eds.), *The anthropology of experience.* Urbana: University of Illinois Press.

Narayan, K. (1989). *Storytellers, saints, and scoundrels: Folk narrative in Hindu religious teaching.* Philadelphia: University of Pennsylvania Press.

Newman, L. (1944). *The Hasidic anthology.* New York: Bloch.

Newman, L. (1962). *Maggidim and Hasidim: Their wisdom.* New York: Bloch.

Nisbet, R. (1969). *Social change and history: Aspects of the Western theory of development.* London: Oxford University Press.

Noy, D. (1963). *Folktales of Israel.* Translated by G. Baharav. Chicago: University of Chicago Press.

O'Flaherty, W. (1988). *Other people's myths: The cave of echoes.* New York: Macmillan.

O'Hanlon, W. (1987). *Taproots: Underlying principles of Milton Erickson's therapy and hypnosis.* New York: W. W. Norton.

O'Hanlon, W., & Weiner-Davis, M. (1989). *In search of solutions: A new direction in psychotherapy.* New York: W. W. Norton.

Orlinsky, H. (Ed.). (1962). *The Torah: The five books of Moses. A new translation of the Holy Scriptures according to the Masoretic text.* Philadelphia: Jewish Publication Society of America.

Ornstein, R. (1972). *The psychology of consciousness.* New York: Viking Press.

Ozick, C. (1986, May). The moral necessity of metaphor. *Harper's Magazine, 272*(1632), 62–68.

Palazzoli, M., Boscolo, L., Cecchin, G., & Prata, G. (1978). *Paradox and counterparadox: A new model in therapy of the family in schizophrenic transaction.* New York: Jason Aronson.

Patai, R. (1980). *Gates to the old city: A book of Jewish legends.* New York: Avon Books.

Pavese, C. (1965). *Dialogues with Leuco.* London: P. Owen.

Peck, F. (1987). *The different drummer: Community making and peace.* New York: Touchstone Press.

Peseschikan, N. (1986). *Oriental stories as tools in psychotherapy: The merchant and the parrot. With 100 case examples for education and self-help.* Berlin: Springer-Verlag.

Petuchowski, J. (1982). *Our masters taught: Rabbinic stories and sayings.* New York: Crossroad.

Piaget, J. (1962). *Play, dreams and imitation in childhood.* Translated by C. Gattegnot & F. Hodgson. New York: W. W. Norton.

Piaget, J. (1977). *The essential Piaget.* Edited by H. Gruber & J. Vonèche. New York: Basic Books.

Porter, W. (O. Henry). (1907). *Tales of O. Henry.* New York: Doubleday.

Prince, R. (1964). Indigenous Yoruba psychiatry. In A. Kiev (Ed.), *Magic, faith, and healing: Studies in primitive psychiatry today.* New York: Free Press.

Pritchard, J. (1958). *The ancient Near East: An anthology of texts and pictures.* Princeton: Princeton University Press.

Prosky, P. (1979, February). *Some thoughts on family life from the field of family therapy.* Paper read at the Ackerman Institute for Family Therapy, New York.

Protinsky, H. (1986). The strategic use of hypnosis in family therapy. In D. Efron (Ed.), *Journeys: Expansion of the strategic systemic therapies*. New York: Brunner/Mazel.

Rahman, F. (1987). *Health and medicine in the Islamic tradition: Change and identity*. New York: Crossroad.

Rajneesh, B. (1978). *Ecstasy: The forgotten language*. Poona, India: Rajneesh Foundation.

Reps, P. (1961). *Zen flesh, Zen bones: A collection of Zen and pre-Zen writings*. New York: Doubleday, Anchor Books.

Richards, A. (1974). List of analogies. In J. Strachey (Ed. & Trans.), *The standard edition of the complete psychological works of Sigmund Freud*, Vol. 24. (pp. 177–183). London: Hogarth Press.

Ricoeur, P. (1975). Biblical hermeneutics. *Semeia, 4*, 29–148.

Riemer, J. (1991). *The world of the high holy days*, Vol. 1. Miami: Bernie Books.

Riemer, J. (1992). *The world of the high holy days*, Vol. 2. Miami: Bernie Books.

Roberts, J. (1990). *Using family storytelling and writing in making transitions*. Audiotape. Washington, DC: American Association for Marriage and Family Therapy.

Roberts, J. (1994). *Tales and transformations: Stories in families and family therapy*. New York: W. W. Norton.

Roberts, M. (Ed. & Trans.). (1979). *Chinese fairy tales and fantasies*. New York: Pantheon Books.

Röhrich, L. (1986). Introduction. In R. Bottigheimer (Ed.), *Fairy tales and society: Illusion, allusion, and paradigm*. Philadelphia: University of Pennsylvania Press.

Rosaldo, R. (1986). Ilongot hunting as story and experience. In V. Turner & E. Bruner (Eds.), *The anthropology of experience*. Urbana: University of Illinois Press.

Rosen, S. (1980). *Ericksonian hypnotherapy—simplified*. Audiotape. Phoenix: Milton H. Erickson Foundation.

Rosen, S. (1982a). *My voice will go with you*. New York: W. W. Norton.

Rosen, S. (1982b). The values and philosophy of Milton H. Erickson. In J. Zeig (Ed.), *Ericksonian approaches to hypnosis and psychotherapy. Proceedings of the First International Congress on Approaches to Ericksonian Hypnosis and Psychotherapy*. New York: Brunner/Mazel.

Rosen, S. (1988). What makes Ericksonian therapy so effective? In J. Zeig & S. Lankton (Eds.), *Developing Ericksonian therapy: State of the art. Proceedings of the Third International Congress on Approaches to Ericksonian Hypnosis and Psychotherapy*. New York: Brunner/Mazel.

Rossi, E. (1972). *Dreams and the growth of personality: Expanding awareness in psychotherapy*. New York: Pergamon Press.

Rossi, E. (1982, January–February). Erickson's creativity. *Family Therapy NetWorker, 6*(5), 5.

Rossi, E., & Cheek, D. (1988). *Mind–body therapy: Methods of ideodynamic healing in hypnosis*. New York: W. W. Norton.

Rubin, R. (1978). Introduction. In R. Rubin (Ed.), *Bibliotherapy sourcebook*. Phoenix: Oryx Press.

Sadeh, P. (1989). *Jewish folktales*. New York: Doubleday.

Sander, D. (1979). *Navaho symbols of healing: A Jungian exploration of ritual, image, and medicine*. Rochester, VT: Healing Arts Press.

Sarbin, T. (1986). The narrative as a root metaphor for psychology. In T. Sarbin (Ed.), *Narrative psychology: The storied nature of human conduct*. New York: Praeger.

Sawyer, R. (1942). *The way of the storyteller*. New York: Viking Penguin.

Scholem, G. (1946). *Major trends in Jewish mysticism*. New York: Schocken Books.

Schwartzman, J., & Restivo, R. (1985). Acting out and staying in: Juvenile probation and the family. In J. Schwartzman (Ed.), *Families and other systems*. New York: Guilford Press.

Scieszka, J., & Smith, L. (1992). *The stinky cheese man and other fairly stupid tales*. New York: Viking Penguin.

Shah, I. (1972). *Thinkers of the East*. New York: Arkana.

Shelton, R. (1992). The stones. In J. Thomas, D. Thomas, & T. Hazuka (Eds.), *Flash fiction: Seventy-two very short stories*. New York: W. W. Norton.

Shiryon, M. (1977). Biblical roots of literatherapy. *Journal of Psychology and Judaism*, *2*(1), 3–11.

Shiryon, M. (1978). Literatherapy: Theory and application. In R. Rubin (Ed.), *Bibliotherapy sourcebook*. Phoenix: Oryx Press.

Shiryon, M. (1992). The stories of Exodus as metaphors for psychotherapy. *Journal of Psychology and Judaism*, *16*(4), 235–244.

Shrodes, C. (1978). Implications for psychotherapy. In R. Rubin (Ed.), *Bibliotherapy sourcebook*. Phoenix: Oryx Press.

Siebers, T. (1992). *Morals and stories*. New York: Columbia University Press.

Silko, L. (1991). Language and literature from a Pueblo Indian perspective. In P. Mariani (Ed.), *Critical fictions: The politics of imaginative writing*. Seattle: Bay Press.

Simms, L. (1983, March). Crosstalk: A retelling of an African Bushman story by Laura Simms. *Psychology Today*, *17*(3), 18.

Slonimsky, H. (1967). *Essays*. Cincinnati: Hebrew Union College Press.

Soskice, J. (1985). *Metaphor and religious language*. Oxford: Clarendon Press.

Sperry, R. (1964). The great cerebral commissure. *Scientific American*, *210*, 42–52.

Steinberg, M. (1951). *A believing Jew: The selected writings of Milton Steinberg*. New York: Harcourt, Brace.

Strenski, I. (1992). *Malinowski and the work of myth*. Princeton: Princeton University Press.

Stern, C. (Ed.). (1975). *Gates of prayer: The new union prayerbook*. New York: Central Conference of American Rabbis.

Stewart, I. (1992, November). Does chaos rule the cosmos? *Discover*, pp. 56–63.

Stiles, N. (1987). Another Cinderella. In M. Thomas (Ed.), *Free to be … a family: A book about all kinds of belonging*. New York: Bantam Books.

Tatar, M. (1987). *The hard facts of the Grimm's fairy tales*. Princeton: Princeton University Press.

TeSelle, S. (1975). *Speaking in parables: A study in metaphor and theology*. Philadelphia: Fortress Press.

Thoma, C., & Wyschogrod, M. (1989). Introduction. In C. Thoma, & M. Wyschogrod, *Parable and story in Judaism and Christianity*. New York: Paulist Press.

Thompson, K. (1985). Almost 1984. In J. Zeig, (Ed.), *Ericksonian psychotherapy. Proceedings of the Second International Congress on Approaches to Ericksonian Hypnosis and Psychotherapy, Vol. 1. Structures*. New York: Brunner/Mazel.

Thompson, K. (1988). *Meaningful messages: The manufacturing of metaphors.* Audiotape. Phoenix: The Milton H. Erickson Foundation.

Thompson, K. (1990). Metaphor: A myth with a method. In J. Zeig, & S. Gilligan, (Eds.), *Brief therapy: Myths, methods and metaphors. Proceedings of the Fourth International Congress on Ericksonian Approaches to Hypnosis and Psychotherapy.* New York: Brunner/Mazel.

Thompson, S. (1946). *The folktale.* New York: Holt, Rinehart & Winston.

Thompson, S. (1955–1958). *Motif-index of folk-literature: A classification of narrative elements in folktales, ballads, myths, fables, mediaeval romances, exempla, fabilaux, jest-books and local legends,* rev. ed. Bloomington: Indiana University Press.

Thompson, S. (1965). Myth and folktales. In T. Sebeok, (Ed.), *Myth: A symposium* (pp. 169–180). Bloomington: Indiana University Press.

Thurber, J. (1939). *Fables for our time and famous poems illustrated.* New York: Harper & Row.

Tolstoy, L. (1962). *Fables and fairy tales.* Translated by A. Dunnigan. New York: New American Library.

Tolstoy, L. (1886/1983). *How much land does a man need?* London: Oxford University Press.

Tracy, D. (1978). Metaphor and religion: The test case of Christian texts. In S. Sacks (Ed.), *On metaphor.* Chicago: University of Chicago Press.

Tracy, D. (1987, December 6). *Myth, sacrifice and the social sciences.* Paper read at the annual meeting of the American Academy of Religion, Boston.

Travers, P. (1989). *What the bee knows.* Northamptonshire: Aquarian Press.

Turner, V. (1974). *Dramas, fields, and metaphors: Symbolic action in human society.* Ithaca: Cornell University Press.

Twain, M. (1876/1991). *Tom Sawyer and Huck Finn.* New York: Knopf.

Umansky, E., & Ashton, D. (1992). *Four centuries of Jewish women's spirituality.* Boston: Beacon Press.

Van Doren, M. (1958). *Autobiography of Mark Van Doren.* New York: Harcourt, Brace.

Visher, J., & Visher, E. (1981). Common problems in stepfamilies. In A. Gurman (Ed.), *Questions and answers in the practice of family therapy, Vol. 1.* New York: Brunner/Mazel.

Wallas, L. (1985). *Stories for the third ear.* New York: W. W. Norton.

Watzlawick, P. (1976). *How real is real? Confusion, disinformation, communication: An anecdotal introduction to communications theory.* New York: Random House.

Watzlawick, P. (1978). *The language of change: Elements of therapeutic communication.* New York: Basic Books.

Watzlawick, P. (1985). Hypnotherapy without trance. In J. Zeig (Ed.), *Ericksonian psychotherapy. Proceedings of the Second International Congress on Approaches to Ericksonian Hypnosis and Psychotherapy, Vol. 1. Structures.* New York: Brunner/Mazel.

Watzlawick, P., Beavin, J., & Jackson, D. (1967). *Pragmatics of human communication: A study of interactional patterns, pathologies, and paradoxes.* New York: W. W. Norton.

Watzlawick, P., Weakland, J., & Fisch, R. (1974). *Change: Principles of problem formation and problem resolution.* New York: W. W. Norton.

Wehse, R. (1986). Past and present folkloristic narrator research. Translated by R. Bottigheimer. In R. Bottigheimer (Ed.), *Fairy tales and society: Illusion, allusion, and paradigm*. Philadelphia: University of Pennsylvania Press.

Whellis, A. (1966). *The illusionless man: Some fantasies and meditations on disillusionment*. New York: W. W. Norton.

Whitaker, C. (1989). *Midnight musings of a family therapist*. M. Ryan (Ed.), New York: W. W. Norton.

White, M. (1989–1990, Summer). Family therapy training and supervision in a world of experience and narrative. *Dulwich Center Newsletter*, 27–38.

White, W. (1982). *Speaking in stories*. Minneapolis: Augsburg Press.

Whitehead, A. (1969). *Process and reality*. New York: Macmillan.

Wiesel, E. (1971). *A beggar in Jerusalem*. New York: Avon.

Wilder, A. (1964). *Early Christian rhetoric*. New York: Harper & Row.

Wilk, J. (1985, March–April). That reminds me of a story: Story-telling and hypnosis have a lot in common. *Family Therapy NetWorker, 9*(2), 45–48.

Williams, L. (1983). *Teaching for the two-sided brain: A guide to right brain–left brain education*. Englewood Cliffs, NJ: Prentice-Hall.

Williams, M. (1926). *The velveteen rabbit*. New York: Doubleday.

Wren, C. (1990). *The end of the line: The failure of Communism in the Soviet Union and China*. New York: Simon & Schuster.

Wylie, M. (1990). Brief therapy on the couch: Analyzing Drs. Erickson and Freud. *Family Therapy NetWorker, 14*(2), 26–35, 66.

Yapko, M. (1990). *Trancework: An introduction to the practice of clinical hypnosis*. New York: Brunner/Mazel.

Yohannan, J. (1968). *Joseph and Potiphar's wife in world literature: An anthology of the story of the chaste youth and the lustful stepmother*. New York: New Directions.

Zeig, J. (1980). *Teaching seminar with Milton H. Erickson*. New York: Brunner/Mazel.

Zeig, J. (1985). *Experiencing Erickson: An introduction to the man and his work*. New York: Brunner/Mazel.

Zeig, J. (1988). An Ericksonian phenomenological approach to therapeutic hypnotic induction and symptom utilization. In J. Zeig & S. Lankton (Eds.). *Developing Ericksonian therapy: State of the art. Proceedings of the Third International Congress on Approaches to Ericksonian Hypnosis and Psychotherapy*. New York: Brunner/Mazel.

Zeig, J. (1989). Using metaphor and the interspersal technique. In S. Lankton & J. Zeig (Eds.), *Extrapolations: Demonstrations of Ericksonian therapy*. Ericksonian Monographs, No. 6. New York: Brunner/Mazel.

Zeig, J. (1990). Seeding. In J. Zeig & S. Gilligan (Eds.), *Brief therapy: Myths, methods and metaphors. Proceedings of the Fourth International Congress on Ericksonian Approaches to Hypnosis and Psychotherapy*. New York: Brunner/Mazel.

Zeig, J. (Ed.). (1994). *Ericksonian methods: The essence of the story. Proceedings of the Fifth International Congress on Ericksonian Approaches to Hypnosis and Psychotherapy*. New York: Brunner/Mazel.

Zimmer, H. (1948). *Hindu medicine*. Baltimore: Johns Hopkins Press.

Zipes, J. (1991). Introduction. In J. Zipes (Ed.), *Spells of enchantment*. New York: Viking.

Author Index

Subject Index

References to pages on which therapeutic narratives appear are in **boldface.**